"While the family therapy literature has recently begun to examine issues of gender in therapy, this new body of literature has tended to focus more on women, creating feminist models of therapy that create a gap for understanding and working with men. *Feminist Approaches for Men in Family Therapy*, one of the newest additions to the growing literature on men in therapy, offers a wide and rich variety of material that both educators and practitioners will find fills this gap. Michele Bograd and her contributors present many of the sociopolitical issues that men bring to therapy. . . . The reader will find this text rich with stories, personal reflections, and clinical vignettes that brings the theoretical material to life."

Richard L. Meth, CISW, Director, Center for Marital and Family Therapy, Marital and Family Therapy Program; Lecturer, School of Family Studies, University of Connecticut, Storrs

"Family systems theory and the practice of family therapy have been seriously gender-blind. One eye, the feminist, has been opening with the assistance of recent writing about the consequences of gender for women in family treatment. This volume of [chapters] are the first eye-openers for the many effects of gender blindness on men in family therapy. . . . We all need increasing gender awareness. . . . These [chapters] address many useful aspects of gender as central treatment issues."

Joan J. Zillbach, MD, Family Therapist in Private Practice, Boston, Massachusetts; Faculty, Fielding Institute, Santa Barbara, California; Training and Supervising Analyst, Boston Psychoanalytic Institute and Society, Boston, Massachusetts

Feminist Approaches for Men in Family Therapy

Feminist Approaches for Men in Family Therapy

Michele Bograd
Editor

Feminist Approaches for Men in Family Therapy was simultaneously issued by The Haworth Press, Inc., under the same title, as a special issue of *Journal of Feminist Family Therapy*, Volume 2, Numbers 3/4 1990, Michele Bograd, guest editor, Lois Braverman, editor.

Harrington Park Press
New York • London

ISBN 1-56023-000-2

Published by

Harrington Park Press, 10 Alice Street, Binghamton, NY 13904-1580
EUROSPAN/Harrington, 3 Henrietta Street, London WC2E 8LU England

Harrington Park Press is a subsidiary of The Haworth Press, Inc., 10 Alice Street, Binghamton, NY 13904-1580.

Feminist Approaches for Men in Family Therapy was originally published as *Journal of Feminist Family Therapy*, Volume 2, Numbers 3/4 1990.

Cover design by Marshall Andrews.

Library of Congress Cataloging-in-Publication Data

Feminist approaches for men in family therapy / Michele Bograd, editor.
p. cm.
ISBN 1-56023-000-2
1. Family psychotherapy. 2. Men – Mental health. 3. Feminist therapy. I. Bograd, Michele Louise, 1952-
RC488.5.F44 1991
616.89'156 – dc20

91-352
CIP

DEDICATION

To Tom Denton, who lovingly, consistently, and fully meets me

To my family – Mom, Larry, and Harvey

To Dorothy Wheeler, Larry Zucker and Dennis Balcolm,
comrades and colleagues

To the memory of my father Nathan

ABOUT THE EDITOR

Michele Bograd, PhD, is a psychologist and marital therapist in private practice in Cambridge, Massachusetts. A highly-skilled teacher and supervisor in family therapy, she has presented widely at family therapy conferences and workshops across America and in Latin America. Dr. Bograd has authored numerous articles and book chapters which address her deep interest in gender and family therapy, specifically concerns about violence against women, the feminist critique of family therapy, sexual issues in the treatment relationship, and issues facing women therapists treating male clients. The co-editor of *Feminist Perspectives on Wife Abuse* (Sage, 1988), Dr. Bograd received her degree in Human Development from the University of Chicago.

CONTENTS

∞ ALL HARRINGTON PARK PRESS BOOKS ARE PRINTED ON CERTIFIED ACID-FREE PAPER

Preface

"A woman-centered perspective inevitably sheds new light on masculinity and maleness"

—H. Eistenstein

". . . what is a giant step to the battler may appear as a wriggle of progress to the beholder"

—J.B. Miller

The feminist critiques of family therapy models and techniques have focused primarily on clinical and theoretical biases against women clients, given the social and historical contexts of current family therapy practices. The feminist perspective on woman's place is essential for creating a foundation of progressive and non-sexist family therapy models. However, to be truly systemic, family therapists must also critically examine men's subjective experiences and their interrelationships with larger social structures and processes.

There is a growing body of literature on men in family therapy, but little of this work is feminist in theoretical orientation. A feminist approach to men's issues is informed by several key premises:

- Gender is a crucial organizing dimension of human life.
- Gender roles limit and constrict the psychological development of men and women, and inhibit the development of rich, mutually satisfying, and non-coercive intimacy.
- Individual and family dysfunction is related to the fulfillment of traditional gender roles.
- Family life reflects, maintains and is perpetuated by the larger social order.
- This social order is fundamentally patriarchal, preserving the interests of men as a group over women.

With these premises as a backdrop, feminist theoreticians and clinicians approach men in therapy with certain key questions in mind. First, what are the experiences of men as men in families? With this question, masculinity itself becomes an object of inquiry. Although feminists have argued that women's experiences have been silenced, distorted, or pathologized when standards about humanity in general are extrapolated from norms of white male experience, it is increasingly evident that dominant theories of psychological and family functioning do not reflect the lived everyday experiences of men as well. Family therapists are in a privileged position to explore this experience and to document its pattern and variety.

Second, how are these experiences structured at the social level? This question guides us to examine men's issues from two frames of reference that encompass the experiences and struggles of individual men: the symbolic order and social organization. Here, we explore how masculinity is constituted in our culture, highlighting dominant conceptions and the many variations of "masculinities" (Brod, 1987). This exploration occurs hand-in-hand with the elaboration of socially constructed ideals of womanhood or femininity—as the definitions of one depend on those of the other. This inquiry is grounded in social and historical analyses of gender relations, which seeks the source of dysfunctional patterns in families in social structures and trends outside of the family boundary, beyond the hearts or personal histories of family members.

Last, the distinguishing question of any feminist analysis is: how do power and domination shape the intimate connections of men and women in families? This question separates out feminist exploration from traditional approaches to men's issues, for it contextualizes the experiences of all men through reference to the reigning social order—regardless of their subjectively felt powerlessness or experiences of victimization by other men and sometimes women. From this frame of reference, we do not simply explore obviously dysfunctional patterns, such as male violence, we also question whether what is defined as "normal" or "appropriate" for men (and so remains unnoticed by many clinicians) is pathogenic to the man himself and to the relationships he depends upon and values. A feminist perspective is characterized by binocular vision that combines awareness of the pain and struggles of individual men with that of their adaptation and unquestioning compliance to cultural dictates that give them power at the cost of a certain humanity.

Common wisdom has it that men are recalcitrant customers of psychotherapy. A recent Andy Capp cartoon captures this sentiment as the lead male character says to his wife, "Look, Flo, you say you're unhappy and you think marriage guidance can help. Fair enough – I'm all for it . . . But there's no point in me coming – I'm perfectly happy." But my experience, and that of many marital and family therapists, is that more and more men are willingly entering therapy, aware of the high costs of their manhood, confused by the paradoxes of intimacy, and frightened by the extraordinary difficulty of change that violates current conceptions of masculinity. The challenges then become how to translate a feminist awareness into caring, effective clinical practice with men; how to extend feminist insights about women to encompass human systems; and how to bring men and women together from their divergent experiences and positions that so conspire against mutual understanding and collaboration. Men and women therapists and clients will struggle with new definitions that have ramifications for more than the outcome of this particular client, but for the personal lives of all members of the therapy system. This process can be angry, confusing, self-righteous, and painful, but it is not without many moments of exhilaration and promise.

–Michele Bograd

REFERENCE

Brod, H. A case for men's studies. In M. Kimmel (Ed.), *Changing men: New directions in research on men and masculinity*. Newbury Park, CA: Sage, 1987.

PART 1: COMBINING POLITICAL AND CLINICAL ANALYSES OF MEN

Feminist Therapy with Male Clients

Anne Ganley

SUMMARY. Traditionally, feminist therapy has been discussed as it applies to women as clients. This article presents a definition of feminist therapy with men, the client issues unique to male clients, and certain process issues relevant to the feminist therapist and the male client. The reality is that the mental health of all persons is severely damaged by sex role socialization and sexism. Feminist therapy with male clients is an important contribution in changing this reality. In this article, feminist therapists are called upon to rethink their understanding of feminist therapy, of men as clients, and of themselves.

INTRODUCTION

For many people, the term feminist therapy is typically associated with the image of a feminist therapist counseling women clients in individual, group, couples, or family sessions. Such an im-

---

Anne Ganley, PhD, is affiliated with the Seattle Veterans Administration Medical Center. Correspondence may be addressed to her at 4408 Sunnyside North Seattle, WA 98103.

This article is reprinted with slight modification, by permission from M. Douglas and L. Walker (Eds.), *Feminist psychotherapies: Integration of therapeutic and feminist systems*. Norwood, NJ: Ablex Publishing Corporation, 1989.

age is based on the assumption that feminist therapy by its nature is solely for the female client. Supposedly, if men are involved at all as clients in the therapy, it is because they are in relationship as lover or family member to a female client. Yet in spite of this image of feminist therapy, the reality is that men are also consumers of this psychotherapeutic approach. Some men intentionally seek out feminist therapists while others are in feminist therapy because it was available. These men may have sought a qualified therapist or, more specifically, a female therapist only to discover later that she is a feminist therapist. At an agency or counseling center these men may have been assigned to their therapist, unaware of the therapeutic approach used by that therapist.

This reality that men are consumers of feminist therapy is not reflected in the literature of the new field of feminist therapy. While there has been much written about feminist therapy and women as well as about feminism and men, there is a noticeable gap in articles about the applications of feminist therapy with male clients. The primary contribution of feminist therapy to therapy with men stems from its power to redefine the norms for the mental health of the adult male and the adult female, and to assert that these norms are the same for both men and women. This androgynous model of mental health for both men and women, by definition, changes the very nature of the therapeutic issues male clients will deal with in feminist therapy. This chapter will consider each of these issues in light of this model. Moreover, it will review the practices and principles in feminist therapy that must be reconsidered to avoid their becoming obstacles to using this approach with male clients.

TRADITIONAL MODELS OF THE MENTALLY HEALTHY ADULT

Traditional approaches to therapy have attempted to address the needs of male clients. The sheer volume of literature that forms the basis of these therapies with men prohibits a detailed review or a feminist critique of each in this chapter. However, the central difference between these nonfeminist approaches to therapy with men and a feminist approach is not so much in the strategies used, but in their definition of what it is to be a mentally healthy adult male or mentally healthy adult female. What traditional approaches have in common are their limited models for normal human behavior. Some approaches rely on a double standard model whereby men and women are treated differently, while others employ an androcentric model for both men and women.

For many years there has been a double standard of mental health, one for men and one for women. Descriptions of the mentally healthy male were considered synonymous with those of the mentally healthy adult. As the Broverman et al. (1972) study revealed, the characteristics seen as appropriate for a mentally healthy woman were not seen as synonymous to being a healthy adult. Furthermore, the adult woman was characterized by more negative qualities. Under this double standard, women either had the characteristics of an adult and were considered "unfeminine" or they had the characteristics associated with being "feminine" and were considered less than an adult. As long as they had the stereotypical masculine qualities, they were considered healthy adults. Unfortunately this double standard is still used as the norm in much clinical practice.

Even when this model is challenged, it is too often replaced by an androcentric model, which endorses stereotypical masculine traits as ideal for all persons (Brown & Liss-Levinson, 1981). The androcentric model defines the healthy adult as being achievement-oriented, rational, instrumental, independent, aggressive, and individualistic, etc. Neither the double standard of the mentally healthy adult nor the androcentric model affirms the typically feminine attributes, such as being relational, interdependent, empathetic, or nurturing. Neither affirms pluralistic models of mental health.

In the past decade and a half, criticisms of the male model for mental health have come from multiple sources. Feminists within psychology (Chesler, 1972; Kaplan, 1976; Rosewater & Walker, 1985) and feminists outside psychology (Ehrenreich, 1983) have questioned the negative impact of the unchallenged androcentric model on both women and men. Some of the challenges to the model have come from writings and research on the psychology of women (Gilligan, 1982; Miller, 1976) where a more complete understanding of women's development underscores the inadequacy of the androcentric model. Building on feminism, the men's liberation movement has also questioned the model's relevance to men, and it has called on men to develop further their "feminine" qualities of being more emotionally expressive, nurturing, and empathetic (Fasteau, 1974; Goldberg, 1976; Pleck & Sawyer, 1974; Welch, 1985). Some of the criticism comes from scholarship outside of feminism where the definition of mental health is expanded by a better understanding of white racism (Schwartz & Disch, 1970), race/ethnicity/culture (McGoldrick, Pearce, & Giordano, 1982), sexualities (Zilbergeld, 1978), economic class (Sennett & Cobb, 1972), aging (Fisher, 1986), and differences in physical abilities. In the face of this ever-growing body of knowledge, the androcentric model for mental health is inadequate at best and is damaging at its worse.

It is not surprising that women's mental health suffered under these standards. Too often, therapy based on such models mislabeled women who had either traditionally masculine or feminine attributes as being deviant, pathological, inappropriate, or irrational. When being measured against such limited models, women in therapy were expected to adjust to the status quo. What is also not surprising is that all who did not fit these narrow models were also stigmatized by those norms of mental health: persons of color, persons of lower economic class, lesbians, gays, bisexuals, the elderly, and those differently abled.

Furthermore, even those who supposedly do fit, i.e., men, are limited by that mental health norm. While the androcentric model reinforces men's positions of economic and social power, it is a mixed blessing. As discussed later in this chapter, such a model also cripples their understanding of themselves in the past and present, and it limits their ability to change in the future. Traditional therapeutic approaches to counseling men reinforce an androcentric norm and assist clients only in adjusting to the status quo. In so doing, they fail to meet the therapeutic needs of both those men who fall outside that norm and those whose issues are the direct result of ascribing to that norm.

AN ANDROGYNOUS MODEL OF MENTAL HEALTH

Feminists look to an androgynous model for mental health to move beyond the deficits of the androcentric model (Bem, 1974; Cox, 1982). Rawlings and Carter suggest that "to think of traits in terms of the masculine-feminine dichotomy perpetuates the old set'' (1977, p. 28). They prefer Bakan's concepts of agency (self-protection, self-assertion, self-expansion) and communion (being at one with the organisms) for their definition of an androgynous model. They stress that Bakan's major contribution is in defining the central developmental task as being the one of integrating and balancing agency with communion. A feminist analysis also brings to this androgynous model an awareness of the pluralism in how this norm of the healthy adult is lived out. This pluralism results from differences in race/ethnicity/culture, age, economic class, sexualities, and physical abilities. The androgynous model for the healthy adult says that men and women can be both relational and achieving, instrumental and expressive, rational and emotional, self-nurturing and other-nurturing, assertive and receptive, independent and dependent, individualistic and collaborative. Androgyny calls for a flexibility of roles and life-styles, egalitarian rather than power-based relationships, and a sensitivity to human rights.

DEFINITION OF FEMINIST THERAPY WITH MEN

Feminist therapy is a philosophy as well as a particular school of therapy. The philosophy, based on feminist theory, guides the use of a wide variety of assessment and therapeutic techniques. Central to the philosophy is the assumption that ideology, social structure, and behavior are interwoven: Hence, women's and men's behavior stem more from socialization and institutional sex roles than from biology (Cammaert & Larsen, 1988). A feminist analysis highlights the harmful effects of such sex role stereotyping for both women and men while also being clear that women's economical and political status is more negatively affected than men's.

Feminist therapy involves the resocialization of women (Forisha, 1981) and of men. It uses the androgynous model of mental health for both men and women to assist clients in identifying goals for therapy. This is a model of health, growth, and development rather than one based on illness. Feminist therapy draws on a variety of personality theories in understanding human behavior. The feminist therapist employs psychoeducational approaches, choosing to incorporate strategies from radical psychiatry, humanistic psychology, cognitive behavioral approaches, etc. Some even attempt to use psychoanalysis within the feminist conceptual framework. In sex role analysis, the external and internal constraints to change are identified. While feminist therapy stresses individual responsibility for change, it deals with the issues of choice, control, and power within the current social structures. The process of feminist therapy draws on the phenomenological experiences of both therapist and clients as women to guide the changes (Brown, 1984). Furthermore, feminist therapy is recognized as not being solely a change process for an individual, since it calls upon both client and therapist to change society's institutions, including the structures of psychotherapy itself.

Such a definition of feminist therapy distinguishes it from two closely related approaches to therapy: nonsexist therapy by male and female therapists and profeminist therapy by male therapists. In nonsexist therapy there is the use of sex role analysis and the androgynous model of the mentally healthy adult. However, little attention is given to the need to restructure social institutions, either by the therapist or the client. Oftentimes nonsexist therapy practice reflects traditional methods and procedures; little attempt is made by the therapist to be accessible to varieties of persons or to empower clients both in therapy and in their communities. Inclusive language may be used, traditional sex roles challenged, and individual change supported, but these nonsexist approaches appear to focus solely on the progress of individuals to the exclusion of social change. The primary difference between feminist therapy and nonsexist approaches is that the nonsexist approach addresses the personal but overlooks the political.

Profeminist therapy is similar to feminist therapy in its sex role analysis of human experience, its understanding and use of power, its use of the androgynous model of mental health, and its recognition of the need for social change. The difference between the two rests solely in the gender of the therapist. In feminist therapy the therapist is a female who uses her phenomenological experiences as a woman to understand her clients and to enrich her therapeutic strategies. In profeminist therapy the therapist is male. Since he does not have the phenomenological experience of being female, he uses his experiences as a male and particularly a male whose understanding of himself, of all men, and of women has been transformed by feminist analysis. The recognition that feminist therapy is a phenomenological process clarifies that men cannot be feminist therapists. Male therapists can and do use feminist analysis to provide nonsexist therapy *and* to bring about social change: In doing so they are profeminist therapists. This description of the difference does not devalue them or their work. At this time and in this social context it is merely different from feminist therapists.

Feminist therapy with men is a particular kind of feminist therapy shaped by the gender of the client. A feminist analysis underscores the point that men in this culture have different experiences than women: This reality alone makes all the difference in the application of feminist therapy to male clients. Rather than discuss all the similarities and differences between feminist therapy with men and that with women, the remainder of the chapter will focus on those particular client and process issues raised by feminist therapy with male clients.

CLIENT ISSUES IN FEMINIST THERAPY WITH MEN

The use of the androgynous model for mental health in therapy with male clients brings into focus certain specific issues which otherwise might not be identified. In addition, such a model reframes some of the traditional counseling issues presented by male clients. To illustrate these points, each of the common themes raised in feminist therapy with male clients are discussed separately, although in practice they are often interwoven. Specifics from a variety of cases and practice settings are used in the examples in order to provide some breadth to the particular theme. The examples also illustrate how a particular theme may appear in a very dysfunctional and obvious way with one client, whereas it would result in less dysfunction for another person. To a greater or lesser degree some combination of these issues are presented by most male clients in feminist therapy.

Relationship/Achievement Values

One of the major developmental tasks for the adult is the integration and balance of relationship and achievement needs in one's life. Sometimes characterized as the balance between love and work, this issue for most men involves the integration of the whole range of relationships: acquaintances, friends, lovers, and family members with multiple aspects of doing work. On no other issue is the impact of sex role socialization so disparate for men and women. As the work of Miller (1976) and Gilligan (1982) reveal, women have been socialized to value relationships and to measure their self-worth and that of others in terms of one's ability to develop and maintain relationships. Men on the other hand are socialized to value achievement and production and to measure their self-worth and that of others accordingly.

Men assess their own worth in terms of their achievements, which in turn are determined by quantitative standards of how much, how many, how often, and how big. Whether it is football, corporate sales, sexual activity, surgical procedures, legal cases, farming, manufacturing, selling illegal drugs, or philanthropic work, the push for men is to be bigger or better than other men. They tend not to value relationships except in terms of the way those relationships improve or detract from their achievement goals. Historically, even family relationships for men signified property relationships. In fact the word family originally means having to do with the property and slaves of a particular man. Relationships are entered into and dissolved according to men's achievement needs. Oftentimes what has been described as great models of male-male friendships have been those of being "comrades in arms," where the relationship is actually a means to a task. In addition to that military setting, the friendships may now take place on the racquetball court or in the pool hall. However, the emphasis still remains on these relationships being vehicles for conducting business rather than being experiences shared between intimates.

The change in times may have modified some of the particulars in the way the theme is manifested, but for men in therapy the struggle between relationship and achievement values remains. Some men describe this conflict solely in terms of a sense of failure about achievement goals. For example, they may be unemployed due to disability, aging, changes in the job market, imprisonment, or by choice. Or they may be employed, but they are filled with anxiety about performance or they are dissatisfied when the work does not fit their dreams. In either case the despair or anxiety is centered solely with discomfort about work and achievement. There is hardly any mention of relationships. Men's emphasis on achievement at expense of relationship usually means that their relational needs are not even acknowledged. Occasionally the theme is expressed solely in terms of relationships: a troubled marriage, a lack of friends, or a sense of alienation. Yet seldom do men recognize their needs to be both relational and achieving.

In feminist therapy, the sex role analysis of the issues as presented by the client make the dimensions of the relationship/achievement conflict apparent. This aspect of feminist therapy allows the individual male client to become aware of the specific nature of his strengths and weaknesses in integrating those two parts of his life. It also encourages a valuing of the relational side of his life as an end in itself. Thus, as he makes changes in one aspect, he will not inadvertently ignore the other. By identifying the gender-specific nature of his conflict, he may be better able to strategize the steps for change. Sometimes this may initially involve developing more realistic expectations in terms of work and then focusing more on developing relationships. Sometimes the approach would be reversed. A feminist analysis contributes a reminder to the resolution of this particular conflict: gender socialization for men emphasizes achievement to the detriment of relationships. Both are needed for a sense of well-being and healthy functioning.

Intimacy Avoidance

For some men one result of the devaluing of relationships in their socialization is their avoidance of intimacy. This intimacy avoidance is manifested in many ways. Men may demonstrate a fear of intimacy through excessive anxiety and/or anger in any relationships which pose even the possibility of intimacy. In such relationships they may swing from times of intense demands for reassurance that a partner "loves" them to times of extreme anger at the partner for inconsequential events. With either behavior the result is to drive the partner away, thus avoiding the possibility or actuality of intimacy. The avoidance of intimacy may also be expressed in the excessive emphasis on sexual behavior in one or multiple relationships. For these men there is the appearance of intimacy through sex but without the emotional involvement. With others this issue is revealed in what they call their anxiety about meeting women. With either the Don Juan or the timid man, the intimacy avoidance is totally focused on their relationships with women or the lack of relationships with women. They do not even express intimacy issues as they pertain to friends, children, or work associates. Others may experience the intimacy avoidance by being the classic workaholic or substance abuser which allows them to avoid all opportunities for intimate relationships with friends, lovers, and family members.

For clients dealing with the issue of intimacy avoidance, feminist therapy is particularly useful. It reframes the issue in terms of gender role socialization, rather than in terms of one particular past negative event, such as abandonment by mother, rejection by previous girl friend, or a bad marriage. A sex role analysis of this particular issue assists both client and therapist in understanding both the social rewards that determine this behavior as well as the negative events that contributed to it. Only then will the changing of intimacy avoidance become more than finding one good woman. In feminist therapy with men the goal becomes the process of increasing intimacy in a variety of relationships: parent-child, friend-friend (both sexes), colleague-colleague, and lover-lover. The change also involves a process of building social reinforcers for being intimate. Intimacy requires a lot of risk taking and one cannot be successful without sometimes failing. Too often traditional therapies have focused exclusively on trying to avoid the failures rather than on how to use them as a learning experience.

Self-Disclosure/Insight/Empathy

Given the emphasis on achievement rather than on relationships in the gender socialization for men, it is not surprising that deficits in relationship skills appear. One such deficit is in self-disclosure. In order to have relationships one must be able to reveal oneself to another. Yet sex role socialization holds up as the ideal for men the man who is strong, nonemotional, striving, achieving, better than others. Here the emphasis becomes revealing only part of the self to avoid the display of any "weaknesses," i.e., emotions. Consequently, men become skilled at avoiding self-disclosure. This serves them well in certain achievement tasks such as war and production. However, this avoidance of self-disclosure has its price, both for the psychological and physical well-being of men as well as for their relationships with others.

Men suffer personally from this constraint on expressing emotions by the self-perception that there is part of who they are that they must keep hidden. This "secret" part is perceived as being negative and not experienced by other normal men. Such thinking leads to decreased self-esteem and to the perception that others would misuse the information against them. Masking and monitoring of thoughts and feelings become the norm and consume physical and psychic energy. Some suggest that this results in stress and stress-related illnesses (Jourard, 1974).

Men's lack of self-disclosure also impairs their relationships with others. As Jourard (1974) points out, men's failure to self-disclose limits their insight into themselves and blocks their ability to empathize with others. Men do not reveal feelings and thus do not get feedback about those emotions or the perceptions that accompany those feelings. They often do not identify certain emotions in themselves. This lack of information about themselves leads them to misperceive the thoughts and feelings of others. Consequently their attempts to respond to another are often inappropriate or miss the mark. Jourard uses the self-disclosure process of therapy itself to illustrate this breakdown in insight and empathy due to the lack of self-disclosure. With increasing self-disclosure (in therapy), the client becomes more aware of feelings and more skilled in labeling them. With this increased insight into self comes the increased ability to identify the feelings and thoughts of others and to consider as real the differences and similarities in the other. This is empathy.

Feminist therapy's sex role analysis of this theme assists men in identifying the multiple ways they are limited by the failure to self-disclose. In supporting changes for men in this characteristic, the value of self-disclosure must be integrated with both achievement and relationship needs. Clients may need to learn to discriminate the type and timing of self-disclosure to use in the workplace and in social relationships. For change to occur, the male client needs to develop a support system with others, which affirms his growing abilities in self-disclosure and in empathizing with others. In feminist therapy this can be accomplished through the encouragement of either therapeutic groups or social change groups which are committed to this process goal.

Anger as Mask/Identifying All Emotions

While much has been written in the men's liberation field about men being socialized to avoid expressing emotions, less attention has been given to the reality that men are oversocialized to use the emotion of anger as a mask for other emotions. The issue is not so much that they do not express feelings, but that they usually express all feelings as anger. Women are socialized to be emotional and men are socialized to be angry. This has particularly serious consequences when this emotional pattern is paired with the behavioral pattern of violence (Ganley, 1981). While all men do not physically batter their partner or children or strangers, most misuse anger. When experiencing the full range of human emotions, such as happiness, sadness, fear, and anger, men tend to identify and express the negative emotions of sadness and fear in all their varying degrees as upset/anger. Consequently, guilt, anxiety, hurt, disappointment, etc., result in inappropriate angry expressions.

Tavris (1982) examines how culture shapes human emotions, specifically anger, and challenges the simplistic acceptance of human emotions as being innate. Men's expression of anger is in keeping with their socialization to be instrumental rather than relational. Anger is used by men to intimidate, to control, and to punish others – to accomplish a task. Women's expression of their emotions is in keeping with their relational priorities. Women express feelings to maintain relationships rather than to accomplish a task.

Given the centrality of this emotion in men's sex role socialization, anger is a major theme in feminist therapy with male clients. The writings of Brown and Liss-Levinson (1981), Forisha (1981) illustrate that the issue of anger is also a central theme for women in feminist therapy. However, this is true for very different reasons and the feminist therapist working with both male and female clients has to deal with the anger theme in very different ways according to the gender of her client. Anger in women is not synonymous with anger in men. Anger is not anger is not anger. A male client's experience and expression of anger must be routinely assessed by the therapist. Because of their gender socialization, men usually do not acknowledge that their anger or its accompanying violence may even be a problem. A routine assessment of anger reveals where an individual male's anger expression is on a continuum of misuse to abuse (Ganley, 1981). Furthermore, the assessment allows both therapist and client to recognize when crisis intervention strategies may be necessary, due to the lethal nature of the way the client is expressing anger. As anger is explored further as a theme in feminist therapy, the male client can learn to identify and to express constructively the other human emotions which lie beneath that mask of anger.

Communication Skills: Listening, Reflecting, and Facilitating

Given the devaluation of relationships in men's socialization, it is understandable that certain communication skills are overdeveloped and others overlooked. Men tend to have the communication skills necessary to their instrumental roles. They give orders, state demands, provide facts, interrupt others, and interrogate others clearly and easily. While there is a cultural myth that women are more verbal, the experience of men in mixed groups is that they dominate the conversation in both length, frequency, and volume of comments. What is evident is that men are verbal, but they use certain verbal skills more than others. They often appear blocked or tongue tied when attempting to use the communication skills that are more typically associated with developing and maintaining intimacy in relationships. In addition to the previously discussed poor self-disclosure skills, men have problems with the listening and facilitating skills due to their sex role socialization. When "listening," men often hear only a portion of the message before interpreting it and preparing their responses. They usually do not ask for clarification nor do they utilize the active listening skills of paraphrasing or reflecting. In groups they do not take the role of facilitating; they don't draw others out or summarize what has happened, or make process comments. They will be very verbal in conversations, but the content and types of comments reflect their gender socialization.

In feminist therapy with men, the issue of these communication deficits needs to be addressed to make the therapeutic process possible. Most therapies will involve the clients in increased self-disclosure and communication of emotions. What is important in feminist therapy with men is the awareness that the men also traditionally have deficits in listening and facilitating skills. Unless this is kept in mind, insight-oriented therapies can occur without assessing for deficits in listening or facilitating communication skills. As with other issues, feminist therapy is useful in identifying the source of the deficits while also promoting client responsibility for developing those skills. The emphasis in feminist therapy on two-way communications between the therapist and the client in individual therapy as well its emphasis on group therapy provide the male client an immediate laboratory for change. Male clients need encouragement to apply these skills in both intimate relationships and work relationships. For some clients, the skills have already been learned in management classes. Here the communication skills are taught to enhance being instrumental, not relational. Without a feminist analysis, the skills are utilized only in the typically masculine world of work and they are not generalized to personal relationships.

Models for Relationships: Mutuality vs. Dominance; Collaborative vs. Competitive

Although men's socialization devalues relationships, it does offer a model for work, social, and family relationships. This model is one of competition and dominance. Since men enter relationships to meet achievement needs, men seek a position of power or control in those relationships. Their primary model for relationships appears to be a hierarchical one. Since each relationship must have a one up and a one down, then each relationship is entered with some jostling for position. No man wants to be in the one-down position, since it becomes a threat to his ideal of being independent. In collegial and social relationships, men are competitive. Even so called male-male bonding develops out of a dominance model in which too often men bond with each other to be against another, e.g., team sports, all-male clubs to be "away from women," military units, gangs, etc.

A feminist analysis not only places value on relationships, but it offers new models for relationships: collaboration rather than competition; mutuality rather than dominance. In collaborative relationships, information, resources, and power are shared. Mutuality in relationships requires respect for the other as having equal worth to oneself as well as the respect for differences in resources. Developing mutuality in work, social, and family relationships becomes a process of maximizing cooperation rather than competition, of giving rather than hoarding, of sharing oneself rather than withholding oneself, and of valuing the differences of the other rather than defending against those differences. Each of the above becomes a theme for reframing many of the issues presented by male clients in feminist therapy.

Nurturing: The Self and The Other

Even though the androcentric model sets a standard for men to show limited emotions and to be independent, men as human beings have emotional and intimacy needs. In the development and maintenance of their sense of self, they, like women, need affirmation and acceptance. Typically they look for and expect this nurturing to come from women but not from men. There are various theories to explain this: the reality of women as the primary nurturers in childhood establishes this pattern, the association of nurturing with emotions and relationships means nurturing is women's work, etc.

What is important in feminist therapy with men is to look at the consequences of this expectation of woman as being the only nurturer: Men do not learn to do this for themselves or for others. Nurturing involves being aware of and responding to emotional needs. In self-nurturing, it is the nourishing of one's spirit. In therapy the male client needs to be challenged to do this for himself. Like the female client in feminist therapy, the male client needs to accept the importance of one's own emotions and the responsibility for attending to them. Unlike the female client, who has been socialized to nurture others and has only to learn to apply this to herself, the male client has to be taught basic nurturing skills. In addition to nurturing oneself, men need to learn to nurture others. To break that self-defeating cycle of always looking to women to do nurturing, men must be expected to give and receive nurturing with other men. In addition they need to develop skills in providing nurturing to women without immediate demand for reciprocity. Men's nurturing skills need to be developed in a variety of relational contexts: work, social, and intimate.

Consensual vs. Nonconsensual/Coercive Sex

Gender socialization has a major impact on men's sexuality. A primary operative assumption in male heterosexuality is that the male take the initiative, be dominant, and overcome the expected resistance of a female partner.[1] The expectation of the female is that she "says 'no' when she means 'yes.'" This expectation can become erotically charged for the male, so that his erotic interest becomes dependent upon the "conquest." Operating with a nonconsensual model of sexual interaction bypasses the need for listening, negotiation and mutual choice, and disregards the lack of interest or ambivalence of the partner. In addition, this sexual interactive style is counterproductive for the male because it emphasizes his sexual performance expectations while it minimizes genuine relational interaction and the benefits of sexual intimacy (Fortune, 1982).

The impact of sex role socialization on sexuality is illustrated by the continuum of resulting dysfunctions. For some men this gender socialization puts them at risk to be sex offenders. David Finkelhor (1984) discusses traditional masculinity and its relationship to child sexual abuse as other authors have done with its relationship to sexual violence against adults, i.e., primarily women (Groth, 1979; Russell, 1982). With male clients the therapeutic issues of sexuality range from the nonconsensual, to the coercive, to violently abusive. A feminist analysis challenges men to develop consensual, relational models for sexuality.

Acceptance of "No": Disappointment vs. Anger

A recurring theme in feminist therapy with men revolves around their perception (real or imagined) of being turned down, hearing no, or being rejected by family members or women. Their typical response is one of anger and a desire to punish the other. And for many this desire to punish is acted upon. This response in part stems from the previously discussed issue of identifying all emotions as anger. However, this issue is also associated with men's socialization to the concept of entitlement in relationships with women or family members. Men expect that things will go their way in such relationships. When they do not, they perceive the other as intentionally harming them and therefore deserving of punishment. Women on the other hand typically experience those no's as a rupture in the relationship and respond with hurt and attempts to re-establish the relationship. Given the nature of adult-adult relationships and family life, there are bound to be many no's and rejections in the course developing intimacy. After all women are adults with their own needs and wants, and relationships of mutuality have to be negotiated. Too often in therapy men's statements of anger about rejection are validated without exploring men's socialization to entitlement. In order to better meet their intimacy needs, men need resocialization to accept no's from women and family members, to experience disappointment rather than anger at those times, and to perceive those no's as being acts of autonomy rather than as acts of attack against them.

Noncoercive Problem Solving

Due to cultural norms of masculinity which socialize men to be solely instrumental rather than instrumental *and* relational, men regard control, coercion, and violence as the only tools available to accomplish problem solving. This is a natural outcome of the overemphasis on achievement to the detriment of relationships. If relationships have equal value to accomplishments, more attention would be given to the problem-solving skills of listening, brainstorming, negotiation, and compromise in order to sustain relationships. The increased interest in mediation, "yes-yes" negotiation, and other such nonadversarial models of problem solving is in part due to the recognition that while coercion or violence may work to accomplish an immediate task, it destroys the relationship in the process.

In feminist therapy, the teaching of any noncoercive, problem-solving skills attends not only to the skills themselves but also to their function, i.e., relationship maintenance. Otherwise the acquisition of these new skills (assertion, mediation, etc.) can simply further enhance the client's ability to control or coerce others. For example, teaching men assertion skills too often has simply increased their ability to exert power over others in order to achieve their goals, disregarding others' needs. In feminist therapy, assertion training would always be viewed as a means to the end of enhancing and sustaining relationship through good communication.

Attitudes and Beliefs About Women

Just as the androcentric model of mental health has misled men in their understanding of themselves, it also misleads them in their understanding of women. Feminist therapy on this issue with men involves re-education of men about who women are now and what their potentials are as adults. This re-education requires the client to utilize resources of books, films, music made by women about women, as well as to listen with a "new ear" to their experiences of the women in their lives. Obviously feminist therapy has a unique contribution to make to men dealing with these issues since the feminist therapist herself has the phenomenological experience of being female, has the knowledge about women in general, and is one model of the androgynous adult embodied as woman.

PROCESS ISSUES IN FEMINIST THERAPY WITH MALE CLIENTS

There are certain process issues typically associated with feminist therapy that have to be reconsidered in light of a male client population. Reconsidering these issues enables the feminist therapist to avoid their becoming obstacles to the therapeutic goals of the male clients. The two primary process issues are the use of therapist as model and the use of power in the therapy. These are complex issues in any type of therapy and it is beyond the scope of this article to delineate them in detail. However, this introductory discussion of them is a reminder that feminist therapy with men is not the same as feminist therapy with women.

Therapist as Model

Therapist as model has been accepted as being important in many therapeutic encounters and particularly so in feminist therapy with women. Here, the feminist therapist as model directly demonstrates with the female client the reality that the personal is political, that being female is valuable, and that growth in the direction of autonomy does not necessarily result in loss of relationships. The client is both taught and affirmed by the therapist as model.

In feminist therapy with men, therapist as model shifts in somewhat different directions, since the feminist therapist is female. Here the therapist can provide modeling of specifics skills, such as communication skills, nurturing skills, and nonviolent, problem-solving skills. However, there are limits to such modeling because males also need to experience other men who have these skills. Furthermore, there is a danger that modeling of certain skills by a female therapist will reinforce a male client's self-defeating cycle of relying solely on women to provide these skills. Obviously these limits can be overcome by doing feminist therapy with men in groups where men can learn from each other's positive gains or by referring the client to a profeminist therapist. Another strategy would be to raise this limitation directly in the therapy and to expect the client to build male support networks for the changes he is seeking. This benefits the client in moving the issues out of the rarefied atmosphere of the therapy sessions and into his daily world.

Female therapist as model provides substantive learnings for men in feminist therapy. First, the client experiences a woman as an androgynous adult who is competent, independent, rational, and instrumental while also demonstrating the more typically feminine qualities of being relational and nurturing which challenges and rectifies the client's sexist attitudes about women. Secondly, the therapy sessions for a male client can be the laboratory where he learns to discard the seductive or dominating interactive patterns of relating to women and to replace them with the communication skills necessary to relate to women as authorities or as valued peers, depending on the circumstances. Gender of therapist is salient to the process issue of therapist as model.

Power

To provide feminist therapy for men, the therapist must be cognizant of a variety of power issues that are manifest in the therapeutic process. Douglas (1985) discusses power and feminist therapy by highlighting the multiple issues related to power: the different bases of power (reward, coercive, informational, expert, legitimate), the inequality inherent in the client-therapist roles in therapy, the use of direct and indirect power, and gender as power. In her discussion she accepts the feminist therapy principle of minimizing the power differential between therapist and client and suggests that implementing this principle must take into consideration all the power issues she raises.

In feminist therapy with women the therapeutic goal is to equalize the power differential between client and therapist by a variety of process strategies (demystifying therapy, psychoeducational approaches, etc.) as well as by the use of particular techniques (having the client call the therapist by the first name, the use of touch, placement of office furniture, etc.). Careful thought is given to these issues because women generally enter therapy feeling very powerless. This powerlessness is at least in part due to their experiences in a culture that devalues women and ascribes differential power solely based on gender.

In feminist therapy with men, the situation is different. Due to sex role socialization, male clients will often assume a position of power over the female therapist even if they feel powerless at that time in other areas of their life. This assumption of power is based on their gender vis-à-vis the female therapist. Even though the roles in therapy between client and therapist would give greater weight to the therapist, the gender power differential is more salient to the client. Utilizing strategies prematurely to de-emphasize therapist's power based on role may inadvertently foster this inappropriate client response and block therapeutic change. It may be more effective with certain male clients to expect them to use titles or other standards of behavior to establish and reinforce the female therapist as authority, i.e., to indicate the differential in power based on role and to de-emphasize power inequality based on gender.

Another therapeutic practice which needs to be reconsidered in light of power and gender is the use of touch in feminist therapy with men. The use of certain kinds of touch can establish power differentials or equality. In feminist therapy with women a hug or touch is used to convey warmth, support, and a sense of being present to the other. These are done in the context of minimizing the power differential between female therapist and female client. In feminist therapy with men these types of touch must be used carefully because of the way men have been socialized to sexualize touch between men and women and/or to use touch from a base of having power over another. One type of touch that restructures power issues with the male client is the handshake initiated by the female therapist. It conveys a feminist therapist's assumption that therapy is both a relational and instrumental process. It also conveys to men that the woman as therapist is there to share equal power with men but not to be intimidated (fear of touch) or to be seduced (sexual touch).

Feminist therapists with male clients must also deal with their own issues of having power over men. In a significant number of situations involving therapy with men (sex offenders, batterers, etc.), it is therapeutic for the client to experience women as having power over them. The major therapeutic issue in therapy with offenders is teaching accountability. That requires having the power to hold the person accountable and being willing to use that power. The feminist therapist who prematurely attempts to equalize the power between the male client and herself can prevent change from occurring. Clearly feminist therapy with men requires a re-evaluation of the practices and procedures generally associated with feminist therapy with women.

CONCLUSION

It is difficult at times to discuss concepts of feminist therapy with male clients without the appearance of reducing the topic to simplistic generalities. It can begin to sound like a paraphrase of comedian Bill Cosby's comment on his 20-year marriage ("my wife has given me a machoectomy''): doing feminist therapy with men is performing a machoectomy. However, the reality is that the mental health of all persons is severely damaged by sex role socialization and sexism. An important contribution to changing this reality is feminist therapy with male clients. To provide this, feminist therapists are called upon to rethink their understanding of feminist therapy, of men as clients, and of themselves. This chapter is one part of that ongoing process.

ACKNOWLEDGEMENTS

The author wishes to acknowledge the substantive contributions to this article by Marie M. Fortune and Laura S. Brown.

NOTE

1. Some of these comments also apply to homosexuality as well, but there are some differences. In order to avoid doing injustice to these variances, space requires the author to limit her comments to heterosexual males.

REFERENCES

Bem, S. (1974). The measurement of psychological androgyny. *Journal of Consulting & Clinical Psychology*, *42*, 155-162.

Broverman, I., Vogel, S., Broverman, D., Clarkson, F., & Rosenkrantz, P. (1972). Sex-role stereotypes: A current appraisal. *Journal of Social Issues*, *28*, 59-78.

Brown, L., & Liss-Levinson, N. (1981). Feminist Therapy I. In R. Corsini (Ed.), *Handbook of innovative psychotherapies*, (pp. 299-314). New York: Wiley-Interscenic Publication.

Brown, L. (1984). Feminist assessment and therapy. Workshop conducted at the Washington State Psychological Association Continuing Education Program.

Cammaert, L. & Larsen, C. Feminist frameworks of psychotherapy. In M. Dutton-Douglas & L. Walker (Eds.), *Feminist psychotherapies: Integration of therapeutic and feminist systems* (pp. 12-36). Norwood, NJ: Ablex Publishing Co.

Chesler, P. (1972). *Women and madness*. New York: Doubleday.

Cox, S. (Ed.). (1982). *Female psychology – The emerging self*. New York: St. Martin's.

Douglas, M. (1985). The role of power in feminist therapy: A reformulation. In

L. Rosewater & L. Walker (Eds.), *Handbook of Feminist therapy: Women's issues in psychotherapy*, (pp. 241-249). New York: Springer.

Ehrenreich, B. (1983). *The hearts of men*. Garden City: Anchor Press/Doubleday.

Fasteau, M. (1974). *The male machine*. New York: McGraw-Hill.

Finkelhor, D. (1984). *Child sexual abuse*. New York: Free Press.

Fisher, K. (1986). Demographics beckon young to maturing field. *APA Monitor*, *17*, 18-19.

Forisha, B. (1981). Feminist Therapy II. In R. Corsini (Ed.), *Handbook of innovative psychotherapies*, (pp. 315-332). New York: Wiley-Interscenic Publications.

Fortune, M. (1982). *Sexual violence: The unmentionable sin*. New York: Pilgrim Press.

Ganley, A. (1981). *Court mandated treatment for men who batter*. Washington, DC: Center for Women Policy Studies.

Gilligan, C. (1982). *In a different voice*. Cambridge: Harvard University Press.

Goldberg, H. (1976). *The hazards of being male*. New York: Signet Books.

Groth, A. N., & Birnbaum, H. J. (1979). *Men who rape*. New York: Plenum Press.

Jourard, S. (1974). Some lethal aspects of the male role. In J. Pleck & J. Sawyer (Eds.), *Men and masculinity*, (pp. 21-29). Englewood Cliffs, NJ: Prentice-Hall.

Kaplan, A. (1976). Androgyny as a model of mental health for women: From theory to therapy. In S. Kaplan & J. Bean (Eds.), *Beyond sex-role stereotypes: Readings toward a psychology of androgyny*. Boston: Little, Brown.

McGoldrick, M., Pearce, J., & Giordano, J. (Eds.). (1982). *Ethnicity and family therapy*. New York: Guilford Press.

Miller, J. (1976). *Toward a new psychology of women*. Boston: Beacon Press.

Pleck, J., & Sawyer, J. (Eds.). (1974). *Men and masculinity*. Englewood Cliffs, NJ: Prentice-Hall.

Rawlings, E., & Carter, D. (Eds.). (1977). *Psychotherapy for women: Treatment toward equality*. Springfield, IL: Charles C Thomas.

Rosewater, L., & Walker, L. E. (Eds.). (1985). *Handbook of feminist therapy: Women's issues in psychotherapy*. New York: Springer.

Russell, D. (1982). *Rape in marriage*. New York: Macmillan.

Schwartz, B., & Disch, R. (1970). *White racism*. New York: Laurel Edition.

Sennett, R., & Cobb, J. (1972). *The hidden injuries of class*. New York: Vintage Books.

Tavris, C. (1982). *Anger–The misunderstood emotion*. New York: Simon & Schuster.

Welch, D. (1985). *Macho isn't enough! Family man in a liberated world*. Atlanta: John Knox.

Zilbergeld, B. (1978). *Male Sexuality–A guide to sexual fulfillment*. Boston: Little, Brown.

Men in Therapy: Exploring Feminist-Informed Alternatives

Anna Dienhart
Judith Myers Avis

SUMMARY. Conventional family therapy models tend to reinforce traditional gender-role socialization in subtle but pernicious ways. A feminist approach to work with men requires therapists to improve their conceptual and perceptual skills by becoming knowledgeable about men's issues and by clarifying personal values concerning the social construction of masculinity. A feminist approach to working with men in families is presented which invites therapists to build a flexible and broad repertoire of skills drawing from several models and to carefully scrutinize interventions for sexist meta-messages. This feminist-informed framework offers therapists working with men considerable room to maneuver within a framework of respect, validation, empowerment, and recognition of the larger social context.

The first waves of the feminist critique of family therapy brought gender into our conscious awareness by focusing our attention on women's experience in families and in family therapy. As we have progressed further in our exploration of gender, however, it has become surprisingly and often painfully clear that the real needs of men have also been disregarded in our traditional conceptualizations of families and of change. This new awareness is somewhat startling since the feminist critique has emphasized the many ways

Anna Dienhart, MSc, is Sessional Lecturer, Department of Family Studies, University of Guelph, Guelph, Ontario, Canada N1G 2W1, and a Marriage and Family Therapist at Guelph-Wellington Counselling Center, Guelph, Ontario. Judith Myers Avis, PhD, is Associate Professor in the Marriage and Family Therapy Program, Department of Family Studies, University of Guelph, Guelph, Ontario, Canada N1G 2W1.

in which male cultural privilege is maintained and reinforced in therapy. With deeper examination, however, we see that family therapy may be at risk of failing men as badly as it has failed women. By failing to challenge their misuse of power and position, and by failing to address their frequently ineffectual emotional and interactional patterns, family therapy may actually prevent men from changing. This article examines some dimensions of male socialization that impact negatively on male development and adult functioning, and that commonly underlie men's difficulties in relationships. It is contended that these issues and needs must be explored in therapy in order to help men change. The article critiques the ways in which five frequently used models of family therapy typically work with men, and highlights some ways in which these models risk perpetuating traditional male roles. Finally, a feminist framework for working with men is outlined, including suggestions for adapting from several family therapy models interventions which offer promise for facilitating change with men.

MALE SOCIALIZATION

> The human animal is divided into two genders, not really very different from one another until one is taught from birth how to be Masculine and the other is taught how to be Feminine. Most people have been taught their gender stereotype so well that they don't remember learning it and assume it is inherent and innate, as if they came into the world wrapped in either a pink or blue blanket, and everything flowed naturally from there. (Pittman, 1985, p. 24)

The social construction of "masculinity" results in particular difficulties for men both in their own adult development and in their family and social relationships. This gender socialization has such a profound impact on the experience of being male that we must examine and understand it in some depth before we can hope to be effective in our therapy with men. The masculine mystique (Doyle, 1983; Farrell, 1974, 1986; Goldberg, 1976, 1987; McGill, 1985; O'Neil, 1981) prevalent in our patriarchal society helps to explain the pervasiveness of sex-role stereotypes. This mystique holds that since men are biologically stronger than women, masculinity is the superior, more valued form of gender identity. The essence of masculinity is anti-feminine: traits of power, dominance, competition, and control are essential to masculinity, while the feminine traits of vulnerability, emotionality, and feelings are to be avoided by any 'real man.' Rational-logical thought is adopted as the superior form of communication; sexual prowess is deemed a primary means to prove one's masculinity; and, man as 'breadwinner' values work and career above family and relationships.

Masculine and feminine mystiques (Brannon, 1976; Brownmiller, 1984; Doyle, 1983; Freidan, 1964; Miller, 1976; Rubin, 1983) promote sexism and make for a world of impossible relationships between men and women, men and men, and women and women. The impossibility of creating satisfying relationships out of these dichotomous gender-stereotypes brings increasing numbers of people into therapy as "we increasingly confront a world full of half people, angrily living out their gender stereotype" (Pittman, 1985, p. 26).

When we work with men in family therapy, their socialized values around relationships and family are of particular interest. While all of the major tenets of the masculine mystique affect a man's values regarding relationships and family, a few especially need to be attended to in therapy.

Separateness

Chodorow (1978) and Dinnerstein (1976) have characterized the core of male socialization as a process of separating from the primary caregiver, who is almost always female. This separation process stresses differences rather than similarities, as boys are taught to leave their mothers (and female control) to enter the world outside the home. The socialization of girls, on the other hand, is a process of remaining connected to the primary same-sex caregiver, leading to a female identity that is relational in orientation. Chodorow (1978) and Dinnerstein (1976) suggest that these gender differences in the process of separating from the primary caregiver typically leave men with a deficit in the relational capacities and skills which their female counterparts have developed.

According to Osherson (1986), male separation involves a search for male models upon which to base a masculine identity. Fathers are the most obvious male model, but as Osherson (1986) poignantly asks, "Who is father?" (p. 6). He points out another side of the separateness dilemma, noting that as men separate from their mothers and look to their fathers, they "often misidentify with [their] fathers, crippling [their] identities as men. Distortions and myths shape normal men's pictures of their fathers, based on the uneasy peripheral place fathers occupied in their own homes" (Osherson, 1986, p. 6). An internalized sense of separateness extends beyond a man's relationship with the original primary caregiver and is confounded by his struggle with an introject of a "wounded father . . . a conflicted inner sense of masculinity rooted in men's experience of their fathers as rejecting, incompetent, or absent" (Osherson, 1986, p. 6). Males take this socialized sense of separateness, superiority, and "submission to the requirements of production" (Chodorow, 1978, p. 180) to their interactions at work, in recreation, and, most importantly, with their families.

Rationality

The over-valuation of rational-logical thought which is central to traditional masculinity precludes interpersonal communication that emphasizes feelings, emotions, intuition, and physical contact. According to the masculine mystique, emotions and vulnerability are signs of femininity, and men who seek help through emotional expressiveness are perceived as weak, dependent, and immature. Since emotional expression, which can reveal inner fears and conflicts, is frequently construed as evidence of instability and unmanliness, many men have considerable difficulty in therapy as well as in their relational lives with self-disclosure, with recognizing and expressing feelings, and with dealing with the complexities of interpersonal life.

Competence

A prominent characteristic of the masculine mystique is the prescribed preoccupation with success, accomplishments and eminence as means to substantiate one's masculinity and personal value

(Doyle, 1983; O'Neil, 1981). Men are supposed to know what to do, how to do it, and be able to make it happen. Any task or event can be turned into an opportunity to prove one's masculinity. Succeeding once is usually not enough. The goal is to accept all challenges and accumulate successes, each bigger than the last. It is success in the world outside, as opposed to in the family, that really counts, so that family obligations are often experienced as role-overload and secondary to work and career (Doyle, 1983; O'Neil, 1981).

Control, Power, and Competitiveness

> Control implies to regulate, restrain, and have others or situations under one's command. Power is to obtain authority, influence, or ascendancy over others. Competition is an act of striving against others to gain something or the comparison of self with others to establish one's superiority in a given situation. (O'Neil, 1981, p. 207)

Men are typically socialized to fit into the larger socio-cultural context, with dominance, control and power essential to proving one's masculinity, and competition being the means to obtaining each. Often control and power are seen as goals in themselves, with all other aspects of interaction and relatedness subordinated to them. When men have difficulty giving up power, control, and competitiveness in relationships, their ability to relate or achieve intimacy is seriously hampered (O'Neil, 1981; Pleck & Sawyer, 1974; Rice, 1978). They lose their ability to be self-aware, spontaneous, honest, and emotionally expressive because of the need to constantly monitor and control the relationship (Nichols, 1975). Family therapists must be acutely aware of these four characteristics of "masculinity" in order to understand and intervene in socialized male behavior.

CRITIQUE OF FAMILY THERAPY PRACTICE: HOW FIVE MODELS WORK WITH MEN

Since systems theory rests on the central tenets of neutrality, complementarity, and circularity, until recently the field has not paid specific attention to how men and women are treated differentially in particular therapeutic models. While most models of family therapy are not explicitly sexist, their therapeutic applications may be. The feminist critique has focused our attention on how traditional gender-roles for women are often subtly reinforced in family therapy. This critique also allows us to examine how family therapy inadvertently reinforces and perpetuates traditional gender-roles and privilege for men. The following discussion examines the ways in which five different family therapy models typically work with men.

Structural Family Therapy

Structural family therapy uses a highly directive-prescriptive style that "accurately and perceptively addresses family organizational-transactional dimensions" (Gurman & Klein, 1980, p. 173), but may completely fail to redress stereotypic gender-roles which lock the family in dysfunctional patterns. Most notably, as structural family therapy restructures the family by bringing father in from the periphery, it can reinforce the male sense of power and hierarchy and, in effect, deify his presence. Hare-Mustin (1978) has noted that Minuchin "sees himself as modeling the male executive functions, forming alliances, most typically with the father, and through competition, rule-setting, and direction, demanding that father resume control of the family and exert leadership" (p. 184). Gurman and Klein (1980) point out that while involving father in this manner strengthens generational boundaries, it may also have "unexamined, negative secondary effects" (p. 173). Haig and Avis (1988) found numerous examples in the family therapy literature of husbands/fathers being brought in as experts to teach their wives how to do something properly, but not a single example of a mother's expertise being used to enhance a father's role repertoire. Seldom is father challenged about his heretofore peripheral role, which essentially leaves a void that the wife/mother fills with her nurturing and concern.

Strategic Therapy

Brief strategic therapy models, such as those stemming from the MRI school, also tend to be highly directive and prescriptive. Their minimalist approach, which is goal-orientated and symptom-focussed, seeks to change problematic behaviors by interrupting clearly delineated transactional sequences. Luepnitz (1988) points out that therapists using brief therapy models tend "to show even less interest than other family therapists in understanding the family as an institution. . . . rather they plunge into questions of how to 'create change' as expeditiously as possible" (p. 76). Strategic therapists do not usually overtly reinforce men's roles, but the mere fact that they focus on treating 'the customer' often means a therapist does not value the inclusion of all family members to the same extent as do therapists working within other family models. This approach may reinforce the cultural message that the family is woman's work and often leaves the distant father unchallenged (Luepnitz, 1988). Although strategic prescriptions do not necessarily reinforce gender stereotyped behaviors, the potential is evident to exploit stereotypical behavior and to reinforce male dominance in order to induce change.

Behavioral Family Therapy

Behavioral Family Therapy (BFT) is based on operant learning principles, social exchange theory and cognitive psychology. BFT is usually highly directive and teaches communication skills to enhance the development of mutually acceptable problem-solving. The skill focus of BFT can inadvertently reinforce the man's instrumental functioning and his stereotypic attitudes and behaviors by its reliance on 'neutral' interventions that focus on trade-offs between the couple to change their interactive patterns. Gurman and Klein (1980, 1984) and Jacobson (1983) alert us to the possibility of reinforcing traditional beliefs by taking requests for changes in behavior at face value. Citing an example where the wife was asked to trade sexual favors for the new home furnishings she wanted, Gurman and Klein (1980) point out "the extent to which a 'hands-off' stance regarding personal values about intimate relationships" can reinforce the man's notion that sexuality equals caring and can perpetuate "exceedingly damaging and demeaning notions about how a woman 'ought' to behave, and what they 'ought' to do, to gain power and influence in marriage" (p. 178). Margolin, Fernandez, Talovic and Onorato (1983) also note the potential for BFT to reinforce stereotypic gender-roles and beliefs. They alert us to the subtleties of the therapist attending to the husband on household financial matters, and to the wife on matters of childcare. Further, the assessment instruments utilized in BFT implicitly assume that household tasks are the responsibility of the woman and that the husband is being cooperative and generous if he helps out (Margolin et al., 1983). Assessing outcome with such criteria leads the couple and the therapist to celebrate apparent changes, while the necessary second-order changes—that is, "who defines the relationship and how its rules are made" (Goldner, 1985a, p. 34)—are not tackled, leaving the man 'in charge' of the family.

Functional Family Therapy

Functional Family Therapy (FFT) draws on theory and technique from two major models—systems theory and behaviorism (Barton & Alexander, 1981). It is reported to be a "relatively well-developed, well-researched and, apparently, effective approach to intervening with delinquent families" (Avis, 1985, p. 128). FFT places particular emphasis on understanding behavior in the relational context, with individuals seen as "simultaneously creat[ing] an interpersonal environment and respond[ing] to that environment" (Barton & Alexander, 1981, p. 407). FFT assumes that all behavior is purposive and adaptive, with the primary functions of behavior being to promote interpersonal closeness and intimacy ("merging functions") or to promote separateness and distance ("distancing functions"). The function of behavior is determined not by the actual behavior, but by examining the outcome, which may be quite different from the verbalized need (Avis, 1985).

As with Behavioral Family Therapy, FFT may perpetuate traditional instrumental behaviors in the husband/father without supplementing his role repertoire with some relational behaviors, thus reinforcing complementary patterns between men and women rather than helping families to learn non-stereotypic behaviors. Since FFT affirms whatever functions are present in the family and in the marital dyad, traditional, gender-socialized relational patterns go unchallenged. Thus, FFT may actually work against the development of other adaptive behaviors, such as emotional expressiveness and empathy in men (Avis, 1985) and assertiveness and mature independence in women.

Transgenerational Therapy

The cornerstone of a transgenerational model is Bowen's Family Systems Theory (Bowen, 1978). This theory is based on the concept of the family as an intergenerational emotional relationship system with forces pulling members toward togetherness and opposing forces pulling toward individuality which tend to be transferred from one generation to the next. According to Bowen's theory, the degree to which a person is 'self-differentiated' is based on his/her ability to discriminate intellectual from emotional functioning. The characteristics of a healthy adult clearly reflect traditional male values: a highly functional adult is described as being more goal-oriented than relationship oriented, having clear boundaries, and valuing intellectual reasoning over intuition or emotional 'hunches' (Hare-Mustin, 1978; Lerner, 1988b).

Family-of-origin therapy that stems from Bowen's Family Systems Theory tends to be directive, calm, objective and detached. The therapist as "coach . . . is an active expert who helps the individual players and the team (family) perform to the best of their abilities" (Goldenberg & Goldenberg, 1985, p. 175). While the therapist may acknowledge that each end of the differentiation continuum -- emotional functioning versus intellectual functioning -- is unbalanced by itself, the theory tends to value 'masculine' behaviors. The bias in the model may lead the therapist to place higher value on the man's pattern of 'de-selfing' as he conforms to cultural pressures to over-function "through relinquishing the experience and expression of dependency, passivity, vulnerability, and other so-called weakness" (Lerner, 1988b, p. 53). That men are "characteristically under-functioners when it comes to attunement with the emotional components of human experience, and the ability to rely on co-operative, rather than aggressive/competitive modes of interaction'' (Lerner, 1988b, p. 53) is seldom, if ever, mentioned in the therapeutic literature, outside of the feminist critique. The Bowenian approach seems to assume that men can easily learn affective connection, ignoring the socio-cultural context of men's traditional alienation from their families and the attendant constraints that make it hard for them to connect or reconnect.

A FEMINIST FRAMEWORK FOR WORKING WITH MEN

Feminist family therapy draws techniques from a variety of extant family therapy approaches, but does so with full awareness of the possible gender biases hidden in these techniques. In assessing theory and therapeutic techniques, a feminist lens emphasizes the social context as a prime determinant of behavior and as a fundamental organizing principle in families (Goldner, 1985b; Goodrich, Rampage, Ellman & Halstead, 1988; McGoldrick, Anderson & Walsh, 1988; Walters, Carter, Papp & Silverstein, 1988; Wheeler, Avis, Miller & Chaney, 1988). A feminist conceptualization of a problem identifies the gender message and social constructs that serve to condition behavior, beliefs, and family roles (Walters et al., 1988) and uses this analysis to formulate interventions that will both challenge and free family members from constricted, stereotypical patterns of behavior and beliefs (Goodrich et al., 1988). A common feature of most feminist approaches to family therapy is the creation of a process that increases family members' sense of having options for themselves and that develops greater reciprocity among family members (Goodrich et al., 1988). Awareness of the implications of gender socialization (especially the impact of family being 'women's work') leads feminist family therapists to confront familial and social barriers to change and to support each client's right to design his or her life outside of culturally prescribed roles (Walters et al., 1988; Wheeler et al., 1988).

Feminist approaches to family therapy tend to emphasize reframing and relabeling techniques to shift the conceptual or emotional perspective on a family problem, while stressing action and behavioral change (Wheeler et al., 1988). While changing presenting behaviors may be a centerpiece of feminist-informed therapy, behavioral change alone is not considered sufficient: the power structures underlying those behaviors must also be addressed. Feminist approaches to family therapy specifically explore the family's division of labor, power, and rewards, and address the inequity of gender arrangements (Goodrich et al., 1988). Inviting the family to change includes supporting each family member in maximizing her/his individuality and autonomy, while sharing more or less equally in accommodating or subordinating individual needs (Wheeler et al., 1988). Feminist therapists recognize the tendency of traditional models to help the family system at the expense of the individual, and therefore work to expand both individual and system role opportunities by addressing personal choice and interpersonal negotiation in a collaborative framework (Wheeler et al., 1988). Expanding individual role repertoires involves giving specific attention to "building, for both men and women, traditional womanly skills—such as empathy, listening, support and nurturing—and traditional manly skills—such as giving clear directives, taking authoritative stances, and displaying competence" (Goodrich et al., 1988, p. 29).

Change is conceptualized as a process of generating alternative behaviors and expanding belief structures beyond traditional sex-role stereotypes (Goodrich et al., 1988; Walters et al., 1988; Wheeler et al., 1988). An interactive therapeutic environment facilitates change: the therapist does not simply instruct clients in new behaviors and attitudes, clients *experience* themselves differently in this context. Goodrich et al. (1988) tell us that clients "first recognize the incongruence between customary expectation and what they now experience, then the therapist helps them integrate these new behaviors" (p. 25). Further, therapeutic outcome is broadened beyond typical first-order (behavioral) change to encompass second-order change (redressing the rule structure). Feminists see therapy as a moral endeavor (Goodrich et al., 1988) in which the therapist exposes the political and socio-cultural influences on the personal and interpersonal lives of the client(s) (Wheeler et al., 1988).

While feminist approaches to family therapy have focussed on issues and strategies to overturn the disadvantaged position of women, the underlying philosophy and structure of a feminist framework is particularly well suited to redressing traditional ways of thinking about and working with men. Feminist family therapists use socio-cultural variables to inform their therapy and to both understand and challenge the special privileges and burdens of men in families, particularly those issues related to control and power. Although addressing men's traditional use and abuse of their power is most obvious in work with abusive men (see Bograd, 1984, 1986a, 1986b; Pressman, 1987, 1989; Wheeler, 1989, 1990), it is an issue in therapy with most men. Feminists therapists assess behaviors and attitudes for their blatant and subtle power plays, and point out the destructive consequences to self and others of maintaining these learned behaviors. Men are encouraged to recognize coercive and illegitimate forms of power and are taught to use alternative ways to express their needs and their caring.

EXPLORING FEMINIST-INFORMED ALTERNATIVES FOR WORKING WITH MEN

A feminist lens enables us to adapt tools and techniques from traditional schools of family therapy and to use them effectively in working with men. Although the following analysis will address males in general terms, it is not intended to suggest that all men are similar and that what works with one man will work with all. Obviously, there are many different types of men and the therapeutic approach must be modified to consider life stage, class, education, and ethno-cultural background. The following section will review several models of therapy for specific tools and techniques which are particularly well suited, or can be modified, to a feminist approach for working with men in family therapy.

Structural Models

Minuchin's (1974) structural model offers a feminist-informed family therapist many tools for working with men. The notions of boundaries and subsystems are particularly useful for conceptualizing men's individualistic and competitive positions in society and in families and for encouraging men to separate their own needs and responsibilities from the needs and responsibilities of others. Structural interventions can also facilitate a man's exploration of being separate *and* connected. Negotiating time and activities as a family, as part of a marital dyad, and as an individual can help a man clarify his personal boundary and encourage a new kind of connectedness while affirming his individuality.

The parental subsystem offers a particularly powerful conceptual framework for inviting the man to increase his activities and responsibilities in the family while minimizing the hierarchy between father and mother. Instead of putting father in charge of the family rules and implicitly subordinating the woman, a feminist-informed structural therapist can facilitate a mutual sharing of parental responsibilities. Further, structural therapy techniques help men distinguish between parental and marital responsibilities and behaviors, enabling them to see their multifaceted roles within the family. Roles, rules and hierarchy can be examined against the backdrop of patriarchal socialization and explored further for their appropriateness and functionality. Alternative roles, rules, and hierarchy can be delineated, examined and experimented with.

Structural interventions within the framework of a feminist perspective have been proposed as particularly powerful in working with special populations, especially family violence and incest. Wheeler (1989) advocates initial physical separation of the offender from the victim and the family. From the feminist perspective, the removal of the offender from the family is both structural and political in that it is a clear message about who has the problem and the responsibility for change. Further, physical separation allows the family to experience a restructuring of interactive patterns without the dominance of the offender (Wheeler, 1989).

Strategic and Systemic Models

The dividing line between the application of brief strategic models and systemic models is no longer clearcut. Several features of both approaches can be integrated in a feminist framework to challenge behaviors without unduly threatening the man. From the brief strategic models, the goal-orientation and symptom-focused approach of these models is likely to appeal to some types of men, thus creating a context for behavioral changes that can be followed by a shift in attitude. The directness of attacking a problem fits within the common male approach to problem-solving and to strategizing, while the directiveness and expert stance of the therapist may appeal to some men's bias toward structure and hierarchy. More 'indirect' intervention approaches, such as restraining change, symptom prescriptions, positive connotation and reframes, may avert power battles between the therapist and the male client.

The tools and techniques introduced by White (1988a, 1988b, 1988c; White & Epston, 1989, 1990) and Epston (1986) blend strategic and systemic perspectives. They are grounded in an empowering, respectful, creative approach that puts the client(s) in charge of change. White's approach shifts the focus of 'the problem' from within the self to an external position with a personality of its own. In this way, the problem is separated from the person or system, heightening a client's sense of control. Change is effected by creative questioning in search for "unique outcomes" and by requiring behavioral adjustments. Unique outcomes are those instances when the client was not oppressed by the problem; that is, moments when the client had more influence over the problem than the problem had over the client. This approach, which captures Bateson's notions of drawing distinctions and emphasizing differences that make a difference, invites the client to capitalize on his own resourcefulness, discovered by acknowledging those instances when he already exercised some control over the problem.

This therapeutic approach helps men expand their self-concept beyond socially constricted roles, attitudes, and behaviors. It seems well suited to the rational-logical bias in men's socialization. White's technique to 'raise the dilemma' – pointing out that the client has at least two options, which include the conservative one of staying the same and the radical one of standing up to the problem and taking control of change – arouses men's risk-taking predilections. Techniques to restrain change may be particularly effective with men as they may evoke the socialized competitive urge in service of the man's change process. Asking the client to be a consultant to the therapist may appeal to a man's need to be in charge and to his desire to be seen as 'the expert,' thus minimizing his anxiety about asking for help. White's rituals of celebration (e.g., certificates, diplomas, letters, biographies, etc.) may be particularly effective with men as they can be used to provide tangible signs of change, presented as awards that appeal to competence.

The Milan systemic model also has powerful tools to contribute to the feminist-informed therapist. The process oriented interventions of Boscolo and Cecchin (Boscolo, Cecchin, Hoffman & Penn, 1987) are thought to facilitate change during the course of the interview (MacKinnon, 1983). Triadic questioning (MacKinnon, 1983), circular questioning, reflexive questioning and lineal questioning (Tomm, 1987a, 1987b, 1988) can all be used to introduce new information into the system and to challenge stereotypic attitudes and beliefs. Specifically, the questioning modality can readily explore people's beliefs about gender in a non-threatening manner. By exploring the constraints of change and what would happen if things changed, the method of questioning engages men differently and asks them to think about gender relationships in new ways without overtly pressuring them to modify behaviors. The Milan model also uses symptom prescriptions, but in a different way from other brief models. Prescriptions are used to give information to the family on the interrelatedness of their behaviors, rather than to have the family react in 'resistance' to the therapist (MacKinnon, 1983). The Milan therapist's use of positive connotation and "no change" may gain leverage with male clients who are reluctant to acknowledge that there is a problem and are resistant to other family members' requests to change. The use of ritual and tasks by the Milan therapist may be particularly effective in helping men step outside of their traditional behaviors.

"Ritual is probably the most potent socialization mechanism available to kin and other groupings for preparing individual members to understand the group's meanings, carry on its traditions, and perform those social roles considered essential to its continuation" (Laird, 1988, p. 333). Deep meaning and role identity are embedded in social and family rituals (Imber-Black, 1988). Rituals are usually such an ingrained part of our daily existence and special celebrations that their subtle yet powerful meta-messages often go unquestioned. Typical male rituals, such as sports, gang fights or promotions, lead to competition and/or antagonism between men, against other men or against women. By designing different rituals, the therapist has another tool to facilitate men's transition from an 'old' way to a different way, which may appeal to men's needs for tangible signs of change. Whiting (1988) offers five types of rituals that can be adapted to work with men. "Letting go" rituals may facilitate men's moves away from power, dominance, control, and competence. Documenting rituals may be used for apologies and to enhance commitment. Giving and receiving rituals can be designed to mark new ways of being in the family: e.g., in a receiving ritual, a man may be asked to appreciate or acknowledge his wife for exchanges other than sex and obedience; in a giving ritual, he may be asked to find new non-material ways of giving to others to expand his view of his role as "provider." Role reversals or odd/even days are types of rituals that can be adapted to highlight difference. Odd/even days interventions, for example, may be useful for interrupting the competitive cycles of some couples. Odd/even days break constricting system rules and can increase the empathic capabilities of men by having him perform the types of roles normally handled by his partner. Ritualizing the game may appeal to men's tendency for gamesmanship and engage them in the confusion, absurdity and humor, which can alter meaning and introduce new options without confronting men with another opportunity to engage in a power struggle.

Behavioral Family Therapy Models (BFT)

Behavioral therapy techniques (see, for example, Epstein, Schlesinger & Dryden, 1988) for concretely tracking behaviors are particularly powerful tools in work with men, as they can serve to slow men down and help them focus on their behavioral choices. The therapist may use a contract with the man to work on his behaviors that subtly and explicitly subvert his intimate connections and perpetuate power imbalances in the family. In doing so, the therapist unbalances the system by legitimizing the woman's/wife's requests for more nurturing behaviors in the marital contract, without the usual *quid pro quo* (Jacobson, 1983). Other techniques, such as coaching, modelling and successive approximation, fit within the feminist framework as they minimize therapeutic hierarchy, empower through small changes, and validate and amplify positive behaviors. Techniques, such as role reversal, role play, caring days, and time-out, can facilitate awareness of the constraints of stereotypical roles, development of alternative roles, and expansion of the behavioral repertoire. These techniques can be used to help men develop competencies that typically go undeveloped because of socially prescribed roles, such as child care, nurturing behaviors, meal preparation, emotional expressiveness. Reciprocal contracting for specific behavioral expectations between the marital partners or other family members, if conceived within a gender-fair framework, may facilitate change in men's typical competitive and controlling behaviors and attitudes. Communication training may be used to teach men new listening skills and increased direct self-expression in the context of mutual exchange. The goal orientation of BFT is well suited for engaging men in the process of therapy. However if BFT is used without a cognitive restructuring component that challenges the socialized beliefs underlying behavior, the likely result will be limited to first order change, leaving the gender-biased structure of the system unaltered.

Transgenerational Therapy

Bowen's theory clearly identifies the family as the context in which we first learn about ourselves and our expected roles. These patterns of interpersonal interaction are transmitted across generations. In his family-of-origin, a man learns to separate (Chodorow, 1978; Osherson, 1986) and to acquire an "orientation to the public sphere and [a] lack of facility and skill in the emotional sphere" (James & McIntyre, 1983, p. 121). Thus, family-of-origin work seems particularly applicable to working with men. Feminist-informed transgenerational therapy approaches gendered beliefs, attitudes and behaviors from a 'social learning' focus within the family context. This allows men to identify and address those patterned behaviors, often learned early in life, on which they rely to camouflage vulnerabilities, disappointments, hurts, losses and needs. Integrating insights from the work of Osherson (1986) can enhance such a feminist-informed model.

Osherson (1986) draws attention to the crucial relationship between fathers and sons in shaping men's lives and their relationships with partners, children, friends and colleagues. He contends that "naming your father – coming to terms with who he really is, stripped of the distortions of childhood – is a key to every man's ability to allow a richer identity to emerge" (Osherson, 1986, p. 16). This naming may begin the process of resolving the guilt, shame, and anger often felt towards the father, but typically expressed in silent or hidden ways and with much ambivalence. Men tend to carry a wounded father within, an "inner image of father that [is] experienced as judgmental and angry, or, depending on [the] relationship with father, as needy and vulnerable" (Osherson, 1986, p. 27). Three aspects of the "wounded father" can be addressed in therapy: (1) a dominating image of father's deep sadness, incompetence or anger; (2) the deep sense of loss evoked by a wounding father as the son experienced being rejected by or disappointing to the father; and, (3) the distorted and idealized images of father epitomizing the masculinity that the son struggles to internalize (Osherson, 1986). Exploring patterns of how men learn to "love from a distance" (Osherson, 1986, p. 30) helps men learn new ways to express their care and nurturing, instead of the typical "performing, being instrumental, and taking care of by protecting and providing" (Osherson, 1986, p. 30). Questions about how a man experienced his relationship with his father, what he learned explicitly and by example from his father, what he longed for but could not ask for, what his father would think of him if he changed his behaviors, etc., can be used to begin to dismantle the defensive, competitive, controlling, and isolating patterns in men's lives.

By shifting the focus of family-of-origin work beyond notions of a highly differentiated self, the therapist can invite men to move away from extremes of attitudes and behaviors and to begin addressing their affective lives. The emerging body of literature coming out of the "men's movement" (see for example Doyle, 1983; Kimmel, 1987; O'Neil, 1981; Osherson, 1986) highlights men's often hidden needs for connectedness, affection, nurturing, comfort, etc. The therapeutic context can focus on family and sociocultural constraints on male affective expression and can enable a man to find validation of his 'feminine' characteristics and needs as normal and important for all adults. Lerner (1985, 1988a, 1988b,

1989), though writing mostly for women, provides a feminist-informed family-of-origin model for exploring learned patterns and neutralizing their impact in ongoing relationships.

'Self-in-the-System' Models

Psychodynamic therapists typically focus on distinct aspects of male personality structure, which family therapists tended to ignore until recently. Nichols (1987) proposes a model that allows individual personality structures to be addressed in a systems approach. He raises the issues of the 'self in the system' and asks family therapists to recognize their discomfort in joining the system sufficiently to build genuine empathy, a challenge that echoes the feminist critique. This critique invites family therapists to recognize that our best therapeutic tools are inadequate without a solid and respectful relationship between client and therapist. He challenges therapists to use their most powerful tool: putting themselves in the room as human beings and observing what they as individuals are doing to the system. The call is for therapists to slow down, take time to appreciate the unique intricacies of the systemic interactions and the individuals in the system, rather than rushing in quickly with generic interventions. Nichols (1987) argues that a truly systemic approach addresses the interaction between the extra-familial, the family, and individual systems, similar to a feminist perspective. Schwartz (1987, 1988) takes the 'self in the system' concept and adds another psychodynamic dimension, that of the individual's 'multiple selves.' He challenges the "Myth of the Monolithic Self—our cultural bias to view individuals as consistent, unitary beings who know their own minds" and introduces the multiplicity paradigm, which embraces the complexity of "inner selves that are activated under different circumstances" (Schwartz, 1988, p. 22).

Introducing, affirming and validating the complexity behind each man's behaviors can help him separate out intent from behavioral choices, minimize defensiveness, multiply the power of positive connotation, and to take responsibility for his behavioral choices. Distinguishing parts of the self may be a potent tool for helping men identify with their more feminine sides, and may serve to decrease the polar extremes in their behavioral repertoire without threatening their 'masculinity.' This can diminish the tyranny of socialized roles by helping a man get in touch with parts of himself that might behave differently. The therapist may form an alliance with one part to help the client get control over other parts. In so doing, the therapist has a powerful tool to normalize negative socialized beliefs and behaviors and to amplify positive alternatives, without casting the man as consisting of only one small aspect of his being—e.g., strong, independent, sexual, needy, greedy, abusive, etc.

This paradigm offers expanded possibilities for working with men in challenging restricted stereotypic attitudes and behaviors, and it may be particularly powerful when working with special populations. Wheeler (1989) incorporates this paradigm in her work with men. She invites an incest offender to expand his views of his competencies and "rediscover himself as someone other than an offender" (Wheeler, 1989, p. 35). Her approach facilitates empathy for the offender, who is tyrannized by his dominating, controlling, and abusive parts, which he can generalize to an empathic understanding of his victims.

CONCLUSION

Recent literature has begun to take a new look at the position of men in families, with several authors (Doyle, 1983; Farrell, 1986; Goldberg, 1987; McGill, 1985; Pittman, 1985; Toomer, 1978) suggesting that gender-stereotypes "operate to shape—and restrict—the values and actions of males in our society" (Toomer, 1978, p. 23). While feminist family therapists maintain a socio-political understanding of male privilege, there seems to be an emerging sense that male privilege is seldom privilege without some burden. Men pay high prices for conforming to a traditional masculine image, as they die earlier, often live in self-imposed isolation, and report an inordinate amount of stress (Meinecek, 1981; Toomer, 1978). When the dictates of masculinity require males to be competent, tough, sure, invulnerable and unafraid, and femininity involves a process of acting delicate and vulnerable to please men and to help them look all the more masculine, both men and women suffer from their socialized roles (Pittman, 1985). Every day in the therapy room we see families playing out traditional roles that hamper the development of marital intimacy, effective problem solving, and functional parenting. We observe traditional gender roles operating in synergistic and mutually reinforcing ways, resulting in the polarization of husband-wife behaviors, in cutting off the expression of needs, and in the escalation of conflict (Feldman, 1982).

Traditional family therapy models tend to reinforce gender-role socialization in subtle but pernicious ways. However, it is important that we do not throw out the proverbial baby with the bath water. Taking a feminist lens to our work with men in families requires therapists to improve their conceptual and perceptual skills by becoming knowledgeable about men's issues and by clarifying personal values concerning gender socialization for both men and women. A feminist approach to working with men in families invites therapists to build a flexible and broad repertoire of executive skills, drawing from several models and carefully scrutinizing interventions for sexist meta-messages. A feminist-informed alternative, as proposed in this article, may offer therapists working with men, both as individuals and as members of family systems, considerable room to maneuver within a framework of respect, validation, empowerment, and recognition of the larger social context. While inviting men to change attitudes and behaviors that are typically based in traditional power and privilege, the therapist working within a feminist-informed model can address the isolation a man feels as he begins to change, the pain and loneliness of going it alone without social support or ready role models, the vulnerability behind his defensive protection, and the fears accompanying his loved ones' changes. The theoretical underpinnings and intervention tools of such a model can be adapted to tackle different stages in men's change process without abandoning the political and moral questions of power imbalances and inequities germane to the feminist approach.

REFERENCES

Avis, J. M. (1985). The politics of functional family therapy: A feminist critique. *Journal of Marital and Family Therapy*, *11*, 127-138.

Barton C. & Alexander, J. F. (1981). Functional family therapy. In A. S. Gurman & D. P. Kniskern (Eds.), *Handbook of family therapy*, (pp. 403-443). New York: Brunner/Mazel.

Bograd, M. (1984). Family systems approaches to wife battering: A feminist critique. *American Journal of Orthopsychiatry*, *54*, 558-568.

Bograd, M. (1986a). A feminist examination of family therapy: What is women's place? *Women and Therapy*, *5*, 95-106.

Bograd, M. (1986b). Holding the line: Confronting the abusive partner. *The Family Therapy Networker*, *10*, 44-47.

Boscolo, L., Cecchin, G., Hoffman, L. & Penn, P. (1987). *Milan systemic family therapy: Conversations in theory and practice*. New York: Basic Books.

Bowen, M. (1978). *Family therapy in clinical practice*. New York: Jason Aronson.

Brannon, R. (1976). The male sex-role: Our culture's blueprint of manhood, and what it's done for us lately. In D. S. David & R. Brannon (Eds.), *The forty-nine percent majority: The male sex-role*, (pp. 1-48). New York: Random House.

Brownmiller, S. (1984). *Femininity*. New York: Linden Press.

Chodorow, N. (1978). *The reproduction of mothering: Psychoanalysis and the sociology of gender*. Berkeley: University of California Press.

Dinnerstein, D. (1976). *The mermaid and the minotaur: Sexual arrangements and the human malaise*. New York: Harper & Row.

Doyle, J.A. (1983). *The male experience*. Dubuque, IA: Wm. C. Brown Co.

Epstein, N., Schlesinger, S.E. & Dryden, W. (1988). Concepts and methods of cognitive-behavioral family treatment. In N. Epstein, S.E. Schlesinger & W. Dryden (Eds.) *Cognitive-behavioral therapy with families*, (pp. 5-48). New York: Brunner/Mazel.

Epston, D. (1986). Writing your biography. *Family Therapy Case Studies*, *1*, 13-18.

Farrell, W. (1974). *The liberated man*. New York: Random House.

Farrell, W. (1986). *Why men are the way they are*. New York: McGraw-Hill.

Feldman, L. (1982). Sex roles and family dynamics. In F. Walsh (Ed.), *Normal family process*, (pp. 354-399). New York: Guilford Press.

Friedan, B. (1964). *The feminine mystique*. New York: Dell Publishing Co., Inc.

Goldenberg, I. & Goldenberg, H. (1985). *Family therapy: An overview*. Monterey, CA: Brooks/Cole.

Goldberg, H. (1976). *The hazards of being male: Surviving the myth of masculine privilege*. New York: Signet Books.

Goldberg, H. (1987). *The inner male: Overcoming roadblocks to intimacy*. New York: Signet Books.

Goldner, V. (1985a). Feminism and family therapy. *Family Process*, *24*, 31-47.

Goldner, V. (1985b). Warning: Family therapy may be dangerous to your health. *The Family Therapy Networker*, *9*, 19-23.

Goodrich, T.J., Rampage, C., Ellman, B. & Halstead, K. (1988). *Feminist family therapy: A casebook*. New York: W.W. Norton.

Gurman, A.S. & Klein, M.H. (1980). Marital and family conflicts. In A.M. Brodsky & R.T. Hare-Mustin (Eds.), *Women and psychotherapy*, (pp. 159-190). New York: Guilford Press.

Gurman, A.S. & Klein, M.H. (1984). Marriage and the family: An unconscious bias in behavioral treatment? In E.A. Blechman (Ed.), *Behavioral modification with women*, (pp. 170-187). New York: Guilford Press.

Haig, C. & Avis, J.M. (1988). *Mother blaming in major therapy journals: A content analysis*. Unpublished Master's Thesis. Department of Family Studies, University of Guelph, Guelph, Ontario, Canada N1G 2W1.

Hare-Mustin, R.T. (1978). A feminist approach to family therapy. *Family Process, 17*, 181-194.

Hare-Mustin, R.T. (1987). The problem of gender in family therapy theory. *Family Process, 26*, 15-27.

Imber-Black, E. (1988). Ritual themes in families and family therapy. In E. Imber-Black, J. Roberts & R. Whiting (Eds.), *Rituals in families and family therapy*, (pp. 47-83). New York: W.W. Norton.

Jacobson, N.S. (1983). Beyond empiricism: The politics of marital therapy. *The American Journal of Family Therapy, 11*, 11-24.

James, K. & McIntyre, D. (1983). The reproduction of families: The social role of family therapy. *Journal of Marital and Family Therapy, 9*, 119-129.

Kimmel, M.S. (Ed.) (1987). *Changing men: New directions in research on men and masculinity*. Newbury Park, CA: Sage Publications.

Laird, J. (1988). Women and rituals in family therapy. In E. Imber-Black, J. Roberts & R. Whiting (Eds.), *Rituals in families and family therapy*, (pp. 331-362). New York: W.W. Norton.

Lerner, H. (1985). *The dance of anger*. New York: Perennial Library – Harper & Row.

Lerner, H. (1988a). *Women in therapy*. Northvale, NJ: Jason Aronson.

Lerner, H.G. (1988b). Is family systems theory really systemic? A feminist communication. In L. Braverman (Ed.), *Women, feminism and family therapy*, (pp. 47-63). New York: The Haworth Press.

Lerner, H.(1989). *The dance of intimacy*. New York: Harper & Row.

Luepnitz, D. (1988). *The family interpreted: Feminist theory in clinical practice*. New York: Basic Books.

MacKinnon, L. (1983). Contrasting strategic and Milan therapies. *Family Process, 22*, 424-441.

Margolin, G., Fernandez, V., Talovic, S. & Onorato, R. (1983). Sex role considerations and behavioral marital therapy: Equal does not mean identical. *Journal of Marital and Family Therapy, 9*, 131-145.

McGill, M.E. (1985). *The McGill report on male intimacy*. New York: Harper & Row.

McGoldrick, M., Anderson, C. & Walsh, F. (Eds.) (1988). *Women in families: A framework for family therapy*. San Francisco, CA: Jossey-Bass.

Meinecke, C.E. (1981). Socialized to die younger? Hypermasculinity and men's health. *Personnel and Guidance Journal, 60*, 241-245.

Miller, J.B. (1976). *Toward a new psychology of women*. Boston, MA: Beacon Press.

Minuchin, S. (1974). *Families and family therapy*. Cambridge, MA: Harvard University Press.

Nichols, J. (1975). *Men's liberation: A new definition of masculinity*. New York: Penguin Books.

Nichols, M.P. (1987). *The self in the system: Expanding the limits of family therapy*. New York: Brunner/Mazel.

O'Neil, J.M. (1981). Patterns of gender role conflict and strain: Sexism and fear of femininity in men's lives. *Personnel and Guidance Journal, 60*, 203-209.

Osherson, S. (1986). *Finding our fathers: How a man's life is shaped by his relationship with his father*. New York: Fawcett Columbine.

Pleck, J. & Sawyer, J. (1974). *Men and masculinity*. Englewood Cliffs, NJ: Prentice Hall.

Pittman, F. (1985). Gender myths: When does gender become pathology? *The Family Therapy Networker, 9*, 24-31.

Pressman, B. (1987). The place of family-of-origin therapy in the treatment of wife abuse. In Hovestadt & M. Fine (Eds.), *Family of origin therapy*, (pp. 45-56). Rockville, MD: Aspen.

Pressman, B. (1989). Wife-abused couples: The need for comprehensive theoretical perspectives and integrated treatment models. *Journal of Feminist Family Therapy, 1*, 23-43.

Rice, D.G. (1978). The male spouse in marital and family therapy. *The Counseling Psychologist, 7*, 64-67.

Rubin, L.B. (1983). *Intimate strangers: Men and women together*. New York: Harper & Row.

Schwartz, R. (1987). Our multiple selves. *The Family Therapy Networker, 11*, 25-31, 80-83.

Schwartz, R. (1988). Know thy selves. *The Family Therapy Networker, 12*, 20-29.

Tomm, K. (1987a). Interventive interviewing. Part I: Strategizing as a fourth guideline for the therapist. *Family Process, 26*, 3-13.

Tomm, K. (1987b). Interventive interviewing. Part II: Reflexive questioning as a means to enable self-healing. *Family Process, 26*, 167-183.

Tomm, K. (1988). Interventive interviewing. Part III: Intending to ask lineal, circular, strategic, or reflexive questions? *Family Process, 27*, 1-15.

Toomer, J.E. (1978). Males in psychotherapy. *The Counseling Psychologist, 7*, 22-25.

Walters, M., Carter, E., Papp, P. & Silverstein, O. (1988). *The invisible web: Gender patterns in family relationships*. New York: Guilford Press.

Wheeler, D. (1989). Faulty fathering: Working ideas on the treatment of male incest perpetrators. *Journal of Feminist Family Therapy, 1*, 27-48.

Wheeler, D. (1990). Father-daughter incest: Considerations for family therapists. In M.P. Mirkin (Ed.), *The social and political contexts of family therapy*, (pp. 139-157). New York: Allyn & Bacon.

Wheeler, D., Avis, J.M., Miller, L. & Chaney, S. (1988). Rethinking family therapy training and supervision: A feminist model. In M. McGoldrick, C.

Anderson & F. Walsh (Eds.), *Women in families: A framework for family therapy*, (pp. 135-151). San Francisco, CA: Jossey-Bass.

White, M. (1988a). Negative explanation, restraint and double description: A template for family therapy. *Family Process, 25*, 169-184.

White, M. (1988b). The process of questioning: A therapy of literary merit? *The Dulwich Center Newsletter, Winter* (Special Edition), 8-14.

White, M. (1988c). Assumptions and therapy. *The Dulwich Center Newsletter, Autumn*, 7-8.

White, M. & Epston, D. (1989). *Literate means to therapeutic ends*. Adelaide: Dulwich Center Publications.

White, M. & Epston, D. (1990). *Narrative means to therapeutic ends*. New York: W.W. Norton.

Whiting, R.A. (1988). Guidelines to designing therapeutic rituals. In. E. Imber-Black, J. Roberts & R.A. Whiting (Eds.), *Rituals in families and family therapy*, (pp. 135-151). New York: W.W. Norton.

Traditional Men in Marital and Family Therapy

Gary R. Brooks

SUMMARY. Recently, psychotherapy approaches sensitive to the role constraints of traditional men have appeared. Marital and family therapists, because of their broader systemic focus, require sensitivity not just to the socialization of each gender, but also to the family as a political institution and to the interactive nature of gender role stereotypes. Case material is presented to suggest avenues for integrating feminist and men's studies insights into gender-sensitive family therapy models.

The growing feminist voice in family therapy has elevated the topic of gender roles from its formerly neglected position to a central place in the field of family therapy. The major thrust of the feminist critique includes charges that family therapy (a) is overly blameful of women and mothers for family pathology; (b) ignores real power inequities of the larger system in which families are embedded; (c) reinforces traditional stereotyped roles; and (d) neglects the political dimension of family life (Bograd, 1986; Goldner, 1985; Hare-Mustin, 1978). The bulk of the attention given to gender issues in family therapy has been focussed on women's perspectives. This is understandable and appropriate considering that women's relatively disadvantaged position in our culture makes

---

Gary R. Brooks is affiliated with the Olin E. Teague Veterans' Center and Texas A & M University, College of Medicine. Correspondence concerning this article should be addressed to Gary R. Brooks, Psychology Service (116B4), O. E. Teague VA Center, Temple, TX 76504.

The author is grateful for valuable case consultation and gender role insights provided by Carol Philpot, Don-David Lusterman, and Roberta Nutt.

them more vulnerable to harm from sexist practices. Recent feminist writers, however, have expanded their focus to consider how one aspect of their critique, reinforcement of stereotyped roles, may also harm men (Avis, 1986; McGoldrick, 1988). Other writers (Brooks, 1990; Pittman, 1985) have looked exclusively at men as potential recipients of sexist family therapy practices.

Successful psychotherapy is a complex interpersonal enterprise that emphasizes cognitive, affective, and behavioral skills that are inconsistent with traditional male socialization. Recent contributions by men's studies writers have markedly enhanced understanding of how the traditional male gender role affects what a man brings to the therapist's office, and how the therapist might benefit from greater gender-awareness in accomodating to traditional men as a special sociocultural group (Brooks, 1990; Scher, 1990; Solomon, 1982a). Family systemic models, with their broader conceptual focus, pose an even greater challenge to the gender-awareness of the therapist. A gender-sensitive focus requires that therapists be knowledgeable about feminist insights into female consciousness, appreciative of the reciprocal interactive nature of male and female gender roles, and attuned to the family as a political institution. The material that follows is both a review of recent observations about traditional men in psychotherapy, as well as an attempt to integrate several interrelated perspectives, previously studied separately, into a conceptually useful systemic view.

WHO IS THE TRADITIONAL MALE?

The traditional male is here defined as a man with strong allegiance to the imperatives of the traditional male gender role. Despite differences of emphasis, there is general concurrence that central features of the role are competitiveness, emotional stoicism, homophobia, distant fathering, emphasis on work and achievement, neglect of health needs, and distrust of women despite overreliance on them for nurturance, emotional expressivness, and validation of masculinity (Doyle, 1989; Goldberg, 1976; Pleck, 1976, 1981; Solomon, 1982b). Having worked for 18 years at a Central Texas Veterans Administration hospital, I suspect that this value system is expressed in a more concentrated form in working-class, non-academic settings in mid-America. Nevertheless, aspects of this value system are probably present in all men and continue to have significant influence on male self-definition and interpersonal conduct.

Contemporary Gender Role-Strain

Gender role stereotypes are reciprocal and interactive (Doyle, 1989; Gilbert, 1985; Hafner, 1986; Kimmel, 1987). The women's movement gains of empowering women and challenging traditional female role stereotypes have presented substantial challenges to traditional men. Though many men have recognized the potential benefits of broadened role definitions, others have responded by rigidifying sexist beliefs and subsequently experiencing considerable "gender-role strain" (O'Neil, 1982).

Gender-role strain, the discomfort resulting from disharmony between early gender socialization and newer role expectations, is the negative fallout from contemporary society's gender role reevaluations. The degree of negative fallout may be dependent upon the precipitating factors. When gender-role transitions are seen as self-initiated and growth-enhancing, the gender-role strain may be minimal. In the case of the traditional man, however, the role challenges are usually experienced as rooted in external (and hostile) forces, such as the women's movement and amorphous social changes. At other times, the challenges may be seen as precipitated by personal failures in meeting masculine role standards. In either case the traditional man's role strain may be more intense, destructive, and devoid of compensatory benefits than the strain experienced by other men.

Evidence supports the apparent rise of gender role-strain in men. Pleck (1987) cited data showing that "men as a group are experiencing more psychological distress than they did three decades ago, both absolutely and relative to women" (p. 20). A dramatic rise in the number of men entering sex therapy programs (Fracher & Kimmel, 1987; LoPiccolo, 1985; Tieffer, 1986) may be evidence of "threatened masculinity" (Doyle, 1989). Increased participation of men in psychotherapy has prompted mental health professionals to address issues of men entering therapy (Brooks, 1990; Scher, 1990;

Silverberg, 1986). Extreme negative reactions to gender role changes may produce the "breadwinner suicides" (Pleck, 1987).

TRADITIONAL MEN IN THERAPY: THE POLITICS OF POWER

Whether the source of men's greater role-strain is women's relative recent empowerment, or the "economic changes undermining the male breadwinner role" (Pleck, 1987, p. 25), it is clear that many features of traditional male-female relationships are increasingly less acceptable to most women. Although traditional women are not unilateral in their endorsement of new gender role definitions, all are subject to the general benefits of increased economic opportunities, alternative definitions of "femininity," challenges to conventional patriarchal leadership, and expectations for more varied male participation in family life. Traditional men, however, rarely perceive a personal benefit from these social changes and, though they may be stressed enough to consider psychotherapy, they do not enter therapy seeking new definitions of masculinity. Some are in sympathy with "masculine reactivity" with its "anti-feminist and pro-male" orientation (Kimmel, 1987, p. 13). Scher (1990) observed that traditional men see few "life-enhancing qualities in psychotherapy and come into therapy because they have no alternative" (p. 3).

Once in therapy, traditional men participate in a manner consistent with their socialization, and in a manner very dissimilar to the "ideal" therapy patient. Rather than acknowledging vulnerability and openly seeking help, they may attempt to control therapy sessions and may provoke intellectual games or compete with the therapist for power (Scher, 1990). They may avoid affective material and focus instead on tangible, instrumental objectives (Hotelling & Forrest, 1985). More critically, they may adopt "superficial changes" (Pleck, 1987) to covertly undercut their spouse's empowerment and to reestablish the old relationship system.

The therapist who is sophisticated about male socialization and male patterns in psychotherapy is better prepared to handle these maneuvers which can be seen as interpersonal power plays, or the "political" aspects of marital and family therapy. Psychotherapists must recognize that their interventions also have political implications—a crucial impact on the interpersonal balance of power. When the traditional man realizes that his female partner wants him to change, he often attempts to ignore the demand or, if he feels it necessary, will attempt to subvert the challenge. Often, the woman threatens to leave him. When the traditional man faces the potential loss of the relationship so vital to his sense of worth, he will commonly respond with desperate measures. Naturally, his response will draw from the repertoire of interpersonal tactics that are a product of his masculine socialization. These tactics, which have the ultimate objective of restoring the status quo through disempowerment of women, may be grouped into four general categories, with several variations. These categories are: (1) coercive control and intimidation; (2) winning favor; (3) creating confusion and manipulating others; and (4) provoking guilt and appealing to feminine nurturance.

Coercive Control and Intimidation

The most desperate and flagrantly offensive tactics attempting to disempower women are those that rely on physical intimidation and assault. The increased public sensitivity to the problem of wife abuse has generated alternatives for women wishing to escape violence in the home. Nevertheless, the psychological paralysis engendered by potential violence (Finklehor & Yllo, 1985), as well as the flawed system of legal protection, severely complicate therapy in these situations.

Less overt, but sometimes almost equally disempowering, are coercive tactics that rely on financial intimidation and scare tactics. In situations where the wife has not been able to establish an adequate financial power base, she is vulnerable to her husband's financial manipulations. He may threaten to "cut her off" from funds for household maintenance, college tuition, child support, or even from legal expenses. In the increasingly common situations where women are employed and less financially vulnerable, the husband may employ more indirect scare tactics. If he has controlled the family's financial affairs, he may exaggerate the danger and complexity of the "cold, cruel world," while simultaneously demeaning his wife's fiscal competence. In extreme cases he may manipulate finances to force her to choose between reconcilation or possible financial devastation.

Winning Favor

In the face of the marital crisis many traditional men will try to avoid the desired egalitarian relationship by offering a more "rewarding" relationship structured along traditional lines. To do this they elevate their commitment to the "good-provider role" (Bernard, 1981) and try to assuage dissatisfaction with gifts—new cars, home remodeling, furniture, or vacations. Many of these men are puzzled and dismayed if their wives construe as "bribes" the gifts the men saw as remediations for male role-failures.

Similar interpersonal tactics are those in which the man escalates the traditional "suitor" or romantic pursuer role (Farrell, 1987) to reestablish the former relationship. Often this takes the form of appeals to rekindle earlier romantic times by "getting away together for a second honeymoon without the distracting influence of meddling others." As part of this maneuver the man may be "a good boy" by adopting superficial changes—not drinking, coming home early, going to church—to demonstrate desire for a better marriage.

Creating Confusion and Manipulating Others

Some disempowering tactics, intellectual and strategic in nature, play upon the woman's uncertainty or ambivalence through arguments, denials, and obfuscation. The husband may insist that her nascent feminist awareness is the product of a confused state of mind, a "phase," a side-effect of the biochemical changes of menopause or pre-menstrual syndrome, or the result of too much association with "women's libbers."

In some cases the husband may adopt a pattern of unpredictable and erratic behavior—conciliatory and supportive one day, angry and vengeful the next. Although this behavior pattern probably should not be conceptualized as a conscious disempowering tactic, and is probably equally reflective of the man's disorientation, it often confuses the woman and impedes rational planning.

In a more deliberate tactic, the man may attempt collusion with significant others to undercut change. Marital therapy, once resisted by the husband, may be sought as a major step toward immediate, and premature, reconciliation. In situations where the wife has achieved geographic separation as a step towards empowerment, the husband may pressure the therapist to recommend that the wife return to cohabitation. This is frequently accompanied by the rationale "Doc, wouldn't it be easier to work on our problems if we see each other more frequently?" In situations where the man has responsibility to pay the therapy bill, there may be subtle pressure to comply with his wishes (or dangers of her being prevented from seeking individual therapy appointments).

A similar collusion takes place when the husband is able to triangulate family members against the woman. In this maneuver the husband enlists traditional role-oriented members of the extended family to "counsel" the woman about the "unappreciated" benefits of her marital situation. Children, naturally fearful of a disruptive divorce, can be encouraged to pressure their mother to stop "rocking the boat." In this scenario, social isolation is especially effective in undermining the woman's resolve. If her friendship network is composed entirely of traditional women, or if she is dependent upon her husband's social network, she is unusually vulnerable to these social pressures.

Provoking Guilt and Appealing to Feminine Nurturing

The most subtle disempowering tactics are those in which the man recognizes the futility of overt power tactics and appeals to traditional feminine nurturing. Many men, unable to conceive of living without their spouse, will openly consider suicide, or adopt functionally similar behaviors such as neglecting self-care, abusing drugs or alcohol, or engaging in high-risk activities. Frequently, by neglecting health needs, mishandling health-damaging stress, or by exaggerating physical problems, the man often is able to assume the "sick" role (Mechanic, 1962), with its accompanying benefit—expectation of female nurturance. Many women, socialized to be caretakers, are unable to resist the pull of a "sick" mate.

In the face of this range of interpersonal tactics from the male, the therapist may have difficulty maintaining enough therapeutic objectivity to work effectively with all parties. Though systemic family therapy has been the justified target of considerable feminist criticism because of its politically naive concepts of "therapeutic neutrality," its perspective may nevertheless have utility in this situation. If the recent empowerment of women is seen as a force which unbalances the traditional homeostatic family system enough to engender reciprocal forces, then the male counterbalancing activities should be viewed as a natural systemic reaction. Since systemic conceptualizations do not assume that members of a system are fully aware of the larger purposes of their actions, the judgement should not automatically be made that the male's behavior is intended to be malevolent. It may be therapeutically useful to view him as a fearful male trying to fulfill his strongly-felt duty to restore patriarchal control. The man's fear and vulnerability, easy to see when he is physically ill or desperately suicidal, is also present even when his coping behaviors are offensive. Needless to say, this recognition of the man's pain must not blind the therapist to his or her responsibility to do everything possible to equalize power and to avoid sabotaging potential "second-order change" (Hoffman, 1981) of the family to a more effective, differentiated, and egalitarian functioning.

TREATMENT MODEL – TRADITIONAL MAN/EMPOWERED WOMAN

In 15 years of family therapy practice in Central Texas, I have repeatedly been contacted by traditional men asking for marital therapy to restore a disrupted relationship. Typically, these men were not believers in the value of therapy, and may have previously refused their wives' requests for conjoint help-seeking. But I usually accepted as genuine their statements that they were willing to consider substantive change. To expedite marital therapy progress, I often complied with the man's request for almost immediate conjoint sessions. However, after several outstanding failures, I have reevaluated my role in these situations. After much reflection, I recognized that sometimes I had unwittingly allowed my therapy to be used by the man as a political manuver to undercut a recently empowered woman. I have subsequently formulated a general treatment model for these situations that includes the following six elements.

First, the therapist deeply appreciates the gender role socialization of men and women, and is capable of conveying empathy for the actions of each spouse, without condoning coercion or intimidation. The therapist's ability to convey understanding of the man's anguish is especially critical, since the male client is usually experiencing a variety of emotions and impulses he poorly understands. The therapist views the marital distress in a sociocultural context, that is, as a traditional marital arrangement poorly suited to contemporary times. This contextual insight helps the male client see cultural value conflicts as part of the problem; excessive self-blame and rage become less problematic. The woman is portrayed as realistic about contemporary social and political facts of life, rather than disloyal; the man is seen as loyal to an older value system undergoing fundamental changes. With better understanding of the socioeconomic realities of the woman's position (through education about divorce rates, feminization of poverty), the inappropriateness of disempowerment and coercion are more clearly understood. The empathy and reassurance displayed by the therapist are vital in promoting the male client's commitment to therapy.

Second, the therapist maintains therapeutic leverage by perpetuating the homeostatic imbalance. Usually, this leverage, a product of the woman's empowerment, is only achieved when she insists upon physical separation, that they live apart. This separation is strongly endorsed by the therapist as vital to successful therapy outcome. The marital partners are seen separately. A woman must understand that premature reconciliation will undercut therapeutic leverage, and might make future change even more difficult. She is encouraged to remain separate from her husband and to resist her culture-bred temptation to befriend or nurture him. Because the man has greater resistance to the separation, he is harder to persuade about the merits of the treatment plan. The therapist, though reliant on the steadfastness of the empowered woman, should not be identified as the instigator of the woman's changes, but as a resource for the man in developing an appropriate response. The immediate crisis is shown to be a manifestation of longstanding marital issues, rather than a phase that will pass or disappear if suppressed. The therapist counsels the husband about the shortcomings of coercion as a problem-solving strategy, particularly in light of his wife's demands for greater autonomy. The male client is reassured that a more conciliatory and cooperative approach, contrary to his fears, will actually make reconciliation more likely. A common troublesome myth, that women secretly desire omnipotent and dominant men, is replaced by a more realistic, autonomy-respecting view of heterosexual relationships. Additionally, the man is encouraged to develop alternative, non-sexual, nurturing relationships and questioned about possible overdependence upon his spouse.

Third, the woman's empowerment is supported. She is advised about the possible disempowering tactics she may face and assisted with appropriate coping strategies. If necessary, more intense intervention for her is arranged (for example, through referral to a feminist therapist and/or a women's support group). The therapist, if challenged for "encouraging" the woman, may counter by pointing out that the woman client, not the therapist, initiated the changes. Further, the therapist does well to show that acknowledgement of the woman's empowerment is the most practical alternative, and that efforts to suppress her will be self-defeating. Equally important is the therapist's reassurance that an enlightened response from the husband may not only salvage the relationship, but make it more rewarding to each partner.

Fourth, the man is enthusiastically supported for his willingness to enter therapy and to consider change, encouraged about his potential for change, and chided for any relapses into male disempowering tactics directed at his wife. Since many traditional men are struggling to accept the necessity of gender role changes, and often have deeply ingrained beliefs about the "rightness" of traditional gender arrangements, the therapist maintains a pragmatic orientation: the male client can't avoid recognition that the women's movement is a reality and that gender role changes are inevitable. Philosophical debates, and righteous arguments, are counterproductive at this point. The man's fuller appreciation of the underlying moral issues comes later.

Fifth, while the man is treated separately from his wife, he is encouraged to discover the intrinsic benefits of broadened gender roles for men. Male consciousness-raising activities and support groups are especially useful for his emotional sustenance and for the development of improved male-male relationships.

Last, the therapist carefully monitors the situation for indications that conjoint therapy may be possible to promote a more highly functional marital relationship. Three conditions should be met before conjoint marital therapy is begun. The woman's empowerment should be secure; the husband should be committed to her continued empowerment and to an egalitarian marital relationship; both parties independently, without coercion, choose to pursue the therapy. When reconciliation is seen as impractical, the therapist helps facilitate dissolution of the marriage and works to promote more enlightened post-divorce functioning for each partner.

Avoiding Gender Blind-Spots with Men in Family Therapy

A welcome bounty of books addressing women's issues in families (Goodrich et al., 1988; Kantor & Okun, 1989; Luepnitz, 1988; McGoldrick, Anderson, & Walsh, 1989; Walters et al., 1988) provides evidence of the growing recognition of the need to prevent gender-blind therapy that victimizes women. A similar interest in family therapy practices that may constrain men is relatively undeveloped, and has been seen by some as unnecessary (Raymond, 1985). Rekers (1988) echoed an argument frequently made in opposition to expansion of men's studies programs by arguing that patriarchal and androcentric psychology has already overstudied male perspectives. She stated "I am offended by the attitude of males that men have not been adequately studied . . . [a] completely ridiculous notion" (p. 3). In response to Pittman's (1985) call for attention to the male perspective, Taffel (1986) argued that women, through their "empathic linkage with unspoken male disadvantages" and their dedication to the protection of fragile male self-esteem, "already know quite enough about the tyranny of masculinity" (p. 11). Okun (1989) claimed that women therapists have an advantage over men therapists in understanding other-gender experiences because women have learned to live in both the "dominant and non-dominant'' cultures'' (p. 144). Though I have been impressed with the sensitivity of many women to male gender role pressures (oftentimes more sensitive than fellow males), this does not seem to obviate the need for greater scholarly study of the male gender role, and of possible gender role blind-spots harming men in family therapy. It is important to note that the potential harm to men is qualitatively different than that for women, since men, from a political and socioeconomic power position, are relatively less vulnerable. The damage to men would more likely take the form of perpetuating traditional role constraints and missing opportunities for expanded role-functioning in family life. Several sources of gender blind-spots are worthy of mention.

Colluding with Male Resistance to Participation in Family Therapy. Since men often see psychotherapy as an "alien" world, and frequently try to handle problems with avoidance, therapists must avoid colluding with men's resistance to entering therapy. Don't assume that men are unwilling to participate in therapy; their initial resistance should not be seen as final. When men present as the identified patient, their efforts to insulate the therapist from the family should be challenged.

Overemphasizing Work, Career, and Success for Men. Many men work long hours and function in stressful occupational environments. Because our culture values accomplished, competitive, hard-working men, therapists are prone to overlook the costs of a man's work schedule. Sometimes therapists take the male breadwinner role for granted and do not address male overcommitment to it. Instead of challenging overly narrow definitions of manhood, therapists too frequently work to help the family support the breadwinner in all occupational decisions. Families should be encouraged to broaden definitions of acceptable male role behavior. Cooperative and affiliative roles need greater emphasis. Men who see work and career as the only possibilities for gratification and self-esteem are more likely to be traumatized by unemployment, disability, or retirement. As men expand their areas of competence they are less likely to be threatened by a career-oriented spouse.

Reinforcing Patterns of Male Dominance and Patriarchal Leadership. Therapists must be careful to avoid double messages to men by first criticizing patriarchal practices, and then subtly encouraging the male client to provide leadership in conventional ways. Expectations that men should "take charge" of difficult parenting situations, assume ultimate financial responsibility for the family, or handle all emotionally taxing extra-familial negotiations only perpetuate traditional male role expectations.

Overemphasizing Rationality and Emotional Self-Control for Men. The socially prescribed male interaction style emphasizing intellectual analysis, rationality, and self-control should not be perpetuated through family therapy interactions; women should not be encouraged to take full responsibility for affective sensitivity. Men can be helped to be more attuned to the emotional cues of families' members if the therapist intervenes with support, reassurance, and coaching. Therapists can help men detect and listen to the affective distress of family members. Frequently, if the therapist sits nearby, encourages, models, and coaches, the male client can become a better empathic listener. Likewise, environments can be made more conducive to male emotional expression. Men's pain is often buried under many layers of bitterness, frustration, and resentment. Those therapists who are facile at eliciting the safe expression of male rage find themselves with an abundance of useful affective material.

Failing to Recognize Male Vulnerabilities. Traditional men, because of their socialization to be "male machines" (Fasteau, 1974) or "sturdy oaks" (David & Brannon, 1976), tend to overextend themselves and deny the physical limitations of their bodies. A range of high-risk activities, such as fighting, high-speed driving, contact sports, and military combat, have been seen as arenas for expression of traditional masculinity. Male refusal to acknowledge fear, weakness, physical vulnerability, and fatigue contribute to men's unwillingness to perform preventive health behaviors (Nathanson, 1977). Corollary to this high-risk aspect of the male role is the expectation that women should act as restraining agents for foolhardy men, as well as nurturers and healers for injured men. Family therapists should be alert to family behaviors that ignore male physical vulnerabilities or delegate nurturing to women. Psychoeducational activities illustrating the association between the male role and premature death (Harrison, 1978) may be helpful in questioning the "heroic" male value system.

Failing to Promote New Models of Fatherhood. Men traditionally have been physically absent, emotionally distant, and decidedly ancillary in parenting activities. Nurturing children has been seen as the role of mothers; strict discipline and patriarchal leadership as the baliwick of fathers. Empowerment of women in roles beyond motherhood needs to be paired with empowerment of fathers into a wider repertoire of parenting roles. The frequent emotional and financial cut-offs of fathers from children after divorce needs to be given greater emphasis by family therapists.

Dehumanizing the Male. The systemic concept of "circular causality," with its implication that family members engage in a repetitive pattern of mutually reinforcing behaviors, has been regarded by feminists as "suspiciously like a hypersophisticated version of blaming the victim and rationalizing the status quo" (Goldner, 1985, p. 33). When applied to problems such as battering, rape, and incest (against women) this concept of circular causation has been seen as subtly removing responsibility from the perpetrator, while implying that the woman is coresponsible (Bograd, 1984). These are important objections to misuse of the circularity concept; men must be held fully accountable for their violent or abusive behavior. Nevertheless, this should not rule out efforts to understand what precedes a man's rage, to examine sequences of behaviors, to appreciate the context of a man's response as well as his inner turmoil. This is a primary step in helping him learn to discover his affective distress so that he may learn acceptable methods for addressing it. Since many men suppress their unhappiness, they are susceptible to cycles of angry outburst, followed by guilt, supplication, and non-assertiveness. Since they are poor monitors of affective states, they find their anger to be a surprising, and sometimes terrifying, reaction to inconsequential actions of family members. To prevent recurrent cycles of emotional build-up and subsequent loss of control, men must become more adept at recognizing precipitants to their outbursts. Though they cannot be excused for violence, they should be helped in giving voice to their feelings of injustice. Exclusive emphasis on blaming the man produces dehumanization.

Failing to Challenge Stoicism. Traditional men have been trained to view expression of emotional needs as "sissy stuff" (David & Brannon, 1976). They overvalue self-reliance and emotional stoicism. Some men experience "emotional constipation" (Farrell, 1987), the inability to express troublesome emotions. Rather than appear weak and "feminine," men sometimes hide their needs through denial, emotional withdrawal, and when frustrated, though passive-aggressive behavior. Other men fear loss of behavioral control, and resultant physical danger to loved ones, if angry feelings are given expression. The therapist, therefore, should not assume that the silent male is untroubled. Helping men detect, label, and appropriately express affect is an important part of the therapist's role.

Ignoring the Need to Promote Emotional Intimacy Among Men. Though men often congregate in male-only environments, they usually resist suggestions that they meet for "expressive" rather than "instrumental" objectives. This type of meeting has greater appeal when the therapist can demonstrate that men, though sharing distinctive gender role experiences, usually isolate themselves from fellow men. Each man's common concerns, such as sexual functioning, occupational adequacy, aging processes, are faced alone, without recognition of their universality. Many men are greatly aided by the recognition that some of their dysfunctional behaviors are not proof of "badness," but are the product of loyalty to anachronistic gender role standards which hamper all men. The male tendency to become overly dependent upon women in the affective sphere will be lessened if closer relationships can be developed between brothers, fathers and sons, male cousins, friends, and so forth. Occasional meetings with male sub-systems may provide opportunities for non-traditional male-male interactions.

CASE ILLUSTRATION–OVERVIEW

A family therapist's intervention style is shaped not only by training, but also by intense experiences with difficult clinical cases. My efforts to incorporate gender-awareness into my family therapy practices have been greatly influenced by reflections on several challenging and meaningful family cases. The following case (with names and other identifying features altered to protect confidentiality) is presented not only because of the variety of gender role issues raised, but because I've been the fortunate recipient of considerable consultation about it. The opportunity for intensive retrospective analysis of this case by a mixed-gender group, familiar with feminist and men's studies perspectives, has been particularly valuable in the detection of gender blind spots. This consultation model, an extension of the one-gender feminist consultation teams described by McGoldrick et al. (1989) and Walters et al. (1988), seems to have considerable potential in facilitating gender-sensitive family therapy.

The illustrative case material is based on two family therapy sessions, one held during the father's VA hospitalization, the second held a week after his discharge. Information about family background is presented first, followed by specific information about two selected therapy sessions. All members of the blended family attended the first session; only the marital couple attended the second. After description of the highlights of each session, a feminist and men's studies critique, based on the gender consultation team's analysis of the session, follows. General implications of the critique are discussed in the final section.

The Brown Family

John and Sandi Brown's marriage was the second marriage for each. John had two sons in his very traditional first marriage; Sandi had two sons and a daughter. John had been an unusually successful athlete; Sandi was a member of the team's "pep squad." John's athletic career was cut short by enlistment in the military, assignment to Vietnam, and severe injury by a land mine in combat. Despite subsequent physical limitations, he hid his deficiencies and managed to continue in the military for several more years, until he was eventually passed over for promotion and given a medical discharge. Judy, his wife at that time, returned to school and completed a respiratory therapy program. Shortly after returning to the work force, she began an affair with a high-level administrator at her hospital, and, in John's words, "took the children and ran off with him."

Sandi's first marriage had been characterized by difficulties for many years. Married at 19 to "escape" a difficult home environment, she quickly regretted her decision, since her first husband was prone to extramarital affairs and was a poor provider. John and Sandi referred to him as "a zero, a real nothing." After obtaining a nursing degree, Sandi filed for a divorce after losing hope for the marriage. Her husband immediately left the geographical area and maintained only minimal contact with his children.

John and Sandi met at church shortly after their divorces, and their early courtship was centered around church activities. Their relationship developed quickly, and they soon married, although Sandi doubted John's emotional separation from his first marriage, since he frequently slipped and addressed her as "Judy." By mutual agreement, Sandi stopped working to "raise the children and be a homemaker." Family income was provided by John's military disability pension, supplemented by modest child support payments. John completed a masters degree program, but his physical limitations prevented him from all but volunteer work through his church.

First Session

John entered the VA inpatient psychiatric facility with the presenting problem of temper outbursts directed primarily at the youngest son. The initial family session was attended by John, Sandi, Jessica (17), Tim (16), and Sean (12). The most immediate issue was the considerable stress all experienced over how to incorporate John into the new blended family. John was upset that the children, particularly Jessica, had not accepted him more readily; the children were troubled by John's erratic behavior towards them. At times, he would take great interest in them, but when frustrated, he would react strongly, sometimes leaving the home and threatening divorce. Jessica was viewed by the family as "overly emotional"; Tim was seen as cool, controlled, unruffled, and a "role-model"—"Jessica should be more like Tim." Sean was seen by Jessica and John as "out-of-control" and needing dramatic intervention, possibly placement at a boarding school. Sean argued that his problematic behavior was the result of Jessica's refusal to treat him as a peer—"she tries to boss me around." Careful exploration of that issue revealed that the parents were giving a double message about hierarchy, authority, and responsibility. Though Jessica was held responsible for Sean's behavior during parental absences, she was not supported in her efforts at maintaining control. In fact, her reactive distress was viewed by Tim and Sean as a product of her "bossiness" and her need to control others, and by the parents as evidence of her over-emotionality. Jessica was berated for trying to be "a little mother to the whole world," while Tim was praised for his emotional calm and stoicism.

As I examined this work with my consultation group, our analysis revealed that some of the interventions were gender-sensitive, while others were not. A positive feature of the first session was my ability to involve the entire family. The commonly reported difficulties in obtaining male participation in family therapy (Kaslow, 1981; Shapiro & Budman, 1973) are partially a product of male efforts to distance themselves from family tension. In the VA, many men try to insulate their families from treatment—"this is my problem, I don't want my family bothered." A second positive feature was my placing Sean's "rebellious" behavior in intrafamiliar and extrafamiliar contexts. His behavior was described as a function of family distress, as well as a function of double messages presented to young men about aggression, activity, and misbehavior (Goldberg, 1976).

The plusses of the first session were outweighed by two serious instances of gender role blindness. First, I did not challenge how the family presented ambiguous messages to the females regarding power and authority. Jessica was expected to assume executive responsibility when the parents were away, but her authority was not respected or supported. This problem was compounded when her reactive distress was dismissed as over-excitability, and she was compared unfavorably with Tim. Second, Jessica was saddled with another "female" burden—taking responsibility for the survival of the family. She was the only one able (and perhaps, expected) to express the logical fear that John's seemingly unpredictable departures would lead to dissolution of this blended family. Regrettably, her expressions of pain were labelled as controlling and noxious, being a "little mother."

Second Session

In a couples meeting one week after John's hospital discharge, the couple began with a heated marital disagreement prompted by Sandi's change of hairstyle. John was annoyed that she changed her hair without "consulting" him. Sandi, firm in her right to control her own appearance, was both bemused and troubled by her husband's reaction. The therapist, rather than assailing the outrageousness of John's position, encouraged him to talk about the meaning he attributed to Sandi's action. What followed was an illuminating exploration of John's fears related to Sandi's return to part-time work as a beauty consultant. He expressed concern that she would become "a feminist of today . . . one of those Virginia Slims girls," instead of "the nice little girl from Kansas" that he married. Further discussion revealed John's worry that Sandi's work would make her less interested in him, would undercut his provider role, and risked a repetition of his earlier marital loss. At this point, Sandi was able to provide John with considerable reassurance by explaining that she was not concerned about his physical limitations, that she greatly valued his past support of her activities, and that she had no desire to meet a new man, especially one who wanted to control or to lead her. This session was immensely useful as it enabled Sandi to see more clearly the sense of powerlessness and insecurity that drove John's attempts to assume control. John was able to see that a patriarchal leadership style was unneccessary, and could productively be replaced with a style emphasizing partnership and support.

Numerous gender role issues arose in the course of work with this traditional man and his family. Some issues were well handled; many were unrecognized until retrospective analysis was conducted. Of particular interest here is the highly interactive quality of these issues. The marriage benefitted when Sandi's empowerment was matched by John's "disempowerment" from his limited masculine role, and re-empowerment in a less restrictive masculine role definition. Jessica's pain from functioning as the emotional barometer of family distress eased as Tim was able to resist pressures to function in an unemotional and stoic fashion. Sean's "boyish" mischievousness was less pronounced as Jessica was given more role latitude and not expected to be so parental, nurturant, and overly mature. An easing of sanctions on intimacy between males (for example, Tim and John) reduced the need for the males to be overly dependent upon women for nurturance and emotional expressiveness. Sandi's higher level of "instrumental" functioning provided John with greater opportunities for "expressive" functioning, among other non-traditional male behaviors.

FEMINISM AND THE TRADITIONAL MAN: THE CLINICAL ATTITUDE

Family therapy, once seriously gender-blind, recently has been enriched by feminist critiques of theory and practices that are insufficiently attuned to female experience. Because of disadvantaged political positions, women have been more vulnerable to sexist practices. Nevertheless, since men also are constrained when family therapy perpetuates the narrow limitations of traditional gender roles, further study of male experience in the family is timely. Gender role stereotypes constrain both men and women; role strain is experienced by both genders. Patriarchy obviously limits women, but in a qualitatively different manner, it also limits men.

A significant obstacle in discourse about feminism and family therapy has been the failure to recognize the complex nature of gender relations. The feminist position has clearly addressed the "complementary" (Hoffman, 1981) or hierarchical aspect of gender relations, in noting that men are historically in a superior political position. From this perspective, the position of women is analogous to that of oppressed minorities. Family therapy that fails to address this basic power inequity has been challenged as an immoral and conservative practice that only accomplishes first-order change – that is, it superficially mollifies the distress, without challenging the inequitable nature of the relationship. Naturally, from this perspective, appeals for the understanding of male pain are met with outrage. True second-order change regarding women's oppression is seen as a more pressing objective, and compassion towards men's positions can be understood as potentially inhibitory to change.

Gender relations, however, unlike other hierarchical relations, have another aspect which seriously complicates the dilemma. In addition to the overt complementarity in patriarchal culture (men dominant, women dominated), there is a covert complementarity that allows gender relations to function as symmetrical relationships—the "battle of the sexes." Symmetrical relationships, in which each party negotiates from a position of equality or sameness (Watzlawick, Jackson, & Beavin, 1967), are imitated in gender relations because of their covert complementarity. This special feature of gender relations makes them, in some ways, totally unlike other relationships between oppressor and oppressed. Despite men's politically advantaged position, in ways poorly understood by women, men feel disadvantaged in relations with women. Men are enormously dependent upon women for validation and emotional expressiveness (Pleck, 1980). A traditional man has great difficulty feeling masculine without validation by a woman. This situation is unique to gender relations; it is not true of other complementary relationships. Plantation owners may have valued the good opinion of their slaves, but they based little of their self-worth on popularity among the slaves.

Because of this special aspect of gender relations, it is possible to adopt binocular vision—to view men both as oppressors and as psychologically vulnerable persons. From this perspective, men can be viewed in a more compassionate light, without losing sight of the primary objective—second-order change from hierarchical to cooperative relations. Ultimately, with fuller recognition of the benefits of this shift to egalitarian relationships, intergender cooperation should become the predominant operating style.

REFERENCES

Avis, J.M. (1986). Feminist issues in family therapy. In F. P. Piercy & D. H. Sprenkle (Eds.), *Family therapy sourcebook*, (pp. 213-242). New York: Guilford.

Bernard, J. (1981). The good-provider role: Its rise and fall. *American Psychologist, 36*, 1-12.

Bograd, M. (1984). Family systems approaches to wife battering: A feminist critique. *American Journal of Orthopsychiatry, 54*, 558-568.

Bograd, M. (1986). A feminist examination of family systems models of violence against women in the family. In M. Ault-Riché (Ed.), *Women in family therapy*. (pp. 34-50). Rockville, MD: Aspen Systems.

Brooks, G.R. (In Press). Psychotherapeutic approaches to traditional men. In P.A. Keller & L.G. Ritt (Eds.), *Innovations in clinical practice: A source book*. Sarasota, FL: Professional Resource Exchange.

David, D.S. & Brannon, R. (1976). *The forty-nine percent majority: The male sex role*. Reading, MA: Addison-Wesley.

Doyle, J.A. (1989). *The male experience*. (Second Edition). Dubuque, IA: Wm. C. Brown Company.

Farrell, W.T. (1987). *Why men are the way they are*. New York: McGraw-Hill.

Fasteau, M.F. (1975). *The male machine*. New York: Dell.

Finkelhor, D. & Yllo, K. (1985). *License to rape: Sexual abuse of wives*. New York: Free Press.

Fracher, J. & Kimmel, M.S. (1987). Hard issue and soft spots: Counseling men about sexuality. In M. Scher, M. Stevens, G. Good, & G. Eichenfield (Eds.), *Handbook of counseling & psychotherapy with men*, (pp. 83-96). Newbury Park, CA: Sage.

Gilbert, L.A. (1985). *Men in dual career families: Current realities and future prospects*. Hillsdale, NJ: Lawrence Erlbaum.

Goldberg, H. (1976). *The hazards of being male*. New York: New American Library.

Goldner, V. (1985). Feminism and family therapy. *Family Process*, *24*, 31-47.

Goodrich, T.J., Rampage, C., Ellman, B., & Halstead, K. (1988). *Feminist family therapy: A casebook*. New York: W.W. Norton.

Hafner, R.T. (1986). *Marriage and mental illness: A sex roles perspective*. New York: Guilford.

Hare-Mustin, R. (1987). The problem of gender in family therapy. *Family Process*, *26*, 15-28.

Harrison, J. (1978). Warning: The male sex-role may be hazardous to your health. *Journal of Social Issues*, *34*, 68-86.

Hoffman, L. (1981). *Foundations of family therapy: A conceptual framework for systems change*. New York: Basic Books, Inc.

Hotelling, K. & Forrest, L. (1985). Gilligan's theory of sex-role development: A perspective for counseling. *Journal of Counseling and Development*, *64*, 183-186.

Kantor, D. & Okun, B.F. (1989). *Intimate environments: Sex, intimacy, and gender in familes*. New York: Guilford Press.

Kaslow, F.W. (1981). Involving the peripheral father in family therapy. In A.S. Gurman (Ed.), *Questions and answers in the practice of family therapy*, (pp. 27-31). New York: Brunner/Mazel.

Kimmel, M.S. (1987). Rethinking masculinity. In Kimmel, M.S. (Ed.), *Changing men: New directions in research on men and masculinity*. (pp. 9-24). Newbury Park, CA: Sage.

LoPiccolo, J. (1985). Diagnosis and treatment of male sexual dysfunction. *Journal of Sexual and Marital Therapy*, *11*, 215-232.

Luepnitz, D.A. (1988). *The family interpreted: Feminist theory in clinical practice*. New York: Basic Books.

McGoldrick, M. (1988). McGoldrick's MT "Rules of Thumb." *Family Therapy News*, *19*, 23.

McGoldrick, M., Anderson, C.M., & Walsh, F. (Eds.), (1989). *Women in families: A framework for family therapy*. New York: W.W. Norton.

Mechanic, D. (1962). The concept of illness behavior. *Journal of Chronic Disease*, *15*, 189-194.

Nathanson, C.A. (1977). Sex roles as variables in preventive health behavior. *Journal of Community Health*, *3*, 142-155.

Okun, B.F. (1989). Therapists' blind spots related to gender socialization. In D. Kantor & B.F. Okun (Eds.), *Intimate environments: Sex, intimacy, and gender in families*, (pp. 129-162). New York: Guilford Press.

O'Neil, J.M. (1982). Gender-role conflict and strain in men's lives. In K. Solomon & N. Levy (Eds.), *Men in transition: Theory and therapy*, (pp. 5-44). New York: Plenum.

Pittman, F. (1985). Gender myths: When does gender become pathology? *Family Therapy Networker*, *9*, 24-33.

Pleck, J.H. (1976). The male sex role: Definitions, problems, and sources of change. *Journal of Social Issues*, *32*, 155-164.

Pleck, J.H. (1980). Men's power with women, other men, and society: A men's movement analysis. In E. Pleck & J.H. Pleck (Eds.), *The American man*, (pp. 417-433). Englewood Cliffs, NJ: Prentice Hall.

Pleck, J.H. (1981). *The myth of masculinity*. Cambridge, MA: MIT Press.

Pleck, J.H. (1987). The contemporary man. In M. Scher et al. (Eds). *Handbook of counseling & psychotherapy with men*, (pp. 16-27). Newbury Park, CA: Sage.

Raymond, J.G. (1985). Women's studies: A knowledge of one's own. In M. Culley & C. Portuges (Eds.), *Gendered subjects: The dynamics of feminist teaching*, (pp. 25-44). London: Routledge & Kegan Paul.

Rekers, G.A. (1988). Letter to the Editor. *The APA Monitor*, *19*, 3.

Scher, M. (1990). Effect of gender-role incongruities on men's experience as clients in psychotherapy. *Psychotherapy*, *27*, 322-326.

Shapiro, R.J. & Budman, S.H. (1973). Defection, termination, and continuation in family therapy and individual therapy. *Family Process*, *12*, 55-67.

Silverberg, R. (1986). *Psychotherapy for men: Transcending the masculine mystique.* Springfield, IL: C. Thomas.

Solomon, K. (1982a). Individual psychotherapy and changing masculine roles: Dimensions of gender-role psychotherapy. In K. Solomon & N.B. Levy (Eds.), *Men in transition: Theory and therapy*, (pp. 247-273). New York: Plenum Press.

Solomon, K. (1982b). The masculine gender role: Description. In K. Solomon & N. B. Levy (Eds.), *Men in transition: Theory and therapy*, (pp. 45-76). New York: Plenum Press.

Taffel, R. (1986). Letter to the editor. *Family Therapy Networker*, *10*, 10-11.

Tieffer, L. (1986). In pursuit of the perfect penis. *American Behavioral Scientist, 29*, 579-599.

Walters, M., Carter, B., Papp, P., & Silverstein, O. (1988). *The invisible web: Gender patterns in family relationships*. New York: Guilford.

Watzlawick, P., Jackson, D., & Beavin, J. (1967). *Pragmatics of human communication*. New York: W.W. Norton.

PART 2: THE SOCIAL CONSTRUCTIONS OF GENDER

Men and Story: Constructing New Narratives in Therapy

JoAnn Allen
Joan Laird

SUMMARY. This paper proposes a meaning metaphor, that of STORY, for family-centered practice. In response to the women's movement, men are recognizing that their own stories as complex, gendered individuals need reworking. The relationship between story and gender is examined, using the concepts of *context* and *coherence* as guides. Implications for practice with men are drawn.

The history of the world is HIStory. History as narrative in every culture has been created and told largely by men about men. The generic pronoun was "he" and woman was seen as "other." The

---

JoAnn Allen, MSW, is Associate Professor at The University of Michigan School of Social Work, Frieze Building, Ann Arbor, MI 48109. Joan Laird, MS, is Professor at Smith College School for Social Work, Northampton, MA 01063.

narratives of women have been largely untold and unwritten, or told through the language of men. Paradoxically, in this society with the growth of the women's movement and the telling of HERstory in new ways, men are recognizing that their own stories also need retelling. For if HIStory has left out women, it has distorted the lives of men, at least of men as complex, gendered individuals.

Feminist researchers have exposed the gendered nature of epistemology, of metaphors for practice, and of the power of males in defining every woman's story, particularly the story of her mental health. Since recognizing that gender is a socially constructed category and not "given" in nature, women are publicly telling their stories and writing their lives, clearly and loudly. But oddly enough, men's stories as stories of private, gendered, and domestic lives, still need telling. We do not even possess a language for describing men as gendered human beings; there is no male counterpart for the word feminism. "Gender-sensitive" perspectives usually refer to women's issues and concerns. Lewis and Sussman (1986), remarking that "the original myths of creation and governance of the universe and heavens by goddesses were changed to portray control and power residing in the hands of men and men gods" (p. xiii), add that the pendulum has swung in our time from an emphasis on male research and male issues to an emphasis on women. While this shift has been a necessary part of women's struggles for gender equity,

> the time is now appropriate . . . to consider the meaning and significance of these gender changes for men; how men are reacting, perceiving, and behaving. What men do will determine the permanency of these gender changes, how deep they are rooted in the consciousness of humankind. (Lewis & Sussman, 1986, p. xiv)

We propose a shift to a meaning metaphor for family-centered practice, that of STORY. Story and meaning, as metaphors for practice, suggest new possibilities for the elusive integration of the psychological and the social, and for forging an alliance between individual, psychoanalytically-inspired thought and the systemic theories that have emerged from the family therapy movement.

These metaphors, like the constructivist stance that has currently taken hold in the family therapy field, serve as an umbrella under which "many styles of therapy that would otherwise compete can crowd together" (Hoffman, 1990, p. 4). Symbols, co-interpretation, the structure and meaning of language, and the narrative or the text, rather than an objectivist search for truth rooted in a single metaphor, move to center stage. Story and meaning allow for the exploration of many individually and socially constructed metaphors.

Family therapy provides one context in which the male story as a gendered story can emerge and, in fact, men's stories are being renarrated in a new way in the family therapy field, in the literature, in clinical practice, and at professional meetings. Family therapists are questioning the meanings of the gendered male experience, masculinity, male development, men in family relationships, as well as the experiences of men in therapy (Meth & Pasick, 1990). Even with this trend, the social category of gender has largely been ignored in the new and so-called "radical" social constructivist movement in family therapy (MacKinnon & Miller, 1987). This is a failure with profound political implications, for many of our public and private stories carry powerful prescriptions for gender role performance and either enrich or constrain our lives in important ways. They tell us, as gendered human beings, who we are to be and how we are to think and act. In a recent work, Laird (1989) explores women's stories, calling attention to the cultural myths and power imbalances that have shaped the narratives of women and proposing that family therapy serve as one resource for the restorying of women's self-constructions. In this article, we extend the argument to men's stories, for the stories of men too can serve as powerful constraints on, among other things, men's identities, life choices, and relational experiences.

We begin with a brief review of the use of story and narrative in the family therapy field, and identify some of the contributions available from other disciplines. This material is followed by a discussion of the relationship between story and gender. As we look at the ways that men's lives have been and are being storied, two concepts serve as guides: *context* and *coherence*. This discussion serves as a framework for examining the use of story with men in therapy.

STORY AND NARRATIVE THEORY: A REVIEW

In the family therapy field, a number of theorists have explored the use of myth in families (Byng-Hall, 1973; Ferreira, 1963; Selvini-Palazzoli, Boscolo, Cecchin, & Prata, 1977; Stierlin, 1973). However, emphasis has been given to the defensive and homeostasis-maintaining aspects of myth in families, decontextualized from any wider understanding of myth and other forms of narrative as social and self-constructing categories of language. Other family therapists have recognized and used playfully and creatively the power of "story" in therapy (e.g., Bowen, 1978; Erickson [Rosen, 1982]; Friedman, 1984; Papp, 1984). Like Bettelheim (1977) in the psychoanalytic field, these therapists have used therapist-invented stories or well-known fables to pose analogies and to propose solutions to human dilemmas. More recently, family therapists are placing language at the center of their conceptions of problem and of change (e.g., Anderson & Goolishian, 1988), others have adopted a conversation metaphor (Hoffman, 1985; 1990), and Keeney (1983) suggested "story" as a central metaphor for thought. Laird (1989), combining gender and narrative ideas, has explored the usefulness of narrative theory in unpacking and reconstructing women's stories in family therapy. And most recently, White (1990), also adopting a story metaphor, explores the relationship between narrative, knowledge, and power. But no one has brought narrative theory fully into the research, theory development, or practice endeavor. It is a rich and largely untapped resource.

In recent years, truth, objectivity, reliability and the metaphors of the "hard" sciences have lost some credibility as the most useful yardsticks for understanding the human experience. As we recognize the limits of "measurement" strategies to capture our lives, scholars from many fields are rediscovering literature, narrative, conversation, discourse, story, myth, folklore and other forms of languaging as primary sources of knowledge. These categories are central to the postmodern epistemological revolution occurring in many fields of study, as a search for "meaning" is replacing the search for "truth." Story, used in a larger sense as an encompassing concept for these modes of languaging and in a narrower sense to refer to the familiar encapsulated narratives we use to describe particular events in our own lives or the lives of others, can serve as an overarching metaphor for family therapy. As we will see, story is a central device in the social and individual construction of gender.

An adequate review of the literature relevant to "story" or even the major trends in the narrative fields is not possible in a brief article. Yet if we are to understand the richly complex ways that individuals and families create and interpret themselves and their lives through story and to use these narratives in the service of self and family reconstruction, we need to know more about the storying process and the uses of language in narrative. The possibilities are staggering. As Agar (1980) points out, the number of disciplines and overlapping quests and interests form the "worst sort of quagmire" (pp. 223-224). It is, nevertheless, an exciting quagmire as scholars from almost every social science discipline have made language the center of focus. Scholars are studying language as story and verbal performance (Bauman, 1977, 1986), life history (Cohler, 1988; Langness, 1965; Mandelbaum. 1973), discourse (Chock & Wyman, 1986), conversation (Tannen, 1982), speech acts (Austin, 1962), and narrative (Labov and Waletsky, 1967).

Several comprehensive reviews are available. Agar (1980) and Agar and Hobbs (1982), whose work we draw heavily upon in this paper, review developments in cognitive psychology, anthropology, and linguistics. Polkinghorne (1988) and Sarbin (1986) offer useful perspectives from narrative psychology, while Mishler's (1984) analysis of doctor-patient interviews and his critique of prevailing research interviewing strategies (1986) have particular relevance for mental health professionals.

Spence (1982) and Schafer (1981) have both revisited psychoanalytic thought with a narrative lens. Spence contrasts narrative truth and historical truth, arguing that Freud's original metaphors, never intended to be taken literally, have become reified. He proposes a hermeneutic process of exegesis in which multiple interpretations are used to unpack the patient's "story." Schafer (1981), interested in redescribing psychoanalysis as an interpretive discipline rather than a positivist science, explores the narrative structure of the psychoanalytic process. For all of these scholars, language is seen as vital to culture, self, and meaning making; our words create us and they create our worlds.

MEN'S STORIES IN CULTURE

What are the wider cultural and historical narratives, the fictional genres that allow men and women to create and recreate themselves, to connect themselves with larger collectivities and their own histories? Where do our individual and family gender stories come from? These narratives, central to all family work, must themselves be understood in historical and environmental context, for the wider cultural narratives constitute the realms of possibility, the available repertoire, from which individuals and families can select the ingredients and forms for their own narratives. These contexts offer the frames of reference within which the individual narrative draws shape and expression and can be understood and reshaped.

One of the most powerful modes for cultural transmission of gender narratives is through the popular media. Films, television, popular novels, and other forms of literature and art bombard our senses and sensibilities with preferred, idealized, and exemplary ways of being men and women, as well as vividly showing us the consequences of choosing the wrong paths. These images, as Ehrenreich (1989) points out, vary by class, ethnicity and race. Working class men, exemplified by Archie Bunker, have been stereotyped as racist, sexist, somewhat illiterate and uncultured caricatures who drink Budweiser and eat Wonder Bread, clearly unappreciative of the finer things in life. Sylvester Stallone, in his Rambo persona, provides the extreme stereotype of the quintessential, working class masculine type: dark, dirty, nonverbal, aggressive. The epitome of the stereotype, Rambo is physical and inarticulate, able to express his emotional life only through violent acts.

Raphael (1988) points out that "the glorification of savage power and primitive survival has become a culturally significant obsession," as many films and popular television shows exemplify the special appeal of life as a jungle and man as "noble savage" (p. 20). Older men shame and brutalize their own sons (*The Great Santini*), desparately struggle to talk to their fathers (*Death of a Salesman, Cat on a Hot Tin Roof, I Never Sang for My Father, Da*), or express physical closeness to other men primarily in ritualized ways (witness the fanny-patting and high-five rituals in football) or in physical fights (*Women in Love*). Such powerful images, which portray men as emotionally anesthetized, aggressive, and physical (among other much more subtle images), repeatedly permeate our consciousness, shaping our expectations for masculinity. These expectations are crucial to men's identities, as many men are socialized to assume exaggerated, hypermasculine identities, as well as to behave in homophobic and misogynist ways, risking social rejection and ostracism if they deviate from traditional expectations (Pleck, 1981).

In more recent years, there has been a series of films that highlight how women take responsibility for mediating men's relationships with others. *The Great Santini* and *On Golden Pond* provide vivid examples (Bepko and Krestan, 1990). Other films portray men's struggles to emotionally connect with their children, their wives, and their fathers. For example, *Kramer vs. Kramer*, *Shoot the Moon*, and *Twice in a Lifetime* all portray the losses that men experience in divorce and the painful struggles they undergo to understand and connect with their children.

In literature about men's experiences, a major theme concerns the extreme distance in contemporary father-son relationships, seen as a source of male difficulty in all relationships. Reconnection with the father is posed as a necessary part of the restorying of the male life. Osherson (1986), for example, borrowing a metaphor from the poet Robert Bly, argues that men must find their fathers, the warriors within. Manhood is "unfinished": men are unable to come to terms with their masculine identities because they are unable to differentiate themselves from the indistinct and distorted childhood images of their fathers, who were often silent, distant, forbidding, critical, or even violent. Raphael (1988) argues that it is very difficult for contemporary males to find clear definitions for manhood or an unambiguous path to masculinity in male America because they lack clearly structured male initiation rituals that move boys from the company of women to the worlds of men. Male rites of initiation in our society exist, but they are haphazard simulations of earlier rituals. In fact, therapy itself has become a modern-day substitution for the puberty rites characteristic of traditional societies (Haley, 1980; Kimball, 1960).

Some stories have found no audiences; they cannot be told. Heilbrun (1988) makes this point brilliantly in her recent book, *Writing a Woman's Life*, illustrating how women have been denied their narratives or have had their narratives usurped by men, sometimes retreating into depression or madness. She points out that "power is the ability to take one's place in whatever discourse is essential to action and the right to have one's part matter. This is true in the Pentagon, in marriage, in friendship, and in politics" (p. 18). But narrative genres dictate the possibilities and the themes. For example, while men write of their powers, their accomplishments, their own importance, women accept full blame for failures, deny ambition, and disclaim accomplishment. Women who achieve success and even fame, if their lives have not centered around men, marriage, and children, are vulnerable to public vilification.

Men, on the other hand, have been denied their domestic stories. We know little of their private thoughts, their places in family life. In fact, men are frequently storied in the media and on television as incompetent buffoons when it comes to family life, understanding women, or parenting their children. If women's public stories have been limited and distorted and if women lack the "proper" language for public discourse, men's domestic stories are virtually unknown, and men are often at a loss for words in the intimate environs of family life.

While no story is ever told twice in quite the same way, since no two contexts are ever identical in relation to time, space, situation, speaker, audience, or states of mind (Bauman, 1977), nevertheless families, like ethnic and other communities, do develop their own folklores. We know that family stories, myths, and legends travel across the generations in our families, as Elizabeth Stone (1988) has so eloquently described in *Black Sheep and Kissing Cousins*. These stories serve many purposes (Laird, 1989), among them providing the possibilities for how we are to be men or women, how we are to present ourselves and to relate to others in same or cross-sex interactions. Other family stories serve as cautionary tales, warning us how *not* to be men or women. In the folklore of one family we know, for example, women repeatedly are storied as incompetent and men as their rescuers, a continuing narrative that has costly consequences for both sexes. In the stories of another family, the males tend to be described as narcissistic, thoughtless, inferior beings, the women as self-sacrificing, caretaking, long-suffering but superior creatures. Such stories, if few forces for change are allowed to penetrate, restrict possibilities for fulfillment for both sexes.

COHERENCE

To enter the realm of story and narrative is to blur the boundary between truth and fiction, to fully embrace both subject and object, to substitute interpretation for objectivity. As Whan (1979) points out, very little of human narrative can ever be verified or falsified in a strict empirical sense. Bauman (1986) argues that fact/fiction, history/myth dichotomies are not useful in understanding narrative. He suggests, contrary to what we have assumed, that perhaps events are not the raw materials from which we construct our stories, but the reverse, that events may be abstractions from narrative. "It is the structures of signification in narrative that give coherence to events in our understanding, that enable us to construct in the interdependent process of narration and interpretation a coherent set of interrelationships that we call an event" (p. 5). Polkinghorne (1988) makes a similar point when he argues that:

> Historical narratives are a test of the capacity of a culture's fictions to endow real events with the kinds of meaning patterns that its stories have fashioned from imagined events. Thus, historical narratives transform a culture's collection of past happenings (its first order references) by shaping them into a second-order pattern of meaning. (p. 62)

Narrative is intentional and thus may be used to confuse, obscure or distort, as well as to clarify.

If objectivity, historical truth, reality-seeking, verification and other means of measurement are not appropriate criteria for understanding the story, what criteria may be substituted? Most students of narrative have borrowed from hermeneutic, linguistic, ethnographic, and literary traditions to interpret the "story." One notion common to all of these traditions is that of *coherence*. Polkinghorne (1988) points out that "the truth of narrative . . . is linked to the more general question of the truth of literary coherence, a truth that has been ignored by formal science in favor of logical coherence" (p. 63). As individuals and as families, we must construct narratives that are coherent enough to make us intelligible to ourselves and to others. As Gergen and Gergen (1983) suggest, as we communicate our personal and familial narratives, we subject them to social alteration and critique. Whether or not a narrative can be maintained depends on our skill in convincing others that our interpretations of ourselves and of the events in our experiences are correct. Thus we interpret and reinterpret, add to, and revise our stories in order to maintain coherence between the personal and the social realms.

For Agar (1980), an ethnographer, to understand the interview means "understanding all of it—the situation that produced it, the person who gave it, and the shared and idiosyncratic knowledge which constitutes the unseen context needed to interpret it" (p. 224). Agar and Hobbs (1982) offer an interpretation of the concept of story or narrative coherence which is threefold: narratives may present *global coherence*, *local coherence*, and *themal coherence*.

Global coherence refers to the goals the participants have in the conversation, the ideas or plans they seem to have for carrying out their goals, and the changes they improvise as the interaction progresses. As the discourse continues, speakers monitor what they are saying, interpret the listeners' responses and, in turn, modify their own responses and change their plans.

Local coherence refers to the ways that speakers link their utterances and segments of conversation to make sense to the listener. Hobbs (1978) has defined a set of formal relations which speakers use to build coherence in their stories. These include an "occasion" continuation, i.e., a strong temporal linking which presents "what happened next," elaboration, contrast, explanation, and consequence. The third dimension of coherence, *themal coherence*, has been elaborated in the work of Agar and Hobbs. *Themal coherence*

> reflects a longstanding anthropological concern with the move from the detailed analysis of ethnographic material to broader statements of individual and cultural pattern—a pointer for the specific piece of text to more general properties of the speaker's world. (Agar & Hobbs, 1982, p. 7)

In their view, these three dimensions of coherence can help us interpret the relevant "cognitive worlds" of the speakers, that is "the unified, possibly formalizable collection of beliefs, goals, and conversational practices and concerns" (p. 8).

This multilevel scheme for narrative analysis holds promise for future theory building and research and as one way of unpacking the language metaphors now taking hold in family therapy. However, presentation of a microanalytic approach to narrative understanding that encompasses multiple levels of context and coherence is not possible in a brief paper such as this. In the section that follows, using clinical narrative vignettes, we comment on some of the issues of context and coherence that seem to shape the stories of men in therapy, drawing implications for practice and research.

THERAPY AND THE MASCULINITY STORY IN CONTEXT

Therapists who work with male clients must be sensitive to the more general public stories of manhood, as well as to the meanings of manhood relevant to the particular individual and family. The sociocultural context in which men's lives are storied is one in which very powerful myths of masculinity exist. Men are expected to be independent, autonomous, logical, and powerful. Men are strong and silent. They should be able to lead, to confront crises and to solve problems without leaning on anyone else, to protect and defend their wives, children, and property. And they are to be courageous, unafraid in the face of threat. The following vignette, a story one of us has told about her father, gives example:

> When I was a teenager and away at school, there was a major gas main explosion in our community. Several homes blew up and others were threatened. My father, who owned an ice cream store in the neighborhood, rushed home to turn off the gas in our house. Several of the neighborhood women, who had rushed out of their homes, screamed for him to come into their homes to turn off the gas. He saved at least a dozen homes. The living room floor buckled as he left one house. The next day his picture was on the front page of the local paper. My father was a hero, and I was terribly proud of him.
>
> I realized recently that my father never told this story, one of the few positive ones available in the family folklore, in which he was much maligned and ridiculed. I asked him why he never talked about it, why that story was never repeated. He said, "I don't tell that story because I was afraid. I didn't want to go into those homes, and I am ashamed."

If Chodorow (1978), Gilligan (1982), and other feminist/developmental theorists are accurate, masculinity also is defined through separateness and individuation, femininity through attachment and connectedness. Men are said to be threatened by intimacy, to have difficulty with relationships. If women define themselves through connectedness and sharing, the male gender story is more likely to be one of competition. As Meth and Pasick (1990) have pointed out, much of male language is punctuated with "scoring" metaphors, scoring with women, at work, and in sports.

While men's stories are of course influenced by ethnicity, race, class, and sexual orientation issues, most men are taught from early childhood that their place will be in the public world, in the world of work and career. Men own most of the public myths, the public domain. A man's identity is, indeed, highly contingent on his work definition and his ability to compete and to provide. One client, Michael, a second-generation Polish-American youth counselor, told how his uncle Leo, his father's brother, was the hero of the family:

> My uncle Leo was something! He and my father were immigrants, ya' know. My dad was a simple man, but Leo rose to the top in one generation. He was really a businessman, very successful, made a lot of money by the time he was 30 and travelled all over the world, really like the American dream, ya' know. My dad, he was different. He painted houses for a living, we got by. He was real quiet, kinda shy, a real family man, very good with us kids, very patient and kind. Ya know, people always compared my father unfavorably to my uncle. But my dad was the one I really admired. He was gentle, he really cared about us, a genuine person.

With tears in his eyes, Michael continued, "I'm not sure I ever told him that before he died, and I think maybe he felt he was a failure. And maybe he even thought that I thought he was a failure." In the work that followed, Michael spent time at the gravesite in conversation with his father, and was gradually able to examine how the family male mythology had influenced his own choices and his sense of himself as a male.

This brief synopsis gives us a glimpse at the larger context of folklore in which family and individual stories about men take shape. The larger story of men provides a measure against which family stories or mythology, as well as the self-story, can be contrasted. Family stories, with their prescriptions, proscriptions and cautionary aspects, like fairy tales, lay out our choices and foretell the dangers of choosing the wrong paths; many of these stories or bodies of folklore are highly gender prescriptive, constraining the possibilities for each sex.

Sets of linked stories in families also can serve the purpose of explaining or rationalizing choices, or even covering over the paradoxes and contradictions. For example, the family stories about one of our grandfathers repeatedly contrasted him with the cultural story of masculinity, highlighting the ways in which he was *not* masculine. His wife, on the other hand, is storied as a heroine, a pillar of strength, extraordinarily bright and competent, someone who could have run General Motors. The stories illustrate how helpless he was, how dependent he was on her, how much he needed her to survive, to get through the day and the periodic crises. (It was she who killed the poisonous snake that was curled up in the garage!) It was her advice that allowed him to succeed in the public world and, indeed, she even drove him to work and back every day or, if the car was being serviced, walked to the bus stop to meet him and take his arm. On the other hand, quiet, passive, rosy-cheeked and sweet, he loved small children and would spend hours telling them fairy tales. Was it she who should have been dropped off at work? Had nature played a cruel trick of sex reversal on this pair? The linked stories in the family seem to point to a sense of the injustice of a world in which the "stronger" sex is confined to the home and kitchen, while the "weaker" sex must thrust himself into the public fray. But they also cover over her fears and insecurities and her resentment about the narrowness of her life choices, and his own anger at her rigid control of his life and the burdens of his responsibility to insure the family's prosperity. He seemed to become more and more indistinct and remote, she more central to every family story.

Therapists need to be sensitive, then, to the family's notions of the gender story for men and how the gender folklore of the family in treatment fits or doesn't fit with the wider ethnic group's narratives for male functioning or, more powerful yet, the wider cultural masculinity narrative.

The Context of Therapy

Therapy itself presents a particular contextual dilemma for many men. Often forced to enter therapy by a spouse, significant other, doctor, or the courts, some men are faced with the loss of an important relationship, their health, or their freedom if they refuse to seek help. While these may be compelling reasons to accept therapy, to do so may represent a loss of another kind. Many men become prisoners of premises that leave little room for help-seeking options and thus, in a sense, render them less open to problem-solving than women. Acknowledging the "need" for therapy can itself be a crisis for many men, discontinuous with their self-concepts and antithetical to larger social meanings of masculinity, as the following example typifies:

> Nate S. requested therapy because his wife of 25 years was threatening to leave him if he didn't change. In the first session, with both present, Nate explained that his wife must be in the mid-life crisis that "many women go through at her age." He could find no other possible explanation for her "sudden" dissatisfaction with him and the marriage. Further, he had been surprised and hurt to learn of her attraction to another man whom she described as "someone who really listened to her."
>
> Nate felt that he had always been a supportive husband who worked hard to care for her and their two grown children. If he had not been available to listen it was because he was trying to "get ahead" so that things would be better for his family. Now that the children were raised, he could begin to think about taking it easier. But just as he was in a position to spend more time with Janice, she was questioning the marriage. Nate suggests that it may be her two years of therapy that has brought this on, because she has "gotten a lot of new ideas that have been upsetting her." He, on the other hand, has not changed. "I am still the same man she fell in love with years ago. I love my wife and will do anything I can to help her through her crisis."

This "why I came to therapy" story reveals a familiar pattern. Men often enter therapy denying their own involvement and holding others responsible. For example, abusive men often claim they were provoked by their wives. When the referral is connected with addiction, a man will often explain that his wife, employer, or doctor is overconcerned and will be angry at the implication he is not in control. Many women, in similar situations, assume blame and ask "What is wrong with me and how can I change?" Nate, for example, looks outside of himself for a logical explanation and offers to help his wife, defining himself in a superior or "one-up" position. The man who accepts the myth of masculinity in a rigid way will necessarily be uncomfortable with the implication that he needs help or could have "emotional" problems.

Building a Coherent Story in Therapy

The therapist who assumes a social constructivist stance focuses the therapeutic process on the client's construction of reality. The initial task for client and therapist is to build a coherent story of the problem situation from the client's point of view. The story metaphor is highly congruent with the social constructivist stance in therapy, for it offers a path into the ways that the client has languaged his situation. A story perspective leads the therapist to inquire about who has influenced the storying of the situation as a problem, how this story fits with the various levels of contextuality for storying, and what meanings he and others give to the story. If story, rather than theory or concept, drives the interview process, we are better able to avoid superimposing our own theoretical templates, that is, making the family fit our own prior text, which is itself often replete with gender-stereotyped notions for individual and family functioning.

We often begin by asking the client to explain how he came to therapy. A client is likely to give a "story" response which provides the therapist with a window into the client's world of meaning. For example, David W. sought help after his wife demanded a divorce and left him. When asked why this event led him to therapy, he told the following story:

> About a week after my wife left, something terrible happened to me. I work nights and am usually so tired when I get home that I fall asleep right away. But this particular night had been awful at work and I was wishing I had someone to talk to at home. Anyone would want that, I guess. Well, I had to force myself to go into the house. When I got inside, I was scared, panicky and ran outside. I went to my parents' house and they took me in. It was late and they must have wondered about me. I told them I just felt sad and they didn't ask questions.

The therapist may of course supply many interpretations for David's story but, using our framework, it is the client who is encouraged to seek its meanings. The therapist asked how this event meant that he should seek help. David said he realized that his panic was connected to his fear of being alone and that in turn stimulated additional fear. He had never lived alone and had never taken care of himself in the domestic sphere. Asked to elaborate, David replied that he feared his dependence on women meant that he could not be "much of a man." He was distressed, in large part, because he could not fit his newly discovered dependency into his life story of the strong, independent male. Part of therapy included the reconstruction of a masculine self through story revisions which could accommodate dependency and interdependency more comfortably. As David's story illustrates, all of us strive to make our stories coherent to ourselves and others; indeed, our very identity depends on our success in this process. Each event in our lives may be thought of as a "side" story that we must somehow fit into the major "life story," reflecting and reinforcing the meanings and values in that larger story and portraying ourselves, to ourselves and to others, as good and well-intentioned people. The client wishes to tell a story that hangs together and portrays him in a positive light; part of that story is to make the referral for therapy itself coherent with his self-concept and with his sense of himself as masculine. In the example above, the client placed his "fear" experience in the context of a difficult day at work. He took pains to make it clear that fear and dependency were not the usual conditions of his life. The therapist, at this point, can underscore the need for a coherent image of masculinity by acknowledging the courage required to come to therapy.

On another level, the story is taking shape and must attain coherence in an interactional context. The male client must tell his story in a way that it can be accepted by the listener, that is, in a way that will achieve global coherence. Nate's story, for example, must be understood and accepted by his wife and by the therapist. In the process, Nate may have to modify the story in such a way that it will retain its coherence and fit into the larger context in which his "self" is storied. This process is clearly more complex in family interviews where the story is more likely to be challenged. While all family members jockey for position and are interested in having their own stories heard, it is not the case that all stories are equal. As Laird (1989) has argued elsewhere, men tend to have more storying power and claim more verbal space (especially in the public world). They also have clearer access to accepted genres for storytelling. However, many men are less comfortable than women with domestic and relationship language, often the center of the "conversation" in the therapeutic context.

Local coherence, as we said earlier, refers to *how* one tells a story, the ways in which the story is structured and the parts sequenced. Note, for example, how David sequenced his story of the "fear" event. He set the context of unusual stress and his "normal" desire for companionship before revealing what he considered unacceptable behavior. The structure of the story can help to reveal the meaning of the event. The therapist's role is to facilitate the telling of the story, to allow it to emerge, to listen for its coherence, without imposing interpretations. Therapists sophisticated in narrative analysis strategies can work with audiotape, videotape, or transcript to unravel the levels of local coherence and layers of meaning in the narrative structure, a process which is time consuming but richly rewarding as the meanings of even the most confusing and inarticulate narratives may be revealed (Riessman, 1990).

Themal coherence is of special importance in stories and in the therapeutic process. It refers to those recurring themes in a narrative that organize and bring unity to the story. In both individual and family therapy, in our view, it is important to identify the themes, their sources, and their significance to the client/family. Gender, and the client's understanding of self as a gendered human being, serves as a powerful organizing force for shaping both men's and women's life stories. As we shall see in the next section, part of the work consists of helping clients to examine how their own stories have been shaped and perhaps constrained by family and societal notions of gender performance.

RESTORYING THE GENDER STORY: A NEW THEMAL COHERENCE

We agree with Hoffman (1985) that a problem does not reside in family organization or inside an individual but may be located in an "ecology of ideas." From a story/meaning stance in therapy with men, then, one of the goals is to surface the public gender story, that ecology of ideas which so often presents obstacles to change in men. Change for men, from our perspective, flows from a process of "restorying" both their public and private beliefs about masculinity.

The story stance helps to create a context in which such change is possible in part because the therapist assumes a respectful and non-blaming attitude, like the ethnographer bracketing his or her own "prior" theories. We begin by listening for the story, that is, that coherent set of ideas in the context of all who are involved in the therapeutic system. With men, masculinity stories are pervasive. The following vignette illustrates the beginning process:

> Bob B. came into therapy on the advice of his physician. His concerns included his overweight, unhappiness at work, and feeling overburdened in his personal life. He loved his wife Meredith and his two step-children, but felt they all expected too much from him. Besides managing his own business, he acted as accountant for Meredith's business. He felt that his wife expected him to do all of the household repairs and would complain if things were not fixed immediately. He also kept his widowed mother's home in good repair. Bob felt valued only for his "services" and indicated that he thought his needs counted for little. On the other hand, he recognized that he rarely expressed his needs and that he liked being regarded as "strong and dependable."

Several stories from Bob's early family life revealed the themal coherence of his life narrative. His father, a carpenter, who often worked a great distance from home, would designate Bob as "the man of the family" in his absence. Bob had vivid memories of his father teaching him how to "fix things" around the home in prepartion for his surrogate duties.

> I remember the time on a Saturday when I was getting ready to play in a very important baseball game. My dad said that I couldn't go because he wanted to teach me how to do some repairs on the car. I complained but my father made it clear that work came first and play second in a man's life. He told me how I needed to learn these things in case my mother had any trouble while he was away at work. My dad said, "After all, you can't expect a woman to know how to take care of a

> car." I remember feeling disappointed and resentful, but also proud that I was so important, the only son, the only one who could do these things. You know, when I think about it, these times when my father was teaching me were practically the only times I got his attention and felt he really approved of me.

Other stories depicted Bob's father as a harsh, rough man who would cruelly ridicule his son about his weight and his lack of "manliness." Bob's gender story cast him in the role of protector and caretaker of women, an "in control" man. Gradually, this role was to alienate him from his father who was a heavy drinker and often abusive.

> My mother used to say to me over and over, "I hope you won't grow up to be like your father and treat *your* wife like this." Once, when I was about 15, I tried to tell my father how I hated his drinking. My dad said, "Yeah, I know you'd like to hit me and you could probably deck me. But if you do, don't ever turn your back on me 'cause I'll get you." I vowed I would never be like my father.

The initial "storying" is followed by a search for cognitive meaning that is congruent with men's needs for logical explanation. Male clients are encouraged to identify their beliefs and their sources in society and in the family. The "restorying" process continues by connecting the premises of the gender story to the problems and stresses experienced by the client. In Bob's case, he was able to link his current life stresses to the "ecology of ideas" about masculinity derived from his early family experiences. His view of himself as protector and problem-solver for women also fit his interpretation of the dominant societal story of the proper relationship between the sexes. There was, however, a tension between this story and his family of origin gender story which depicted "real men" as hard-drinking, emotionally underresponsible, and abusive toward women. This differentiated him but also distanced him from his father and other men in his extended family and, in his view, limited his choice of male friends.

These initial steps create a positive context for change, as the power of the public story and the courage required for differentiating from it are acknowledged. While it is important for the therapist to facilitate the storying process, it is also essential to encourage alternative stories, to create a context in which meanings can be expanded, and to challenge the dominant societal definition of masculinity as the only viable one for this particular male client. Change comes about through the co-construction of new meanings.

In Bob's case, for example, the therapist was eventually able to question his belief that it would be unmanly to express his needs and concerns to his family. Bob gradually came to acknowledge that his job of benevolent caretaker was also a way of controlling others, of "being-in-charge," and of discounting women. As time went on, Bob began to ask his step-children for help with repairs, to ask his mother to hire outside help, and to re-negotiate role responsibilities with Meredith. As Bob discovered that he did not lose respect and that family members welcomed his expressions of need and feeling, he could begin to reconstruct some of his ideas about "masculinity." At a more playful level, Bob "restoried" his sense of self as "father" by spending more time with his four-year-old nephew, his namesake, playing with him in ways that his own father had not been able to do with him.

Thus, at the heart of therapeutic change is a restorying process which, for the male client, may involve the co-invention of a more workable story of masculinity. This quest for "narrative truth" is a deconstructive process in the sense that some of the values and meanings attached to the masculinity myth are unpacked and reconstituted. The masculine code for behavior can be interpreted to mean freedom and independence but it can also be emotionally and behaviorally restrictive. A deconstructive reading of the client's story may "disrupt the frame of reference within which the client sees the world" (Hare-Mustin and Maracek, 1988, p. 461). When that happens, the restorying begins and change is inevitable.

The deconstruction and reconstruction of a man's gender story is often accelerated by introducing the notion that he may have exercised little choice in the construction of self as man. This idea can be unsettling for many men but useful in the change process because men can bring the logical thought processes and problem-solving efforts they have been socialized in to draw upon to a new and different sort of challenge. The idea of gender as a social construction, a notion at the heart of the women's movement, comes as news to most men; it can spur a man toward change simply to realize he has echoed the dominant gender story without ever seriously examining its effects on his life. As in Bob's story, such a shift in perception makes it possible for the male client to consider choices which may fit his life in more functional and satisfying ways.

One of the most important steps in the restorying process is to surface the private story of the male client. In fact, it is the possibility of exposing the private arena of feeling that makes therapy such a threatening context for most men. Male socialization requires that men keep constant vigil against feelings of dependency, vulnerability, emotionality, or fear. Yet when therapy successfully elicits the private story, many men reveal a deep longing for connectedness and nurturing, as well as frustration with their lack of language to express these needs. For example, one of our clients had considerable talent as an amateur actor. He was very proud of the range of emotions he could express on stage, including crying. In his private life he was cold and unemotional, unable to express affection to his wife or children. He felt haunted by his fears of being seen as weak, or of losing control. Many men have strong, unexpressed fears of inadequacy, of not measuring up, fears that are hidden in competitiveness and bravado. Expressions of sadness and grief, sometimes even tears, are heard in the private stories, while the public repertoire is often limited to silence or anger.

One goal of therapy is to help a man to construct a reality in which he can comfortably incorporate these more "feminine" parts of himself into his life story. The process involves a shift in his model of rigid autonomy to one which includes connectedness. As Goodrich, Rampage, Ellman, and Halstead (1988) point out, "There is no self without an other, and the challenge is to integrate autonomy and connection. The reason a man can look so enviably strong and separate is because women are playing out the other side for him" (p. 19).

A crucial part of the restorying process with male clients is to help them to reconnect with members of the family of origin. Many men know little of the stories of their fathers and grandfathers, men who may have been absent physically and/or emotionally during their childhoods. Part of therapy for Bob, for example, centered on the search for a more coherent and complete story of his father. This process led to the reconstruction of a father who possessed some positive characteristics with which Bob could comfortably identify and a reinterpretation of some of the more troublesome aspects of his father. These Bob began to restory as he thought about the context for male development in which his father had grown. Bob not only rediscovered his father's reputation as a skilled craftsman, but also as a man who could have fun, who "brightened the days of all he met." He heard stories of his father as a helpful, sensitive person. As Bob began to "unpack" the hidden dimensions of his father, he gained new appreciation for parts of himself, experiencing a new and more positive bond with the lost father. He also began to attach new meanings to old stories. For example, Bob had always blamed his father for being overweight. He described many "cruel" scenes in which his father would load his son's plate with enormous quantities of food, insisting that Bob eat every bite. Bob anxiously learned to "inhale" food in order to escape the wrath of his father. In therapy, he reinterpreted this memory in the context of his father's distaste for his own nickname of "Skinny." He wanted Bob to be spared similar ridicule by growing up "with some meat on his bones" and "able to handle himself in a fight." As Bob reinterpreted these stories, he considered the possibility that his father's intentions were caring, even though his behavior was not. This sense of a different and more positive connectedness with his father helped Bob to develop a reshaped story in which his masculine sense of self was more acceptable.

In this process of restorying a life, as a "best text" is co-constructed, new levels of meaning and coherence are achieved. The new story will contain parts of the old, and old and new premises and meanings will blend to link past and present into a reinterpreted narrative. One challenge the male client then faces is how to reveal to others his changed story in a way that makes him coherent to and accepted by others, both men and women.

REFERENCES

Agar, M. (1980). Stories, background knowledge and themes: Problems in the analysis of life history narrative. *American Ethnologist*, *7*, 223-229.

Agar, M. & Hobbs, J. (1982). Interpreting discourse: Coherence and the analysis of ethnographic interviews. *Discourse Processes*, *5*, 1-32.

Austin, J. (1962). *How to do things with words*. Oxford: Oxford University Press.

Anderson, H. & Goolishian, H. (1988). Human systems as linguistic systems: Preliminary and evolving ideas about the implications for clinical theory. *Family Process*, *27*, 371-393.

Bauman, R. (1977). *Verbal art as performance*. Prospect Heights, IL: Waveland Press.

Bauman, R. (1986). *Story, performance, and event: Contextual studies of oral narrative*. Cambridge, England: Cambridge University Press.

Bepko, C. & Krestan, J. (1990). *Too good for her own good*. New York: Harper & Row.

Bettelheim, B. (1977). *The uses of enchantment*. New York: Vintage Books.

Bowen, M. (1978). *Family therapy in clinical practice*. New York: Jason Aronson.

Byng-Hall, J. (1973). Family myths used as defence in conjoint family therapy. *British Journal of Medical Psychology*, *46*, 239-250.

Chock, P. & Wyman, J. (Eds.). *Discourse and the social life of meaning*. Washington, DC: Smithsonian Institution Press.

Chodorow, N. (1978). *The reproduction of mothering*. Berkeley: University of California Press.

Cohler, B. (1988). The human studies and the life history: The *Social Service Review* lecture. *Social Service Review*, *62*, 552-575.

Draeger, J. (1983). The problem of truth in psychotherapy: A phenomenological approach to treatment. *Social Science Medicine*, *17*, 371-78.

Ehrenreich, B. (1989). *Fear of falling: The inner life of the middle class*: New York: Pantheon Books.

Ferreira, A. (1963). Family myth and homeostasis. *Archives of General Psychiatry*, *9*, 456-463.

Friedman, E. (1984). Friedman's fables. *Family Therapy Networker*, *8*, 30-35.

Gergen, K. & Gergen, M. (1983). Narratives of the self. In T. Sarbin and K. Scheibe (Eds.), *Studies in social identity*, (pp. 254-273). New York: Praeger.

Gilligan, C. (1982). *In a different voice: Psychological theory and women's development*. Cambridge, MA: Harvard University Press.

Goodrich, T. J., Rampage, C., Ellman, B., & Halstead, C. (1988). *Feminist family therapy: A casebook*. New York: Norton.

Haley, J. (1980). *Leaving home: The therapy of disturbed young people*. New York: McGraw-Hill.

Hare-Mustin, R. & Maracek, J. (1988). The meaning of difference. *American Psychologist*, *43*, 455-464.

Heilbrun, C. (1988). *Writing a woman's life*. New York: Ballantine Books.

Hobbs, J. (1978). Coherence and coreference. *Cognitive Science*, *3*, 67-90.

Hoffman, L. (1985). Beyond power and control: Toward a second-order family systems therapy. *Family Systems Medicine*, *3*, 381-396.

Hoffman, L. (1990). Constructing realities: An art of lenses. *Family Process*, *29*, 1-12.

Keeney, B. (1983). *The aesthetics of change*. New York: Guilford Press.

Kimball, S. (1960). Introduction. In A. van Gennep, *The rites of passage*. (pp. v-xix). Chicago: University of Chicago Press.

Labov, W. & Waletzky, J. (1967). Narrative analysis: Oral versions of personal experience. In J. Helms (Ed.), *Essays on the verbal and visual arts*, (pp. 12-44). Seattle: University of Washington Press.

Laird, J. (1989). Women and stories: Restorying women's self-constructions. In M. McGoldrick, C. Anderson, & F. Walsh (Eds.), *Women in families*, (pp. 428-449). New York: Norton.

Langness, L. (1965). *The life history in anthropological science*. New York: Holt, Rinehart, & Winston.

Lewis, R. & Sussman, M. (1986). Preface. In R. Lewis & M. Sussman (Eds.), *Men's changing roles in the family*, (pp. xiii-xvi). New York: Haworth Press.

Mandelbaum, D. (1973). The study of life history: Gandhi. *Current Anthropology*, *14*, 177-196.

MacKinnon, L. & Miller, D. (1987). The new epistemology and the Milan approach: Feminist and sociopolitical considerations. *Journal of Marital and Family Therapy*, *13*, 139-155.

Meth, R. & Pasick, R. (1990). *Men in therapy: The challenge of change*. New York: Guilford Press.

Mishler, E. (1984). *The discourse of medicine: Dialectics of medical interviews*. Norwood, NJ: Ablex Publishing Corporation.

Mishler, E. (1986). *Research interviewing: Context and narrative*. Cambridge, MA: Harvard University Press.

Osherson, S. (1986). *Finding our fathers: The unfinished business of manhood*. New York: The Free Press.

Papp, P. (1984). The creative leap. *Family Therapy Networker*, *8*, 20-29.

Pleck, J. (1981). *The male myth*. Cambridge, MA: MIT Press.

Polkinghorne, D. (1988). *Narrative knowing and the human sciences*. Albany: State University of New York Press.

Raphael, R. (1988). *The men from the boys: Rites of passage in male America*. Lincoln, NB: University of Nebraska Press.

Riessman, C. (1990). *Divorce talk: Women and men make sense of personal relationships*. New Brunswick, NJ: Rutgers University Press.

Rosen, S. (Ed.). (1982). *My voice will go with you: The teaching tales of Milton H. Erickson*. New York: Norton.

Sarbin, T. (Ed.). (1986). *Narrative psychology: The storied nature of human conduct*. New York: Praeger.

Schafer, R. (1981). *Narrative actions in psychoanalysis*. Worcester, MA: Clark University Press.

Selvini-Palazzoli, M., Boscolo, L., Cecchin, G. & Prata, G. (1977). Family rituals: A powerful tool in family therapy. *Family Process*, *16*, 445-463.

Spence, D. (1982). *Narrative truth and historical truth: Meaning and interpretation in psychoanalysis*. New York: Norton.

Stierlin, H. (1973). Group fantasies and family myths. Some theoretical and practical aspects. *Family Process*, *12*, 111-125.

Stone, E. (1988). *Black sheep and kissing cousins: How our family stories shape us*. New York: Times Books.

Tannen, D. (1982). *Spoken and written language*. Norwood, NJ: Ablex.

Whan, M. (1979). Accounts, narrative and case history. *British Journal of Social Work*, *9*, 489-499.

White, M. & Epston, D. (1990). *Narrative means to therapeutic ends*. New York: Norton.

Reclaiming Men's Experience in Couples Therapy

John H. Neal
Alan J. Slobodnik

SUMMARY. This paper describes an approach to addressing men in couples therapy based on cybernetic explanation and social constructivism. The approach is designed to validate men's experience of themselves as men while also challenging the cultural prescriptions for masculinity that men have traditionally embraced. It is argued that contemporary challenges to masculinity that devalue men's experience as men serve only to invert the hierarchy of "acceptable" ideas, but do not facilitate an escape from traditional gender practices. Central to our model is the premise that male gender be considered not in terms of differences between men and women, but in terms of how it is constituted through ideas, beliefs, and cultural practices that specify ideal forms of masculinity.

The impetus for this paper on treating men in couples originated from three sources. First, discussions about our dilemmas as professional men, husbands, and fathers left us feeling that a male perspective on gender is not well developed. Feminist thinking invites men to question how we think about and treat women and to question who and what we are. Given what we have learned from women about ourselves and other men, how do we, as men, come to terms with ourselves? How does our changed understanding affect our relationships with our wives, our children, and other men?

John H. Neal, PhD, is on the faculty, Family Therapy Externship, Mental Research Institute, Palo Alto, CA and in private practice, 555 Middlefield Road, Palo Alto, CA 94301 and Santa Cruz, CA. Alan J. Slobodnik, MSW, is Co-Director, Kantor Family Institute, Cambridge, MA and in private practice, 76 Bedford Street, Suite 25, Lexington, MA 02173.

How do we reconcile our feelings of enjoying our masculinity with the realities of the ways men objectify and oppress women? What do we do with our "politically incorrect" feelings? We are not satisfied with the answer that the difficulties characterizing men would be solved if we became more like women. We embrace feminist challenges to the social and cultural "specifications" which structure the subjective experience and beliefs of men (e.g., a patriarchal attitude toward women, strength without vulnerability, etc.). We would add that these social and cultural "specifications" must be critically considered from a male perspective as well. That this paper appears in this publication attests to the validity of the position that this is an important direction of inquiry.

The second impetus for this paper emerged from our observations of how men in therapy make sense of their masculinity. We believe gender is most usefully understood as a socially constructed phenomenon. Men's subjective experience of our masculinity and the role specifications that we follow are inseparable from the messages we receive from our social context about how to be men. Yet most men do not consider how social and cultural notions of "masculinity" dovetail with their personal and professional dilemmas. And most men do not understand that their sense of personal adequacy is inseparable from the ideas that they and others hold about how to be a man. Our approach to treating men in couples challenges many of the habits and interpersonal practices stemming from how masculinity is defined in our culture.

On the other hand, we do not believe that masculinity should be completely devalued. Some of the ideas that constitute men's experience of their masculinity are quite constructive. We suggest that there is tremendous value in providing men the opportunity to explore their experiences of themselves as men, both positive and negative, for themselves and their partners. The alternative, for men to take a feminist perspective toward themselves, is somewhat problematic, since it makes the experience of women privileged over the experience of men. In short, this only inverts the hierarchy of "acceptable" ideas. We do not believe this is an adequate solution to the difficulties posed by male gender.

The clinical approach we advocate requires the therapist to engage men and their partners in exploring the ideas that organize the man's feelings and beliefs about what he must do to feel adequate in his work and relationships. It is important that the therapist grasp how these "specifications" are experienced by men both as exhilarating and exciting while also as intoxicating, addictive, and oppressive. When this understanding is communicated to the man by the therapist, a number of important events follow. The man begins to separate himself as an individual from these ideas and begins to experience gender role specifications as something imposed upon him (and his partner) by the culture. Second, by experiencing these specifications as external to himself, it becomes easier for a man to clarify how he wants to be masculine, as well as to challenge those practices which create problems for him individually and interpersonally.

CYBERNETIC EXPLANATION AND RESTRAINTS

Our approach draws heavily on a perspective most commonly called "cybernetic explanation" or "negative explanation" (Bateson, 1972), and borrows from some of the clinical techniques derived from this perspective by Michael White (1986, 1989, 1990; White & Epston, 1990). The perspective focuses on the restraining influence of *ideas* on persons and is an integral element of many systemically based therapies (e.g., MRI's brief therapy, Milan systemic family therapy, strategic therapy, etc.). These therapists explore their clients' difficulties from the perspective of negative explanation, or how clients' explanations prevent them from noticing information that would lead them to take alternative courses of action. Clients' explanations are referred to by many names: family myths or legacies, versions of reality, or the "attempted solution." Systemic therapists are sensitive to how clients' explanations make sense, are reasonable, and reliably interpret their experience. Information that would lead the clients to alternative explanations and behaviors is experienced as incoherent or irrelevant, since its relevance can only be understood from a different context of explanation.

Individuals vary to the degree they are restrained from noticing information at odds with their explanatory frameworks, and this is strongly influenced by the system in which they are embedded.

Men are often highly restrained from noticing how their ideas about being men prevent them from considering information that would lead them to understand themselves and organize their relationships differently. Some men require a crisis in their lives to notice how their ideas about masculinity affect them: a heart attack or friend's sudden death challenges their workaholism; their wife's decision to leave them pushes them into terror, psychotherapy, and self-examination. Negative explanation can sensitize us to the phenomenon that men's (and women's) ideas about how to be men, what we are calling "male gender," operate to prevent men from noticing information that would enable them to think, feel, and behave differently.

When therapists pursue this course of inquiry with their male clients, they inevitably discover understandable "systemic" or "contextual" reasons for why men behave in the ways they behave. When a man is allowed to explore what he enjoys and dislikes about being a man, or when therapists utilize crises in men's lives to enable them to reconsider how they have been influenced by the specifications for how to be men, an important change takes place. Men examine their own experience on their own terms and a different kind of dialogue is created between a man and his partner and/or his children. The result is greater personal choice and less restraint from cultural gender practices. This approach leads to greater intimacy between men and women, between fathers and their children, and between male friends. A significant advantage of proceeding in this fashion with male clients is that it provides space for men to construct alternatives that are "masculine" solutions to their dilemmas, rather than for them to try to imitate "feminine" solutions or to avoid the issues altogether. We believe this to be true regardless of whether the therapist is male or female.

One result of men taking a feminist approach to male gender has been described critically by many, including Robert Bly (1989), as the "new age man." New age men, for one reason or another, noticed that men have had negative effects on women, children, and other men, and came to the understandable conclusion that it must have something to do with being a man. The most obvious and understandable reaction to this discovery, the one you come to first, is the idea that men are inherently defective, evil, and/or bad.[1]

Thus, the right thing to do is to avoid or oppose masculine ideas and practices. For example, "softness" in men (i.e., the avoidance of aggressiveness, anger, or excessive assertiveness) is often attractive to women who are fed up with men who believe that they are inadequate when they are not "strong." However, some of these women later become frustrated when they discover the softness is not masculine tenderness, but a rejection of the man's own feelings and beliefs in favor of a "one down" position ("passivity") that forces the woman into a hierarchically superior stance. A problem develops when she becomes unhappy that she must take care of him and misses the partnership of equals that she experiences with her female peers. For other couples, this arrangement is experienced as a satisfying alternative to either patriarchal or more egalitarian relationships.

According to Bly, new age men appear at his workshops for men over and over again and are typically depressed and dissatisfied with their relationships without understanding why. New age men often look down on traditional men for not yet giving up those attitudes and practices that are destructive and demeaning to others. On the other hand, traditional men feel equally uneasy with the new age men for rejecting the qualities through which they define their sense of adequacy. For us, both stances are understandable, though not helpful for making sense of male gender in a way that maintains respect for a masculine point of view while escaping the negative effects of some of the practices that accompany it.

GENDER, DIFFERENCE, AND SPECIFICATIONS FOR MASCULINITY

Traditionally, masculinity and femininity have been conceptualized in terms of how they are opposites or different (Hare-Mustin, 1987). Men are more autonomous and women are more related. Men distance from their feelings, women express them. Men do, women feel. However, defining gender in terms of its opposite, that feminine is the opposite of masculine or vice versa, is in complete contradiction to everything we know about constructivism and second order cybernetics. Working with families from a systemic or cybernetic perspective provides continuous confirmation that either-or definitions never capture the complexities of individuals or relationships. Always there are multipie realities, and whatever view one constructs, there is always another view which is equally valid.

Hare-Mustin (1987) argues that when we conceptualize gender in terms of difference, we are "explaining" gender in a way that errs by doing "more of the same." It is absurd, for instance, to assume that because a woman is emotionally expressive and relates well to others, she cannot be assertive or independent. Similarly, that a man is independent and assertive does not preclude an ability to be emotionally expressive and related. So what is the alternative? How does one conceptualize gender if not in terms of differences between men and women?

Our answer is to combine a social construction perspective on gender (cf. Berger & Luckmann, 1966; Gergen, 1985; Kessler & McKenna, 1978) with cybernetic explanation or a "second order view" (cf. Hare-Mustin, 1987; Hoffman, 1990). From a social constructionist perspective, gender consists of persons' methods for attributing and constructing what it means to be masculine or feminine (Kessler & McKenna, 1978). That is, the ways gender influences a man's personal experience and relationships is not reducible to the biological differences between men and women. Instead, gender must be construed in terms of what it means to be male or female. Borrowing from Foucault (1979), White (White & Epston, 1990) observes that cultural "truths" provoke persons to organize themselves and their relationships according to the descriptions of individuality they specify. This does not negate the existence of biological differences, but provides an alternative source for the explanation of "gender" phenomena. Thus, men's experience of masculinity, the ways men organize their interpersonal relationships, and their subjective experience of themselves can be explored from the perspective of socially constructed realities.

White further observes that individuals who experience continuous appraisals of themselves in relation to a set of ideals, and who are isolated in their experience of this condition, become imprisoned by these self-appraisals. In other words, the cultural specifications of how I am "supposed to" be a "man" compel me and others to continuously appraise my success or failure as a person by these standards alone. That I know I am a man suggests to me, for example, that I should handle my feelings in some ways and not in others; that to be an adequate person I must be "successful" in my work; that to be desirable to women I must be emotionally strong and physically a "protector" (i.e., that I can build a fence, repair the lawn mower, figure out what is wrong with the car, if not be able to fix it, etc.). These are "specifications" for masculinity that we and others use to measure our adequacy. They are so pervasive and so ingrained in our culture that we believe them to be "natural." And although these specifications are "only in our mind" and in the minds of others, they translate into very real events in the lives of men and women. They direct us and others to organize our relationships in certain ways.

An additional twist is that the specifications for masculinity support the avoidance of self-expression and examination of our masculinity. Men who "wonder" about their masculinity often are experienced by themselves and others as less adequate men. This has two critical consequences. By avoiding self-awareness, self-expression, and the sharing of our experience as men with other men, men do not pay much attention to the nature of the prescriptions they follow. Paraphrasing Foucault's (1979) argument, the effect of remaining isolated in their experience is that men become the source of their own imprisonment to these specifications. The elaboration of women's experience that has occurred in the recent past (e.g., Gilligan, 1982) has been useful for facilitating challenges to specifications that have constrained women. The equivalent work on men's experience is only beginning (cf. Erkel, 1990).

White (1989) has applied this perspective to understanding and treating men who physically abuse their wives. His analysis suggests that the experience of men who hit their wives is typically characterized by certain ideas. To treat these men, White actively challenges these ideas. The first idea is the notion of patriarchy and the second related idea is that women are the physical property of men. When one considers patriarchy from the perspective of cybernetic explanation, it becomes evident that these ideas prevent men from experiencing women as persons. White observes, "it is not usual practice for people to draw distinctions between their own experience of an event and their property's experience of the same event'' (p. 102).

Typically, approaches to examining men and masculinity (e.g., Brittan, 1989; Ehrenreich, 1984) are quick to critique the obvious flaws in "traditional" (i.e., the "John Wayne brand") masculinity and at least imply that traditional imagery of what constitutes masculinity must be discarded. Yet, in private, many men would say there *is* something positive about being a man, even something positive in John Wayne's brand of masculinity. Not many men want to discard their masculinity. Nor will many men be won over by therapists who take the stance that current notions of masculinity, be they biological or social in origin, have no redeeming value. Do not construe this to mean we are advocating for patriarchy. We are saying only that there is something, for instance, about the male strength that Wayne personified with which many men resonate. The more important question is whether men can experience strength without it being at the expense of women.

One strength of the present approach is that it enables consideration of both positive and negative effects of the varied ways the culture defines masculinity. That is, cybernetic explanation is equally useful for considering specifications which are constructive or destructive. In fact, the distinction between the two is probably more contextual than many of us would like to acknowledge. The specifications which organize men's experience are limited only by the contexts which we as observers choose to examine. The following examples are offered as an attempt to begin to articulate some of the ideas men experience as the basis for appraising their sense of adequacy as men. The source for these observations is our personal experience, our clinical work with men, and recent descriptive research on "successful men" (Weiss, 1989). Consider them as examples of the kinds of information that can be obtained about men's experience of their masculinity and how this is related to the dilemmas for which they seek therapy.

Primarily, men define their sense of adequacy as inextricable from their work. We work to gain self-respect and the respect of our peers and superiors, to demonstrate that we can be counted on in a pinch, and to prove that we do not wilt under pressure. For instance, during training, one of us observed a department chair at a medical school comment that he knew he was working hard enough when he felt that his heart was about to explode out of his chest. Until he felt this degree of pressure, he experienced himself as "sluffing off." Now on the one hand, we can look at this and say it is sick, that the costs of this kind of lifestyle are too great. (He did die of a heart attack a few years later.) On the other hand, this man became a widely published, successful, and highly respected academician. Many of us believe that to be "successful" we must work at this pace until we retire. Our expectation is that we will then feel successful and at ease with ourselves. Certainly, this has always been the "promise" that men have held out for themselves. Ask your male clients if this kind of message permeates their work context and they will tell you that it does.[2]

A second theme around which men examine their self-adequacy also concerns the context of work. Weiss (1989) describes this as the issue of "place." Following a workshop on men, Weiss (1989) posed a question to one of the participants about how he imagined others in the group experienced his place in the group. The man reported that he immediately knew. Weiss was making the point that each man had some notion of their "position" or place in the group relative to each other. The participants might not agree on their respective "rankings," and they might disagree about the most important criterion with which to rank their places, but they would each have some sense of their position. In paying attention to these matters, men will report feeling anxious, a little depressed, or excited, confident, and validated. Men's sense of their place is closely tied to their experiences of themselves as adequate. Most of us know our position in groups without even having to think about it. It is information that we simply attend to without knowing that we are attending to it. It is an important source of self-esteem, as well as a burden. It is like the workplace is one big contest and we are all getting an appraisal of our adequacy depending on how we finish. Sometimes this is made explicit and sometimes men pretend that it doesn't matter. Still, most men are subliminally aware of it, but may never have articulated it to themselves or others.

THE CLINICAL APPROACH

We have mapped out a way of thinking which, we hope, constrains therapists to examine men and gender in certain ways. First, by considering gender from the perspective of second order cybernetics and social constructionism, we have highlighted the ideas that we term gender specifications. These ideas, beliefs, feelings, and habits are central to a man's personal sense of adequacy and central to many of his personal dilemmas. Describing gender from this perspective enables the therapist to escape thinking about gender in terms of differences between men and women and, thus, as inherent characteristics.

Second, we have suggested that therapists must organize their thinking in certain ways in order to apply this approach. Using cybernetic explanation, the therapist must combine the identification and understanding of "vicious cycles" (the repetitive interactional sequences which surround problems) with the exploration of how individuals' participation with the problem is restrained by their ideas about gender. For example, following his son's chronic illness, a man is prevented from responding to the boy's fear and vulnerability (which is acted out aggressively) because he feels that he should not express these kinds of feelings. He believes that he must be "strong" and so he tries to hide his fear and sadness. His son senses his father's sadness and personalizes it as paternal disappointment in him. Hence, because the father believes that he should be "strong" for his son, the boy is left to feel that there is something wrong with him. The cultural prescriptions about what constitutes masculine "strength" restrained this man from noticing other ways he might be strong. We believe many of the "knots" in which men typically experience themselves are traceable to ideas that the culture defines as "masculine."

So how does all this translate into what you do in the room with your clients? And how do you take into account this perspective if you are a male as opposed to female therapist? How can men utilize this "gender sensitive" framework we are advocating in their work with the women in the couples they are treating? How can women make use of this framework in their clinical work with couples?

The overall clinical strategy suggests that the therapist begin in a particular way. Often, the man comes into therapy believing that he is inarticulate or that his view of the problem will not be heard and respected, since many traditional men view therapy as the province of women. We are making the assumption here that the man is the less articulate member of the couple. When the reverse is true, it is important to shift the emphasis onto validating the woman's experience first and early in the interview. Crucial to the engagement process is the therapist's belief that the man can be expressive of his own experience, and that this experience will be given equal weight. Many "resistant" men will respond well when approached in this way, sharing things that surprise spouse and therapist alike.

Also, because men generally are less articulate about their personal experience and more suspicious of therapy than women, it is probably easier for men to join with and listen to a male therapist. However, because both male and female therapists work with both men and women, both genders can develop gender-sensitive stances. In order to accomplish this, we suggest that the therapist explicitly acknowledge gender difference early in the therapy, preferably in the first session. Further, the therapist should communicate his or her understanding that the person of opposite gender knows more about his (her) own gender experience than the therapist, and that the therapist will attempt to make certain that something important about these gender differences is not neglected. This "one down position" is not a ploy, but a stance of respect for what the client knows. The essential point is that the client's experience of his or her gender must be given more weight than the therapist's experience. Female therapists who have used this approach in their clinical work with couples report that they immediately begin to obtain information about men that surprises them and helps them to make sense of men's experience and dilemmas.

After validating the man's and woman's experience of the problem, we attempt to identify (or construct) the circularity in the couple's struggles and to separate the individual man (and woman) from the the gender specifications restraining both partners' ideas and feelings. That is, by taking the position that cultural specifications for masculinity restrain men from certain options, we are organizing our clinical exploration of how gender is linked to the couple's difficulties in a fashion that *creates* a distinction between the individual man and the ideas and cultural practices which have been organizing his experience of himself and his female partner. By separating the man personally from the cultural ideas, feelings, and/or imagery that constrain him from operating differently, he is no longer individually blamed for destructive or oppressive cultural gender practices. Nor is he released from responsibility for the effects of his behavior.

This process of separating the person from these ideas, imagery, and practices can be done in a number of ways, but has been succinctly described by White (1990) as progressively "externalizing" the problem. The process involves what White refers to as "relative influence questioning" and encompasses two sets of questions. The first set of questions maps the influence of the presenting problem on the person and couple's relationship. The second set of questions maps the influence of each member of the couple on the "life" of the problem. In combination, the two sets of questions enable the couple to discover "unique exceptions," or instances which are inconsistent with their understanding and descriptions of each other and the problem. These exceptions are then used to build new accounts of the individuals' abilities to "escape" the effects of the problem. It should be added that the process of externalizing the problem is contingent upon the therapist holding the view that "problems" are separate from the clients as individuals and that cultural ideology and practices operate as symbolic systems that restrain individuals from information that would enable them to think, feel, and behave differently.

Some of the typical beliefs, habits, and practices which restrain men and which warrant externalization in couples therapy are an exaggerated sense of entitlement and status in relation to his female partner and children, an avoidance of social and emotional responsibilities, and reliance on others to face social and emotional responsibilities (Jenkins, 1990). Once these aspects are "externalized," or abstracted out from the individual and made into a "thing," the man becomes more able to examine them and the practices which accompany them. This strategy results in the man beginning to challenge his ideas of masculinity and to choose which behaviors to retain or discard. The pressures of how to behave in the culture and the workplace make the element of choice a crucial factor to a successful treatment outcome.

Following is an example of one way to begin a dialogue with a couple about gender specifications that leads to the externalizing of restraining gender specifications. In the face of a wife's claim that her husband is married to his work and unavailable to her and the children, the therapist can acknowledge his understanding of the man's strategies for balancing work and family in the context of current socio-cultural expectations and male traditions. If the therapist, whether male or female, feels unfamiliar with these, he or she should explore them, acknowledging ignorance and asking the man to inform him or her of the constraints under which he operates. Once these factors have been identified and validated as powerful, the therapist continues by exploring their effects on the man and his relationships. The therapist might say, for example, ''What effects has this expectation that you must keep on striving to become more and more successful been having on you personally?'' ''What effects has it been having on your relationship with your wife?'' ''Which of these concern you most?'' ''What kinds of habits has this expectation for unending success encouraged you to develop?'' ''What kinds of behavior have these habits encouraged in other family members?'' Asked in a context in which the man's dilemmas and experience are respected, these questions often provoke surprising openness.

In the course of this inquiry, it is inevitable that exceptions will be found to the clients' experience of the pervasiveness of the problem. The therapist expects to find these ''unique events'' and looks for opportunities to highlight them. These events are not noticed by the clients, because they do not fit their descriptions, or what White and Epston (1990) call the clients' ''story.'' For example, the therapist expects to find instances in which the man is emotionally expressive. The therapist explores these instances in which the man has been able to avoid or escape some of the prescriptions he experiences. ''How is it that you are able to relax with your wife on vacations and Sundays and put your work out of your mind?'' ''Given the pressures you are under, I am wondering what has prevented you from working more?'' These and other questions that explore instances in which the man has resisted ''giving in'' to the problem create a context in which the man discovers and is validated for having the capacity to operate differently.[3] The "externalization" of the problem, separating the man individually from the specifications, is achieved as a product of this interview process.

For example, one man stated that he had "lost interest" in sex, but not because he found his wife unattractive (as she had thought). The real reason was the surprise: He withdrew because he had felt sexually rejected by her years ago. The tremendous shame and inadequacy he felt as a man had prevented him from ever sharing this with her before. Exploring the ways this man felt "burdened" and "pushed around" by ideas that men must always be good sexual performers and should never communicate about sex enabled him to oppose these pressures and express himself on these and other issues. That is, once he understood that he was being pressured by certain cultural specifications, he was, in effect, separated as an individual from them. He could then choose to oppose them.

In another example, a man expressed his anger to his partner for her "financial irresponsibility," which "required" him to be the financial provider. Inquiry into the specifications he experienced revealed that he needed to be the provider in order to feel good about himself. If he wasn't the primary provider, how could he feel that he was pulling his weight as a man? Following this discovery, he experienced a choice that previously had not been evident. Not only did he not mind being the provider, he was well suited for it. The things he got from this complementary arrangement with his partner made it worthwhile. This enabled him to escape his fears of being burdened and to commit to marriage.

DIALOGUES ABOUT CHOICES

Even after the gender specifications have been identified, explored, and externalized, many men have difficulty seeing or choosing alternatives. Simply identifying and externalizing specifications is not adequate for change. The therapist must engage the man in continuing conversation, or dialogue, that enables the man to understand how previously unseen options, once taken, redefine him as a person. Taking a stand against patriarchy, the idea, for instance, that the man's rational judgement is better than his wife's judgement, changes his experience of himself as a person, her experience of him as a person, and their relationship. Taking a stand against a patriarchal family structure changes our experience of ourselves and, our clients tell us, how we operate as male therapists.

The power of old habits, ideas, and cultural traditions may give men the idea that it is virtually impossible to consider other factors in making a decision. In the absence of alternative realities, the specifications dominate. At this point, the therapist has many options for challenging the ideas and practices which restrain the man and woman from other options. These "dialogues" may take many forms and are not limited to only certain techniques or schools of therapy. One strategy is for the therapist to take a neutral stance towards the prospect of change. The dilemma between the now identified gender specifications and other possibilities for behaving are openly explored as a systemic/strategic therapist might balance exploration between a change/no change stance, genuinely empathizing with the difficulties of either changing or remaining the same (cf. Papp, 1983). None of the choices are judged better or worse than the others per se, but are evaluated as to their potential outcomes and consequences. The responsibility for choice clearly rests with the client.

A prime example of the use of this approach was in the couples therapy of a self-described "corporate quarterback." Although his live-in partner was hurt, angry, and dissatisfied with his unavailability, he felt incapable of giving up the "high" he got from being the "corporate quarterback," even if it meant the end of the relationship. When the therapist explored what prevented him from cutting back at work, he explained that work made him feel like "Joe Montana in the Superbowl.[4] Every day I go out there and everything is riding on what I do. Everyone is watching me, and you know what? I win. It's a total high." As the therapist encouraged him to be really honest with his partner about who he really was, he told her he wasn't willing to reduce his commitment to his work life, even though he knew it was physically destroying him. While he wanted very badly for her to stay, he would support her decision to leave the relationship if she felt the arrangement was not good for her. This honest interaction resulted in increased closeness between them. After a few weeks of thought, she decided to stay. This "proof" that she loved him for who he was prompted him to propose marriage and limit his work schedule. Of course, not every couple has this kind of ending. However, by mapping out the effects of his work on his physical health and on his relationship with his partner and by exploring why he was prevented from choosing to organize his life differently, this man discovered he could be honest about his choices. The irony, of course, was that this created the circumstances which enabled him to make a different choice.

In contrast, the therapist may actively side against the problematic gender specifications, challenging the client to make a different choice. In this case, the therapist takes a position, explicitly or implicitly, that some choices are healthier than others, and that the client has the power to defeat the oppressive specifications. In one example, the therapist was called upon by both members of a couple to agree that the man was "inadequate" in his response to his wife's needs and his use of therapy. The therapist did not believe that men are inherently less capable of emotional expression than women. Consequently, the therapist challenged the man's adherence to the cultural notion that men are incapable of responding emotionally. Instead of protecting him like his wife and others did, the therapist challenged him to do better, questioning whether he were "really" unable to be emotionally available. This approach, while often effective, should be used with caution. One potential danger is that the man will perceive the challenge as another in a long series of expectations for him to get closer and do better, which his wife has been doing for years. As Hoffman (1990) argues, a second danger is that the therapist sets up another set of gender specifications for the man to meet, again wresting the choice away from the client, and producing further alienation.

We wish to emphasize here that this approach does not necessarily require the therapist to maintain "neutrality" (cf. Boscolo et al., 1987). From our perspective, "neutrality" describes a technique through which therapists *attempt* to remain neutral as well as to give the impression to the clients that they are neutral. As MacKinnon and Miller (1987) have pointed out, however, this "neutrality" often has the unintentional effect of suggesting that clients are not responsible for the effects of their behaviors on others, or that "the system" causes behavior. We believe the approach advanced here avoids one of the main problems of a cybernetic approach which have lead some feminists (cf. Luepnitz, 1988; MacKinnon & Miller, 1987) to question cybernetics as the theoretical foundation for family therapy. We would agree that explanations that imply equal responsibility for destructive arrangements in relationships between men and women are unhelpful. Equally unhelpful are explanations that blame men for operating in ways which they were taught to operate in order to feel adequate as persons. In short, we believe cybernetic explanation can be useful for *constraining* therapists into stances that are non-blaming and that enhance increased responsibility for the effects of their behavior. Hoffman (1990) presents a similar argument for the usefulness of what she calls a "second order" approach to "gender sensitive therapy," as does Jenkins (1990) regarding the treatment of violent and abusive men.

The following is an example of remaining non-blaming. A couple comes in for therapy as they are about to move due to the husband's latest promotion. The husband has only excitement about the move, contemplating the new increased career challenges, responsibility, salary and status. Men often give little weight to emotional factors when making a decision, as the importance of emotion is rarely included in cultural specifications for masculinity. The husband cannot understand his wife's depression and anger at having to leave her friends, pull the kids out of school, and set up another home for the third time in six years. He accuses her of being "unsupportive." After all, just as he sees himself responsible for the economic status of the family, he views his wife as responsible for the family's emotional support. It may be a revelation to him when the therapist, not opposing the move or his excitement, asks him to consider the emotional impact of the move on him as well as on his family: increased stress, anxiety, loss, etc. Is asking himself and his family to "tough it out" the only solution to the problem, or is that simply a dictate of masculine gender specifications?

Another alternative for challenging the effects of gender specifications is for the therapist to take a more indirect or strategic approach to the therapeutic construction of alternative realities. For instance, "following the resistance," the therapist can strategically side with the current choice, both agreeing that the alternative choice is unacceptable for whatever reasons the client experiences and highlighting the consequences of taking one or the other option. As this idea has developed over the past twenty years, it has been known as paradox, or more recently, when the therapist sincerely believes that the client's choice should be supported, as taking the "conservative option" (White, 1990).

For example, a man looked ashamed when his wife criticized him for working late at night. As usual, he promised to cut down as "soon as this next project is finished." Paradoxically, the therapist suggested that perhaps there were things that he really liked about working late, and things he didn't like about unstructured time at home. Surprised by the question, the man agreed that he got a feeling of accomplishment at work which he did not get at home, where he often felt "antsy." He was surprised to discover the following gender specification, "Somewhere I got the idea that if you're not bearing down, if it doesn't hurt, you're not doing enough." He became so upset over how this idea constrained his options that he requested the next phase of therapy be devoted to helping him explore this issue.

One reason the indirect approach is so useful is that it supports the man's right to say no to his spouse's emotional (and other) demands, even if they are reasonable, without feeling inadequate. This firmly takes the man out of the "fix it" mode, and allows him to control his own participation. It supports the idea that his giving is up to him, not something he must produce on demand without choice. It is difficult for a man to support his partner's initiative, or to initiate for himself in a relationship, until he is secure in his ability to say no.

Lastly, using action-oriented techniques the therapist can highlight choices for the male client by setting up a drama between different externalized parts of the client's experience. While there are many ways to do this (cf. Papp, 1983), for these purposes, one player in the drama is personified as the externalized specifications. In one example, the specifications, which the client named "Ballbuster," kept telling the man that he wasn't enough, that he was "bad" for making mistakes, that he had to be perfect, etc. The client's task was to mediate between Ballbuster and his inner feelings and needs, making choices about what to believe and what to change.

STRENGTHENING NEW REALITIES

If the client decides in favor of new behaviors, there are things the therapist can do to support and strengthen them. Again, how the therapist chooses to do this depends on his or her orientation and the needs of the clients. Below are three ways to accomplish this.

First, explore instances when the man or couple has had success against the problem specifications, and how in these instances he had more relative influence over the problem than is usual (White, 1986). By remaining sensitive over the course of therapy to events that are incompatible with the problem specifications, the therapist can support and build upon them, developing them into a new "account" or description of self (White, 1990).

Second, the anticipation of relapses are time-honored methods in systemic therapy for supporting change and avoiding a sense of failure in the face of a reappearance of the problem. It is important for clients to understand that the process of change usually involves "relapses" that do not signify a return to "square one." The therapist may choose to not react calmly when a previously abusive man slips and hits his child. However, if the therapist also inquires into what prevented the man from taking responsibility for not hitting the child, acknowledges the durability of old ways, and reinforces the necessity of standing up to them, a new round of inadequacy may be avoided. Nor does a relapse necessarily mean that no progress has been made. The therapist may wish to explore how it was that the man avoided hitting the child on the other occasions that he felt angry. The gains can still be supported while plans are made to reduce future problems.

Last, homework assignments and rituals are useful techniques for expanding and elaborating new accounts of self and relationships. Typical assignments might be: a couple is asked to spend one-half hour talking with each other about anything of concern, alternating talking and listening; a husband is instructed to plan a weekend away for the couple as a surprise; or a couple is coached to ceremoniously burn the account book of how much money the wife "owes" the husband. As should be obvious, we are suggesting that the technique itself is secondary to an understanding of how to escape the restraints of gender specifications. We leave it to the therapist's theoretical orientation and clinical creativity to invent techniques that help to achieve this.

CONCLUSION

This paper grew out of our attempt to reconcile feminist perspectives on men with our beliefs that our experience of being men also must be articulated and accepted. We wanted to consider how men and women can come to terms with men's experience of themselves given the realities that feminists have enabled us to see: that men objectify and oppress women; that men are cut off from their vulnerability; that a patriarchal ideology entraps men as well as women. Yet we do not think masculinity is something that must be suppressed or avoided in order to support egalitarian relationships. Men must be helped/challenged to think about what they want to keep of traditional male gender and what they want to discard and escape.

Important to the clinical method advocated here is that gender be considered not in terms of differences between men and women, but in terms of how it is constituted through the ideas, beliefs, and cultural practices that specify ideal forms of masculinity. Men organize their identities and sense of self-adequacy through these notions of how men are "supposed to be." And men and women alike evaluate men on the basis of the specifications.

We believe our approach is a valid addition, not an alternative, to feminist interpretations of couples and families. The perspective enables us to enumerate key ideas that constitute men's experience of being men, ideas that have not been well articulated nor understood. Cybernetic explanation represents one way of operationalizing what Hare-Mustin (1987) and Hoffman (1990) refer to as a "second order view" on gender. Without this form of explanation, we cannot transcend the polemic of whether masculine or feminine is "better." Such polemics are a sign that the debate is only "more of the same" (Auerswald, 1987). Instead, we advocate that men's experience of masculinity be explored, men's dilemmas as men respected, and men be challenged to take responsibility for their behavior and to separate themselves from restraining cultural beliefs, habits, and practices.

NOTES

1. As men it is difficult to validate this stance, for to do so is to take a position which supports self hate. On the other hand, women's experience of the practices perpetuated by men make it difficult to avoid.

2. There is the question of social class here. How much are these specifications linked to upper middle class professional work culture? In our experience, they are not unique to this social class, but are important across the whole socio-economic range. Preliminary impressions of R. Weiss (1989) are consistent with this interpretation.

3. For a more comprehensive description of relative influence questioning, see White (1986, 1989a).

4. For those of you who are unfamiliar with professional football, Joe Montana is the quarterback for the San Francisco Forty-Niners football team which has won four Superbowls in the past eight years.

REFERENCES

Auerswald, E. H. (1987). Response to "The problem of gender in family therapy theory." *Family Process, 26*, 29-31.

Bateson, G. (1972). *Steps to an ecology of mind*. New York: Ballantine.

Bateson, G. (1979). *Mind and nature: A necessary unity*. New York: Dutton.

Berger, P., & Luckmann, T. (1966). *The social construction of reality*. New York: Doubleday.

Boscolo, L., Cecchin, G., Hoffman, L., & Penn, P. (1987). *Milan systemic therapy*. New York: Basic Books.

Bly, R. (1989, August). *A day for men*. Workshop on men, Monterey, CA.

Brittan, A. (1989). *Masculinity and power*. Oxford: Basil Blackwell Ltd.

Ehrenreich, B. (1984). *The hearts of men: American dreams and the flight from commitment*. New York: Doubleday.

Erkel, R. T. (1990). The birth of a movement. *The Family Therapy Networker, 14*, (3), 26-35.

Foucault, M. (1979). *Discipline and punish: The birth of the prison* (A. Sheridan, Trans.). New York: Random House.

Gergen, K. (1985). The social constructionist movement in modern psychology. *American Psychologist, 40*, 266-275.

Gilligan, C. (1982). *In a different voice: Psychological theory and women's development*. Cambridge: Harvard University Press.

Hare-Mustin, R. C. (1987). The problem of gender in family therapy. *Family Process, 26*, 15-27.

Hoffman, L. (1990). Constructing realities: An art of lenses. *Family Process, 29*, 1-12.

Jenkins, A. (1990). *Invitations to responsibility*. Adelaide, South Australia: Dulwich Centre Publications.

Kessler, S. J. & McKenna, W. (1978). *Gender: An ethnomethodological approach*. Chicago: University of Chicago Press.

Luepnitz, D. A. (1988). *The family interpreted: Feminist theory in clinical practice*. New York: Basic Books.

MacKinnon, L. K. & Miller, D. (1987). The new epistemology and the Milan approach: Feminist sociopolitical considerations. *Journal of Marital and Family Therapy, 13*, 139-155.

Papp, P. (1983). *The process of change*. New York: Guilford Press.

Weiss, R. (1989). Workshop on the characteristics of successful men: Report of research. Department of Continuing Education, University of California, Santa Cruz, CA.

White, M. (1986). Negative explanation, restraint, and double description: A template for family therapy. *Family Process, 25*, 169-184.

White, M. (1989). The conjoint therapy of men who are violent and the women with whom they live. *Selected Papers*. Adelaide, South Australia: Dulwich Centre Publications, 101-106.

White, M. (1990). The externalizing of the problem and the re-authoring of lives and relationships. In M. White & D. Epston, *Narrative means to therapeutic ends*. New York: Brunner/Mazel.

White, M. & Epston, D. (1990). *Narrative means to therapeutic ends*. New York: Brunner/Mazel.

Female Therapist/Male Client: Considerations About Belief Systems

Michele Bograd

SUMMARY. Although family therapists are examining gender in families, there has been little exploration of gender dynamics between the therapist and family members. From a social constructivist position, this paper explores the hypothesis that certain repetitive patterns or impasses emerge between women family therapists and male clients, related to dominant cultural understandings about male and female nature. Special attention is paid to beliefs about differences between men and women; relational responsibility and the world of feelings; gender and anger; and power.

My work with a young couple had reached an impasse. The wife was threatening to leave her relatively traditional marriage, feeling despairing, lonely, exhausted and angry. Her husband earnestly denied that he was unhappy in the marriage, but was willing to change "for her sake." I felt he quietly but angrily resisted change. My head-on approach with him resulted in an open and non-productive struggle.

I turned to my peer supervision group. "You're working too hard," one said, "He hasn't really made a commitment to work with you." As my colleagues explored why I couldn't reposition myself, I finally concluded, "Listen. His wife is so desperate. You expect me to wait for him to engage? He won't do that on his own without someone pushing him. He can't figure out what he wants without help. And he won't change

---

Michele Bograd, PhD, is a clinical psychologist in private practice in Cambridge, MA. Correspondence should be addressed to the author at 63 Stowecroft Road, Arlington, MA 02174.

An earlier version of this paper appeared in *The Family Therapy Networker*, 1990, *14*, 54-58.

> unless he's forced to." My male colleague retorted, "What makes you think all men are that way? I'm insulted, and you're wrong. I have chosen to think about my life, get help, and struggle with things without a woman making me."
>
> I sat, stunned. I simply didn't believe him, or my female colleague who articulated beliefs about men that were somewhat different from mine. I felt caught between my intellectual curiosity about how I think about men, and my subjective panic that the world just isn't what I thought it was.

A male client. A female therapist. Most of us think immediately of the differences between them. Beliefs about gender and sex roles can be key variables influencing information processing or clinical judgments, particularly when clinicians are assessing or treating clients of the other sex (Fisher, 1989; Hare-Mustin, 1978; Yogev & Shadish, 1982). Does it make a difference that I am a female therapist? How do my thoughts about men and women color my therapy and interact with my clients' thoughts about their own gender and mine? Although family therapists are examining gender as an organizing dimension of family life (Goldner, 1985, 1988; Goodrich, Rampage, Ellman & Halstead, 1988; Hare-Mustin & Marecek, 1986; Luepnitz, 1988; Meth & Pasick, 1990; Mirkin, 1990; McGoldrick, Anderson & Walsh, 1988; Walters, Carter, Papp & Silverstein, 1988), we have yet to explore how gender dynamics enliven, complicate or influence the relationship between therapist and family members. In the family therapy literature, there are no published empirical studies on the relation of therapist gender to treatment outcome or process, although there is a growing body of literature outside of the field on gender effects in psychotherapy (see, for example, Fisher, 1989; Kaplan, 1979, 1984). While family therapists have begun to examine clinical challenges specific to female therapists, particularly those of power (Caust, Libow & Raskin, 1981; Libow, 1986; Libow, Raskin & Caust, 1982; Okun, 1983, 1989; Reid, McDaniel, Donaldson & Tollers, 1987; Sheeley, 1982; Wheeler, Avis, Miller & Chaney, 1986), there is little commentary on how these issues influence therapy with clients of different genders. Gender dynamics derive from a variety of sources ranging from social stereotypes to idiosyncratic personal experience. Gender dynamics manifest themselves in a variety of ways, including behavioral patterns, affective reactions, interpersonal expectations, intrapsychic structures, and cognitive systems. In this article, I provide beginning conceptualizations about one piece of this fascinating puzzle: What are the ways that female therapists' belief systems about male clients contribute to impasses and complications in marital and family therapy?

A CAUTIONARY NOTE

Throughout this article, I sound warnings to remind myself and the reader that I am articulating my beliefs about beliefs. In an effort to point out how beliefs about gender can be too limiting or constricting, it may appear that I, too, reinforce them. At the same time that I critique the dualism that characterizes our thinking about gender, I employ it to help illuminate some common patterns between women therapists and male clients. Critical here is my awareness that I am choosing to use a dualistic model as a way of thinking about gender, rather than assuming it exists in the world.

I focus on only one aspect of gender relations: cognition. But relationships between men and women are not simply cognitive constructions. They are based in material, economic, and status inequities and are expressed and maintained in a variety of ways, including non-verbal communication, intrapsychic structures, norms of behavior and acts of force. Changing cognition is not sufficient for changing current gender relations: we cannot simply think ourselves out of oppressive gender patterns.

Belief systems, the focus of this paper, are not the only relevant dimension for understanding treatment relationships of female therapists and male clients. When I refer to a belief system, I am not implying that this system or collection of ideas is coherent or consistent. Ideas about gender continually evolve in response to changing historical, social, and economic conditions. Contradictory or inconsistent ideas co-exist within cultural or personal belief systems. Gaps occur between cultural ideals and personal experiences (Gerson, 1987; Rubin, 1983). Individuals can feel one thing and think another about gender. Although I systematize a set of ideas in this paper, in experience, these ideas rarely form a seamless whole.

Furthermore, men and women are not homogenous groups. My generalizations—although grounded in extensive clinical, supervisory and personal experience—will not capture any one person's reality. My goal is not to give a different version of what is (though my own belief system is obviously revealed), but to provide some sensitizing considerations to help family therapists begin to explore the beneficial or limiting consequences of certain ways of construing gender, and to understand how those constructions relate to the politics of gender relations.

Lastly, I focus primarily on women therapists' beliefs about male clients. A complete analysis must include the male client's beliefs, as well as those of other family members who participate in the treatment system, and description of their reciprocal interaction and development.

WORKING HYPOTHESES

Gender is socially constructed. This article is based on the belief that gender is socially constructed and mediated through symbols (Goldner, 1985, 1988; Hare-Mustin, 1987; Hare-Mustin & Marecek, 1986, 1988; James, 1984; James & McIntyre, 1989; MacKinnon & Miller, 1987; Spender, 1980). Although biological differences between men and women are undeniable, masculinity and femininity are not simply discovered in nature, but created through social understandings and agreements that evolve over time in response to the changing socio-historical context. Our culture teaches us the kinds of distinctions we should draw between men and women, but we don't experience these distinctions as learned, arbitrary, or modifiable. Instead, we experience them as "how men and women are," as real, undeniable, and taken for granted. Experiential vertigo results as we try to absorb what it really means to acknowledge that these differences are socially constructed, but it can lead to hope about changing gender relations. As Herek (1987) states, "What has been constructed can be reconstructed, albeit with considerable effort. Gender and sexual orientation thus should be understandable as changeable ideologies rather than as biological facts" (p. 72).

There are political ramifications to how gender is constructed. We are born into a symbolic order that reflects and maintains a social order that, in turn, reinforces how gender is constructed. This social order is still fundamentally patriarchal: it promotes the dominance of white middle class men over women and over men and women of color (James, 1984; James & McIntyre, 1983, 1989; Spender, 1980; Taggart, 1989). Power differences between men and women as groups are not always experienced at the individual level. This is due to the kinds of social relations that exist between men and women. Unlike other dominant and subordinate groups, strong emotional attachment, mutual caring, and shared dependence link individual men and women—so complicating experiences of power and domination for both (Gerson, 1987; Goode, 1982; Kahn, 1984; Pleck, 1984). The social construction of gender is one way the prevailing social order is maintained. For example, if men are defined as inherently rational, strong and aggressive, and women are defined as inherently nurturant, intuitive, and dependent, this belief system provides a rationale for maintaining the status quo. Even our efforts to redefine it rely, of necessity, on language that perpetuates the very system we are trying to change (Spender, 1980). Although the symbolic order may distort, render invisible, or deny the subjective experiences of men and women, we cannot escape it. As Schaef (1981) states " . . . because we all live in a white male culture, the question is not one of *whether* we are sexist, but of *how* we are sexist. (This is true for women as well as for men, by the way)" [p. 4].

Psychotherapy is a gendered system. When we employ the lens of gender to examine the psychotherapy system, we no longer view "elements" in the system, but human beings for whom gender concepts are a fundamental way of dividing up the world, ascribing meaning to the behaviors and reactions of self and others, and understanding the complex flow of human interaction. Gender beliefs are but one facet of the gendered psychotherapeutic system, among other dimensions such as developmental histories, divergent intrapsychic structures, and social location. In therapy, as in all human interactions, female therapist and male client mutually respond to the gendered self-presentation of each other, which is strongly (if unconsciously) influenced by our ideas about men and women. For our purposes, key ideas include expectations about women caregivers or experts, definitions of "appropriate" kinds of emotions permitted men and women, beliefs about men's capacities to change, and how men and women "should" relate to each other in intimate relationships. Although relatively stable, gender beliefs are not unchanging, static ideas that reside inside each person, but are reinforced, modified, or contradicted by ongoing social exchange. Because of this, gender beliefs are an inevitable and unavoidable aspect of the therapy system, but do not exert a simple, straightforward, invariant, or universal influence.

Clinical impasses are linked to beliefs about gender. "Stuck places" or impasses in therapy are typically attributed to the therapist's skill deficits or family-of-origin issues. I propose that clinical impasses between female therapist and male client also emerge either when there is a significant and unrecognized mismatch between their gendered belief systems, or when their shared belief systems maintain a dysfunctional status quo (Feldman, 1982; Meth & Pasick, 1990) or compromise hopefulness about change. Clients and therapists alike bring gendered maps into the clinical hour that guide us in our perception, evaluation and understanding of self and other. Goodrich et al. (1988) suggest that clients begin interacting with the therapist on the basis of traditional gender stereotypes. Difficulties may emerge when an outspoken directive woman therapist violates some of these conventional standards. More commonly, differences between belief systems of clients and therapist are neither acknowledged nor explored, leading to confusion, tension or misunderstanding. On the other hand, "matched" or compatible belief systems do not insure a problem free therapy. Female therapist and male client may adhere to conventional ideas about gender that reduce their behavioral flexibility, their ability to conceptualize alternatives, or their empathic capacity. From this frame of reference, the goal is neither to erase differences that can stimulate change nor to threaten compatible belief systems that promote mutual understanding. It is to explore how female therapist and male client are each employing dominant ideas about gender to construct understandings of self, other, and the treatment relationship and to challenge those beliefs that inhibit clinical progress.

WOMEN THERAPISTS' BELIEFS ABOUT MALE CLIENTS

Through leading workshops, teaching, supervision, and my own self-examination, I've elicited the belief systems of many women therapists about male clients with whom they are at a therapeutic impasse. These clinicians—of varying age, clinical experience and professional affiliation— work in a wide range of contexts and follow a variety of systemic models. In abstracting a set of themes, I simplify their complexity and separate them in ways that do not occur in practice. Discussion will focus on: (1) Stereotypic notions of differences between male clients and female therapists; (2) Relational responsibility and the world of feelings; (3) Men, women and anger; (4) Beliefs about power.

Remember, this is my construction of their constructions. I use a dualistic model and speak of who women "are" and who men "are" as a way of highlighting beliefs and patterns that shape the therapy relationship. I focus primarily on the belief systems of the woman therapist, but her beliefs alone are not solely responsible for the impasse. Clinical impasses are relational phenomena that occur at the interface between the belief systems of all members of the treatment system.

Stereotypic Notions of Differences Between Male Clients and Female Therapists

> A vivacious, theatrical woman married an emotionally isolated son of a Holocaust survivor. Their female marital therapist patiently tried to enter the husband's inner world, which he described as "barren as the lunar landscape." In one session, he burst into dry sobs and wailed, "What do you two want from me? I'm trying to feel. I'm doing the best I can!" As his wife hurriedly handed him a tissue, the therapist felt overwhelmed with helplessness. Later a male colleague asked, "Why did you stop there? I would have said to him, 'You can and must go farther, just as your wife does.' You let him get away with too much." The female therapist replied, "It never occurred to me to push him. I guess I accepted that men just can't do more."

A colleague announces, "I just gave your name to someone. He'll give you a call soon." For most female therapists, the knowledge that an unknown client is male immediately sets up a network of ideas, images and reactions. We barely notice them, unless we learn that our clients are wife batterers or incest perpetrators—then powerful images intrude. Usually, our beliefs about men seem benign or unimportant. We tend not to notice them when the client fulfills our expectations, as when male clients are intellectualized or emotionally inexpressive. Our belief systems are somewhat more obvious in those moments when we notice that the male client is different from what we anticipated, perhaps he says something that strikes us as "more sensitive than most men" or we see him as "the exception to the rule." Although we don't articulate what the rule is, we easily can. The images of men seem to crystallize, however, when female therapists experience an impasse in the treatment.

In a series of workshops, I asked women therapists, "Imagine a male client with whom you feel really stuck. Without censoring your response, make a list of adjectives to describe him." Female therapists from differing theoretical orientations and with varying degrees of experience generated surprisingly similar lists. At difficult points in the treatment, women therapists perceive the male client as distant, rigid, challenging, childlike, dominant, not interested in change, intimidating, hostile, intellectualizing, controlling, angry, passive/aggressive, weak, and dependent.

Interacting with our beliefs about male clients are the men's beliefs about female therapists—many of which we share. At first glance, these images are positive. But when a female therapist feels compelled to fill her client's image of her or finds it difficult to challenge that image because it mirrors her own belief system of "how women should be," the golden image becomes a gilded cage. I asked a number of my male clients why they had chosen to work with a woman. Not surprisingly, most expected that a woman would be empathic, emotional, understanding, accepting of feelings, and comfortable. These beliefs were almost always embedded in a network of assumptions about male therapists and expectations about the kind of relationship that would evolve with a therapist of one gender or the other. For these men, women therapists felt safer emotionally and even physically: several commented spontaneously that they felt reassured by my petite stature.

> I trust women can give me something different than I'd get from a man. They are more real and also willing to connect on an intimate level. I trust they value vulnerability, at least, stereotypically they do. With men, we'd both end up squirming and getting nervous.
>
> I don't know if I've felt at times that a man would understand me better. Most guys don't understand my issues, even though they're men's issues. Other men aren't that intellectual, not that self-analytical or preoccupied. Most other men have found their groove. I didn't. They have a script, I'm adlibbing.
>
> With a male therapist, at best, it's shoulder to shoulder. But with a woman therapist, it's face to face. It's more a dance. I can't dance with a man. With another man, it's like we're looking together at a picture—out there.
>
> Even though I had a very sensitive male therapist before, I believe that women are more matched intellectually, more emotionally attuned. I want to underline it's my *expectation,* not just a neutral observation.

Are the female therapists' views of male clients or the male clients' views of female therapists correct? From a social constructionist perspective, we cannot answer this question, since we can never know Truth or Reality directly (Hare-Mustin, 1987; Hare-Mustin & Marecek, 1986, 1988). Instead, we can ask, is it useful to employ traditional stereotypes that highlight the differences between male clients and female therapists?

At first glance, it does seem useful. We can explore the personal experiences of men and women with curiosity, not taking for granted that we know the "opposite sex." We can examine the special constraints of each gender with its presumed strengths and limitations. For example, Kaplan (1984) suggests that female therapists bring into their work a sense of self that is relational and an internalized experience of being a member of a subordinate class, while male therapists bring into their work a sense of self that is autonomous and an internalized experience of being a member of a dominant class. Given this theoretical assumption, she goes on to speculate that male and female therapists face different challenges in their therapeutic role and specific dilemmas with clients of the opposite sex.

But taking for granted gender differences also carries potential costs. First, global generalizations of the mutually exclusive characteristics of male clients and female therapists oversimplify complex human experience and overlook important commonalities between men and women (Hare-Mustin, 1987). In perceiving my client as a man like all others, I can lose sight of his particularity. I may highlight those aspects of his experience that fit the cultural stereotype and miss the exceptions. Our culture provides us with a limited set of types of men, each of which is comprised of a constellation of characteristics. We believe that these stereotypes reflect reality, that certain traits empirically co-occur in everyday life. Thus, we perceive one quality, and often assume the presence of others. A male client is coded as "domineering": we expect him to be controlling, opinionated, insensitive—not caring, gentle, and curious about others. When we see evidence of less domineering qualities, it can be discounted as "not who he really is" or as a surprising but not believable deviation from his typical behavior. We are so accustomed to certain descriptions of men that we don't question how many men really fit dominant definitions (Goode, 1982). These images of men, shared by men and women alike, can lead therapists to preconceived but erroneous views of male clients' problems (Ipsaro, 1986).

Second, because our culture gives us models of men and women as "naturally" different, we shift our focus away from historical and social conditions that help maintain or constrain a man's way of being. Ignoring these conditions or reifying gender differences can preserve the status quo. Instead of being realistic but optimistic while inviting and struggling with male clients to be different, female therapists can settle for smaller changes than many men are able to accomplish. If we believe gender differences are irreversible, we face the paradoxical task of treating a man we believe can never change. Understandably, male clients are sensitive to our pessimism, and it often reinforces their own. Although it can be useful to view female therapists and male clients as sharing the task of bridging two fundamentally distinct gendered ways of being, in times of frustration or struggle, we often focus on the chasm and not on the bridge. In other words, the shared belief that men and women are presumably different leads each person in the therapeutic system to assume that mutual understanding cannot be reached.

Third, in our culture, the construction of differences is never descriptively neutral. It is value-laden: we imply that one way is better than another (Hare-Mustin, 1987; Hare-Mustin & Marecek, 1986, 1988; Meth & Pasick, 1990). For example, at least among a certain class of men and women, cultural beliefs about the value of certain stereotypic gendered traits are changing. Women's previously devalued emotional expressivity and relational sensitivity are being recognized as complex interpersonal skills, while men's self-sufficiency and stoicism are being redefined as isolation, relational incompetence, and constricted emotionality. In the clinical, popular, and feminist literature, we lack positive images of men and their capacity for change. The belief that "(t)he primary experience of American men is now the experience of being inadequate" (poet Robert Bly cited in Simon, 1990, p. 27) is coupled with the "myths" that women are good at expressing feelings and so know more than men about living life well (Meth & Pasick, 1990). A poignant and complicated emotional stage is set when male client and female therapist share a belief system that

> men do not have personal skills to nurture relationships and that women do; that women are overinvolved in their relationships and men too distant; . . . that women need intimacy and men fear it. This shared belief system makes men feel incompetent in relationships and makes women feel crazy because they are constantly seeking to get what *both* of them believe is not there to be had.
>
> *–Walters et al., 1988, p. 242*

Relational Responsibility and the World of Feelings

> In live supervision, a trainee found it difficult to probe a husband's role in a marital spat. I directed her to explore his feelings before a typical outburst. After delicately posing the question, she immediately offered an array of responses, filling the airtime, while he sat mostly silent except for a few monosyllabic answers. During the break, I asked if she realized that she was having a conversation with herself. Even with careful supervision, it was hard for her to ask a question and wait for the man's slow, clumsy reply, without rushing to his rescue.

> Over lunch, a colleague described a powerful session in which her male client thanked her profusely for helping him really grieve his mother who had died years before. "He said that no other therapist had gotten him to this point," she reported, obviously moved. "No one knows him like I do, including his wife."

Feminist analyses of male/female relationships emphasize that female caretaking of men reflects and maintains an unequal distribution of power between men and women as social groups (Bernardez, 1982; Carlson, 1987; Lerner, 1983; Miller, 1976, 1982; Schaef, 1981; Spender, 1980; Stiver, 1984), since subordinate groups are often more attuned to the needs of the dominant group than vice versa. Thus, a feminist family therapist faces basic dilemmas. Given that she is in a caretaking relationship with her client, how to take care of him in ways that don't replicate restrictive patterns? How to be full of care without being too careful? How to be responsible to the relationship without being responsible for it?

For many women therapists, the initial answers lie, not in technical strategies, but in the transformation of a set of beliefs about men, feelings, and relationships. These include: (1) Men, and so male clients, do not know their feelings; (2) Men can be overwhelmed by feelings; (3) Men are not motivated to understand themselves; (4) Men do not and cannot nurture relationships; (5) Women are experts on relationships; (6) The right woman can liberate a man's feelings and teach him about relationships.

Given these beliefs, female therapists can err by doing too much emotional work for the male client, conveying that he cannot do it alone (Bepko & Krestan, 1985). This protects him from struggling to learn the skills of emotional expressivity or empathy. Our beliefs that we know men better than they know themselves can be presumptuous or infantilizing, as is our message that men need women to handle their feelings for them—as if men can't tolerate knowing themselves. Although the woman therapist is in a formally hierarchical position to the male client, she reinforces conventional male/female hierarchies if she caretakes the male client without holding him accountable for his half of the relationship. We are not taught to do this with men in general (Bograd, 1990; Lerner, 1983), and there are often high and real costs when a woman therapist demands that a male client meet her fully in the therapy relationship: his anger, disappointment, distance, rejection.

Faced with such reactions, many women therapists are too ready to believe they have failed in their nurturing role. This is itself a function of cultural beliefs that lead to a common but dangerous attributional error. In a study of how clients and therapists understood treatment difficulties, Fisher (1989) found that women therapists perceived themselves as responsible for impasses with male clients while male therapists perceived their female clients as responsible. In other words, whether she was the therapist or the client, the woman was seen—and experienced herself—as responsible for negative events in the treatment!! Because of this belief system shared by men and women, the woman therapist can fail to understand that the male client's disappointment is not an accurate description of her clinical ability but a function of his beliefs and expectations about women (Carlson, 1987). In personalizing his disappointment, she can fail to challenge the gendered assumptions that fuel it.

> I reflected back to my client what he had just said. "That's not right," he replied. I tried again. "You're telling me what I'm feeling," he complained. I asked him to tell me again, and repeated back his words. "You're not understanding my experience," he said, growing irritated. I felt anxious, confused, small, and tentative. Only later did I realize that *my* experience

> got lost in this interaction. I had entered into his belief that women should attend to him perfectly, rather than working with him about how he needed to stay connected to me and tolerate my human imperfection.

For many women, our identity is tied to being superlative nurturers and to our relationships with men (James, 1984). We internalize cultural beliefs about femininity and so equate confrontation or a loving distance with aggression (Stiver, 1985) and caring or support with overfunctioning (Bepko & Krestan, 1985; Carlson, 1987; Caust et al., 1981; Libow, 1986; Libow, Raskin & Caust, 1982; Okun, 1983, 1989; Reid et al., 1987; Walters et al., 1989; Wheeler et al., 1986). Thus, we can feel mean, cold, or distant as we wait until the male client experiences his lack of emotionality as a problem (Goodrich et al., 1988), if we allow him to struggle with his feelings, if we resist the urge to figure it out for him, if we do not immediately console and contain as he starts to feel more. This stems in part from our beliefs about how women should relate to men, as well as from culturally constructed beliefs that lead women to value our relationships with men over those with women (James, 1984; Okun, 1983; Robbins, 1983). As Goodrich et al. (1988) point out:

> Therapists often pay disproportionate attention to any efforts a man does make to change, while letting the woman accommodate on her own. Thus, his effort to become more expressive is seen by the therapist as the psychological equivalent of climbing Mt. Everest, while her effort to enter the workplace after twenty years as a homemaker is seen as a privilege. (p. 27)

* * *

> I supervised a trainee who cherished being "daddy's girl." In a case presentation she pointed out that the wife was insensitive to her husband, careless about housework, and resentful that he made less money than she did. The husband was described as sweetly eccentric, a "hurting puppy." We eventually learned that he had suffered a major depression a year ago, during which time his wife had fully supported the family

> in many ways. This trainee felt little compassion for her and organized her case presentations around the man's vulnerabilities and the small changes he was making, while the wife struggled to maintain the family without his active engagement.

In this case, the therapist experienced no conflict about her treatment relationship with the husband. It felt good to the both of them, although it excluded his wife. But the issue of how men and women get taken care of in relationships remained unaddressed (Stiver, 1984). The man never learned to articulate his needs, because the therapist moved so quickly to respond to them. The woman therapist felt gratified that he was letting her take care of him, and so did not experience the many ways that he was not attending to the treatment relationship. She was vulnerable to the pitfall of "coming down with terminal gratitude" (Goodrich et al., 1988, p. 132): thankful that he had given her something, she didn't expect or require more from him.

Many female therapists are quite successful at helping male clients feel, and we attend well to their pain. But we cannot construct new ways for men and women to be from old positions. For example, we soothe the man's pain and attend less to his beliefs about masculinity (Bernardez, 1982). We explore his anguish without posing the question of whether he is going to defy role assumptions or maintain compliance with them (Bernardez, 1982). We protect the male client from the very anxiety or discomfort that can increase his motivation to change. We confirm that men can find connection and support only in a special relationship with a woman, rather than through the creation of new kinds of relationships with other men as well. The goal here is not for the woman therapist to disengage but to expect that male clients *can* engage and be successfully challenged (Walters et al., 1988).

This challenge destabilizes the system and is distressing for client and therapist alike. The woman therapist must weather the man's distress as he faces himself in a different way in a different kind of relationship with a woman. She must also be prepared for a variety of ways that he will try to re-establish the status quo—be it through anger, withdrawal, devaluation, passivity, seduction, or helplessness. For many women, these moves reactivate their beliefs that they are failing, uncaring, or unresponsive. Women therapists, too, feel a loss when they shift their positions. After all, we work hard to make ourselves indispensible to men and need to learn that we can be valued even when we don't give so much (Schaef, 1981).

It is helpful to remember that this is not just a personal struggle. We are each following deeply ingrained cultural scripts about how things are and should be. But unless basic belief systems of both therapist and client are challenged, change occurs within conventional ideas about male/female relationships (Walters et al., 1988). "The woman therapist, therefore, has an obligation to grow beyond the sex role that traps women into limiting behavior that in turn does not challenge the male client and presumes a power imbalance in his favor and a caregiver role for her" (Carlson, 1987, p. 47).

Male and Female Anger

> In a recent live supervision, a group of female therapists watched a man respond to a simple question with an unexpected outburst against his wife. The therapist and wife froze. After a moment, the clinician turned to the wife and asked her about a different subject. No one commented on the husband's anger. Afterwards, the group observing the session consoled their colleague. All described having similar responses to men's anger: "I freeze," "I go blank," "I just want to be out of there," "I feel like I did when my father yelled at me as a child."
>
> A passive, depressed man entered therapy with his enraged and bitter wife. Sessions deteriorated as their bile poured out and recriminations were hurled back and forth for events that were now twenty years old. My strongest feeling was anger at the sharp-tongued wife, although the husband's rage disrupted our sessions frequently, leaving me exhausted and anxious. Before seeking consultation, I helplessly set limits on the battles, yet patiently and miserably sat through them.
>
> A female colleague complained about a male client. "This guy has issues with women like you can't believe. I sat and listened to him talk about a dream that women were birds, and

> he was shooting them off a limb one-by-one." "What did you say to him?" I inquired. "Nothing directly. I was too angry and didn't want my feelings to interfere. But I ended up being sarcastic and distant."

Nothing intimidates many female therapists more than their male clients' anger, true for male therapists as well (Meth & Pasick, 1990). Some men try to control therapy by yelling, storming out of sessions, refusing to speak, or aggressively engaging in intellectual arguments. Given that many male clients struggle with anger and don't understand its impact on others, female therapists' inability to tolerate and work with male anger can be a serious obstacle to our effectiveness as clinicians. Women's fear of men's anger has a realistic base; our physical vulnerability to men is not a figment of the imagination. But sometimes our beliefs about anger significantly limit our ability to conceptualize therapy with men in novel ways or to take a stance that helps us feel safely in control of the treatment. These beliefs include: (1) Men can't control their anger; (2) Women must create situations that contain or neutralize men's anger; (3) Women's anger is destructive, sick or wrong; (4) A caring woman never expresses anger; (5) Anger, for men and women, is a personal problem (Bernardez, 1988; Kaplan, Brooks, McComb, Shapiro & Sodano, 1983; Miller, 1983).

In my dissertation research (Bograd, 1983), I studied the belief systems of battered women and abusive men. I found that both utilized culturally constructed rationalizations that excused or explained away the man's violence: "he just exploded," "men need to vent," "it's his childhood," "he didn't mean it," "every man has his limit." Since, in our culture, men are defined as not responsible for their anger and its consequences, it falls upon women to modulate, contain, anticipate, and steer clear of male rage. In contrast, women's anger is perceived as more sick, irrational, destructive, pathological (Bernardez, 1988; Miller, 1983). Additionally, for women in our culture, nurturance and anger are defined as mutually exclusive emotions.

When the female therapist is faced with an angry male client, a range of scenarios can occur, partially determined by these beliefs. She may find it hard to set limits on his anger, concerned that he will reject or abandon her. She may begin to work more tentatively, fearful that she will become the brunt of his fury. She may suppress her own feelings of anger or fear, worried that her anger will escalate the situation or compromise the therapeutic alliance. She may try to work with him on the feelings underlying his anger (such as sadness, isolation, vulnerability) without addressing the ongoing impact of his angry behavior. She may be openly cold, irritated or hostile. A feminist sensitivity to the many manifestations of male domination may intensify her anger. The result of all these scenarios is that the male client is not held accountable for the feelings fueling his anger, the anger itself, or his behavior.

There are a variety of technical solutions for the woman therapist, depending on her clinical style and theoretical allegiance. But first she must rethink her beliefs about men, women and anger. Her attention needs to shift from monitoring the man's anger to her internal state, based on the belief that her personal comfort and felt safety are crucial and legitimate elements of the treatment relationship. Few women can provide effective therapy when they are frightened or intimidated. But given the beliefs many of us hold about gender and anger, it is often difficult for the woman therapist to set clear parameters to what she will tolerate of her male client's anger. These parameters are essential, and provide the male client with important and necessary feedback about the consequences of his actions, regardless of his intention. When women therapists begin to believe that the male client is equally responsible for the nurturance and maintenance of the treatment relationship, it often reduces our self-blame if the client chooses to leave therapy. Last, hindered by our belief that commenting on the man's anger will only exacerbate it, we do not learn that many male clients appreciate and respond well to clear and strong feedback, firm limits, and a challenging but compassionate dialogue about their anger.

Therapist and client alike will need to grapple together towards a new definition of anger. Miller (1983) and Bernardez (1988) speculate that the patriarchal conditions of our culture have distorted the experience of anger for both men and women. The constricting and damaging demands of their respective social positions generate anger for men and women. As members of the dominant group, men are trained away from more vulnerable feelings and towards the controlling and aggressive expression of anger towards women and other men. As members of the subordinate group, women are taught to suppress and devalue their anger as a means to preserve relationships upon which they feel economically and emotionally dependent. Women's anger is pathologized and denigrated as a way of subverting collective action because it threatens the social order. Men's anger perpetuates this order, but at extremely high cost to them. Bernardez (1988) suggests a radically different conception of anger in a context of equals, where anger is coupled with vulnerability, expressed without domination or competition, deepens not threatens connection, and leads to personal and shared empowerment, self-respect, healthy rebellion, and change.

These words are inspiring, but their realization is founded on hours of struggle and clarification. I believe that our culture structures male/female relationships in such a way that longing and rage exist hand-in-hand for both sexes. In therapy, it is incumbent upon the female therapist to legitimate her own sense of anger, and to learn to employ it artfully and care-fully, in order to help her male client engage in a different kind of relationship with her and with others in his life. As Bernardez (1988) reminds us, " . . . a pacifist is a person who, through loving indignation, has transcended her own violence, not one who is afraid to fight" (p. 9).

Beliefs About Power

By definition, power is a central analytical dimension in any feminist analysis of the dynamics between female therapist and male client. But it is difficult to track and demonstrate pervasive but elusive gendered power dynamics in therapy. For example, when I asked male clients whether our hierarchical structure was problematic for them, all replied "no," explaining they often turned for nurturance to women who were more powerful than them, such as mothers or grandmothers. The picture grew more complicated with subsequent discussion as they noted: "Your intellectuality is really unusual for a woman"; "I was taken aback by your facile verbalization of sex"; "You are different from most women. You have a sense of presence that most women don't have – like taking up two seats in a subway. I'm used to that in men and I like it, find it stimulating. You model something different. Still it sometimes annoys me when you're too direct and move in too fast on me." I needed to rethink my belief that my position of power was clearly and straightforwardly problematic for my male clients. They needed to rethink their beliefs that it was not problematic at all, since they responded with curiosity, admiration, discomfort, or annoyance when I deviated from their ideas about women and women therapists.

Theoretically, the female therapist/male client treatment system is characterized by several paradoxes. First, a man is dependent on a woman who is hierarchically superior to him within the therapy room, but who often occupies a subordinate position to him in other domains. Women are still socially devalued in our culture, and it is not uncommon for a woman clinician to earn less than her male clients. Second, he is paying her for services he is accustomed to receiving for free from women; she takes care of him in familiar ways, but from the unaccustomed position of acknowledged expertise. These structural conditions are reinforced and complicated by two prevalant beliefs about power: (1) Power is a limited resource; (2) Men and women can choose to change their relationship to power.

Power is a limited resource. Male client and female therapist alike are constrained by certain ideas about power, specifically that power is a limited commodity. Within this belief system, one person is powerful at the expense of another. Given this belief, powerful and nurturant behaviors are often perceived as mutually exclusive (Kaplan, 1979; Miller, 1982; Okun, 1983). Since being nurturant is so primary to many women therapists' personal and professional identities, many experience themselves as uncaring, destructive, dangerous, or selfish when they are openly powerful with male clients (Caust et al., 1981; Libow, 1986; Miller, 1976, 1982; Okun, 1983, 1989; Reid et al., 1987; Sheely, 1982; Wheeler et al., 1985). They have learned that women have the power to influence men by acting less powerful than them (Kahn, 1974; Lerner, 1983; Miller, 1982; Sheely, 1982). But, as Carlson (1987) notes, "[d]eference to male thinking, as inexperienced female therapists often discover, precipitates neither movement for the client nor a sense of competence in the therapist" (p. 44).

In contrast, other women therapists respond to the belief that one person has primary power in the relationship by taking active control of the treatment, but sometimes in adversarial or combative ways (Meth & Pasick, 1990). Many women grow up with little experience in wielding authority and are extremely sensitive to widespread messages that their power is neither legitimate nor important. Our initial, unfamiliar attempts at taking control are often clumsy, and we can remain reactive to challenges by the male client. While some women therapists give up too much power and others insist upon it, few of us believe that men and women can share power equally. This contributes to our feeling threatened or angry, even when the male client is understandably trying to achieve a comfortable form of some control in the therapy (Rice, 1978).

On their part, male clients often fear abdicating power to a woman and so try to control the clinical interaction (Bernardez, 1982; Carlson, 1987)—be it through seduction (Bograd, 1988, 1989), anger, debate, or withdrawal. As one male client told me, "I initially chose to work with a woman because men are more threatening to me. I've manipulated women, successfully, since I was knee-high to a grasshopper." On the other hand, male clients can capitulate any control of their progress to the woman therapist, approaching her from positions of extreme passivity and compliance. Male clients' manipulations of women therapists have complex roots. Bernardez (1982) suggests that men devalue and control women as a way of defending against their emotional dependency upon them, which is fueled by their "irrational belief" in women's power. Other authors have noted that men feel subjectively powerless, in spite of their greater objective social power (Meth & Pasick, 1990).

Men and women can choose to change their relationship to power. In the intimacy of the clinical relationship, we often believe that—as two individuals—we have the ability to choose how to create our system. Our subjective experiences convince us that we are exceptions to broader social patterns. The woman therapist often feels personally empowered and not oppressed; the male client often feels powerless and not dominant. Yet as female therapist and male client try to create a different kind of relationship, each will run up against important barriers or limits. The belief that we are free to change our relationship to broader social conditions—that these limits are internal and personal—can contribute to key impasses in the psychotherapy of men. When a woman therapist is frustrated with a male client's progress, she can attribute this to his lack of will, motivation or effort. Not uncommonly, women therapists believe that male clients don't want to change and sacrifice their power (Meth & Pasick, 1990). This belief can lead to impatience, disdain, or despair in the woman therapist, which is heightened for many feminists (Bernardez, 1982; Goodrich et al. 1988; Ipsaro, 1986). Although Berger (1984) here speaks about husbands and wives, his thoughts seem relevant to the therapy system as well:

> Out of legitimate anger at past inequities, out of anger at oneself for having tolerated these inequities, and out of a fear that clumsiness in the new roles is a sign that men "really" do not want to take on the new roles, wives [read: women therapists] may punish their husbands [read: male clients] for these failures. (p. 323)

In minimizing the massive social forces that constrain or complicate individual choice, we ignore the systemic component to female therapist/male client relationships. Although each woman therapist may believe that her relationships with men in general and male clients in particular are privately and personally created, at the aggregate or social level, women's impasses with male clients may be neither accidental nor idiosyncratic but patterned and rooted in more general gender dynamics (Gerson, 1987). When a male client slowly or imperceptibly changes, this is not simply a question of choice, personality traits, obstinacy, or entitlement. When we view male "resistance" as contextual, we can move from anger that men are simply unwilling to give up privileges to one of greater compassion. Similarly, when female therapists struggle with issues of power, legitimacy or visibility, this is related less to intrapsychic or family of origin issues than to the professional, institutional and cultural contexts of our work (Caust et al., 1981; Hare-Mustin, 1978; Lerner, 1983; Reid et al., 1987; Sheely, 1982).

Predominant beliefs about power are fundamentally conservative. The belief that power is a limited commodity inhibits men and women from experimenting with different models of power. The belief that we can simply choose to change our relationship to power diverts attention away from personal and collective action to modify social conditions. A feminist approach to the therapy of men keeps power at the center of personal and clinical concern. Such an approach enriches conventional therapeutic models of working with men through an analysis of the social context of gender relations and of the psychological costs of men's social privilege. As Sternbach (1989) suggests, feminist informed work with men faces them with a fundamental choice between finding their humanity or maintaining their domination. As a microcosm of larger social conditions, the relationship between female therapist and male client can replicate dominant gender patterns or challenge them. Both sexes have been deprived of interacting with equals (Walters et al., 1988), since our culture does not provide us with a model of shared power where each participant is enhanced and benefitted by the other (Kahn, 1984). In this context, woman therapist and male client together need to struggle with fundamental dilemmas of relevance in and out of the therapy session: How to control without dominating and how to accomodate without sacrificing too much.

CONCLUSION

In this article, I have articulated one woman's belief systems about belief systems, with recognition that cognition is but one dimension of gender patterns in therapy and that full description of treatment impasses requires elaboration of the belief systems of all members of the system. In exploring how gendered beliefs can lead to impasses or non-productive patterns between male clients and female therapists, my language has shifted between talking about how things are and questioning that things are "really" that way, between description and elucidation of the belief systems that shape that description. I have used a language of gender differences, while inquiring into the utility of a dualistic model. I have highlighted both the relative stability of belief systems about gender, while pointing to their evolutionary relationship with the changing social context. This recursive process is both frustrating and necessary, as feminist family therapists try to critique a system in the terms of the system—the only language we have at our disposal (Spender, 1980).

As feminist family therapists, it is essential that we continually question the underpinnings of our beliefs that shape how we approach men in therapy, what we expect from them, how we interact with them, and how we conceptualize the therapeutic task. Although male client and female therapist reciprocally influence each other, I believe it is incumbent upon the feminist family therapist to take the initiative in questioning and challenging taken for granted beliefs about gender. Embedded in the prevailing symbolic order, many of our clients will not question it. Although this symbolic order is larger than any individual, we can choose to maintain or transform it. As Spender (1980) suggests regarding the "man-made categories of masculinity and femininity,"

> (t)hese categories which are complex constructions represent the virtual obsession of the dominant group with dichotomies and hierarchies, for these are fundamental premises in an order based on the supremacy of one group over another . . . It depends upon women playing their part as a muted group, voluntarily suppressing the evidence that exposes the false and arbitrary nature of man-made categories and the reality which is built on those categories. (pp. 101-102)

This will be threatening to us, and to the men (and women) we treat. Towards this end, women therapists will need to learn over and over that we have the power as women and as therapists to help free men from the constrictions of gender, rather than colluding in maintaining them (Carlson, 1987). In challenging these categories, both women therapists and male clients will be required to use previously forbidden aspects of themselves (Miller, 1976). There are high personal and social costs to such profound change for both.

I have also suggested that belief systems are not created randomly, but serve a social function of maintaining a social context that is oppressive to both men and women. Although individuals adhere to the dominant belief system in varying degrees, none of us can transcend the cultural context. Thus, we can neither deny individual differences nor the extrapersonal factors that constrain or interact with individual differences. We can articulate the kinds of contradictions and conflicts that female therapists and male clients may experience as they struggle with how to apply constantly evolving gender ideologies to constantly evolving social situations. The difficult but necessary task is how to honor the particularity of each man and woman, while maintaining a political or gender sensitive analysis (see James & McIntyre, 1989, for a special application of "double description" to this dilemma). By examining beliefs about gender and their relation to material and social conditions, we can also be hopeful about the possibility of individual change while painfully aware of the social constraints that limit it. As Gerson (1987) writes,

> Whatever the form or content, women's relationships with men are neither the result of universal, unchanging predispositions nor passive reactions to male dominance. Rather, a changing structure of gender relations is creating new possibilities—for cooperation and conflict—in male-female relationships. Larger social changes are providing women with new sources of power, but they are also creating new insecurities and vulnerabilities. Only in this context of altered constraints and opportunities can women's varied views of men be understood. (p. 128)

Lastly, female therapist and male client, if each agree to the task, are setting out on an uncharted course. Men and women alike have made adaptations to the social conditions of domination that have limited personal development and possibility (Miller, 1982). Both sexes share beliefs that do not do justice to male or female experience. But how does one create something different? At the beginning, we can only trust that "(w)hen we begin to select, pattern and interpret according to the rule that the sexes are equal, we will construct a very different reality, we will make very different ideas 'come true'" (Spender, 1980, p. 2).

REFERENCES

Bepko, C., & Krestan, J. (1985). *The responsibility trap.* New York: The Free Press.

Berger, M. (1984). Men's new family roles: Some implications for therapists. In P. Rieker & E.H. Carmen (Eds.), *The gender gap in psychotherapy: Social realities and psychological processes,* (pp. 319-335). New York: Plenum Press.

Bernardez, T. (1982). The female therapist in relation to male roles. In K. Solomon & N. Levy (Eds.), *Men in transition: Theory and therapy,* (pp. 439-461). New York: Plenum.

Bernardez, T. (1988). Women and anger – Cultural prohibitions and the feminine ideal. Stone Center Work in Progress, No. 31. Stone Center, Wellesley College, Wellesley, MA 02181.

Bograd, M. (1983). Domestic violence: Perceptions of battered women, abusive men, and non-violent men and women. Unpublished doctoral dissertation, University of Chicago, Chicago, IL.

Bograd, M. (1988). Behind the mask: Sexuality in the therapeutic relationship. *Family Therapy Networker, 12*, 31-34.

Bograd, M. (1989). Passions of therapy: Hidden sexual dimensions. In D. Kantor & B. Okun (Eds.), *Intimate environments: Sex, intimacy and gender in families,* (pp. 163-195). New York: Guilford Press.

Bograd, M. (1990). Women treating men: Confronting our gender assumptions. *Family Therapy Networker, 14,* 54-58.

Carlson, N. (1987). Woman therapist: Male client. In M. Scher, M. Stevens, G. Good, & G. Eichenfield (Eds.), *Handbook of counseling and psychotherapy with men*, (pp. 39-50). Newbury Park, CA: Sage Publications.

Caust, B., Libow, J., & Raskin, P. (1981). Challenges and promises of training women as family systems therapists. *Family Process, 20*, 439-447.

Feldman, L. (1982). Sex roles and family dynamics. In F. Walsh (Ed.), *Normal family processes*, (pp. 354-379). New York: Guilford Press.

Fisher, E. (1989). Gender bias in therapy? An analysis of patient and therapist causal explanations. *Psychotherapy: Theory, Research and Practice, 26,* 389-401.

Gerson, K. (1987). What do women want from men? Men's influence on women's work and family choices. In M. Kimmel (Ed.), *Changing men: New directions on men and masculinity*, (pp. 115-130). Newbury Park, CA: Sage.

Goldner, V. (1985). Feminism and family therapy. *Family Process, 24,* 31-47.

Goldner, V. (1988). Generation and gender: Normative and covert hierarchies. *Family Process, 27*, 17-33.

Goode, W. (1982). Why men resist. In B. Thorne & M. Yalom (Eds.), *Rethinking the family: Some feminist questions*, (pp. 131-150). New York: Longman.

Goodrich, T., Rampage, C., Ellman, B., & Halstead, K. (1988). *Feminist family therapy: A casebook*. New York: W.W. Norton.

Hare-Mustin, R. (1978). A feminist approach to family therapy. *Family Process, 17*, 181-194.

Hare-Mustin, R. (1987). The problem of gender in family therapy theory. *Family Process, 26*, 15-27.

Hare-Mustin, R. & Marecek, J. (1986). Autonomy and gender: Some questions for therapists. *Psychotherapy, 23*, 205-212.

Hare-Mustin, R., & Marecek, J. (1988). The meaning of difference: Gender theory, postmodernism and psychology. *American Psychologist, 43*, 455-464.

Herek, G. (1987). On heterosexual masculinity: Some psychical consequences of the social construction of gender and sexuality. In M. Kimmel (Ed.), *Changing men: New directions on men and masculinity*, (pp. 68-82). Newbury Park, CA: Sage.

Ipsaro, A. (1986). Male client-male therapist: Issues in a therapeutic alliance. *Psychotherapy, 23*, 257-266.

James, K. (1984). Breaking the chains of gender: Family therapy's position? *Australian Journal of Family Therapy, 5*, 241-248.

James, K., & McIntyre, D. (1983). The reproduction of families: The social role of family therapy? *Journal of Marital and Family Therapy, 9*, 119-129.

James, K., & McIntyre, D. (1989). "A momentary gleam of enlightenment": Towards a model of feminist family therapy. *Journal of Feminist Family Therapy, 1*, 3-24.

Kahn, A. (1984). The power war: Male response to power loss under equality. *Psychology of Women Quarterly, 9*, 234-247.

Kaplan, A. (1979). Toward an analysis of sex-role related issues in the therapeutic relationship. *Psychiatry, 42,* 112-120.

Kaplan, A. (1984). Female or male therapists for women: New formulations. Stone Center Work in Progress, No. 83-02. Stone Center, Wellesley College, Wellesley, MA 02181.

Kaplan, A., Brooks, B., McComb, A., Shapiro, E., & Sodano, A. (1983). Women and anger in psychotherapy. In J. Robbins & R. Siegel (Eds.), *Women changing therapy*, (pp.29-49). New York: Haworth.

Lerner, H. (1983). Female dependency in context: Some theoretical and technical considerations. *American Journal of Orthopsychiatry, 53*, 697-705.

Libow, J. (1986). Training family therapists as feminists. In M. Ault-Riche (Ed.), *Women and family therapy*, (pp. 16-24). Rockville, MD: Aspen Systems Corp.

Libow, J., Raskin, P., & Caust, B. (1982). Feminist and family systems therapy: Are they irreconcilable? *American Journal of Family Therapy, 10,* 3-12.

Luepnitz, D. (1988). *The family interpreted: Feminist theory in clinical practice.* New York: Basic Books.

MacKinnon, L, & Miller, D. (1987). The new epistemology and the Milan approach: Feminist and socio-political implications. *Journal of Marital and Family Therapy, 13*, 139-155.

McGoldrick, M., Anderson, C., & Walsh, F. (Eds). (1988). *Women in families: A framework for family therapy*. New York: W.W. Norton.

Meth, R. & Pasick, R. (1990). *Men in therapy: The challenge of change*. New York: Guilford Press.

Miller, J.B. (1976). *Toward a new psychology of women.* Boston: Beacon Press.

Miller, J.B. (1982). Women and power. Stone Center Work in Progress, No. 82-01. Stone Center, Wellesley College, Wellesley, MA 02181.

Miller, J.B. (1983). The construction of anger in women and men. Stone Center Work in Progress, No. 83-01. Stone Center, Wellesley College, Wellesley, MA 02181.

Mirkin, M. (Ed.). (1990). *The social and political contexts of family therapy.* Boston: Allyn & Bacon.

Okun, B. (1983). Gender issues of family systems therapists. In B. Okun & S. Gladding (Eds.), *Issues in training marriage and family therapists*, (pp. 43-57). Ann Arbor: ERIC-CAPS.

Okun, B. (1989). Therapists' blind spots related to gender socialization. In D. Kantor & B. Okun (Eds.), *Intimate environments: Sex, intimacy, and gender in families*, pp. 129-162. New York: Guilford Press.

Pleck, J. (1984). Men's power with women, other men, and society: A men's movement analysis. In P. Ricker & E.H. Carmen (Eds.), *The gender gap in psychotherapy: Social realities and psychological processes, (pp. 79-89).* New York: Plenum Press.

Reid, E., McDaniel, S., Donaldson, C., & Tollers, M. (1987). Taking it personally: Issues of personal authority and competence for the female in family therapy training. *Journal of Marital and Family Therapy, 13*, 157-165.

Rice, D. (1978). The male spouse in marital and family therapy. *Counseling Psychologist, 7*, 64-67.

Robbins, J. (1983). Complex triangles: Uncovering sexist bias in relationship counseling. In J. Robbins & R. Siegel (Eds.), *Women changing therapy, (pp. 159-169)*. New York: Haworth.

Rubin, L. (1983). *Intimate strangers: Men and women together*. New York: Harper Colophon Books.

Schaef, A. (1981). *Women's reality: An emerging female system in the white male society.* Minneapolis: Winston Press.

Sheely, M. (1982). The dilemma of personal authority for the female family therapist. In A. Gurman (Ed.), *Questions and answers in the practice of family therapy, Volume 2*, (pp. 287-292). New York: Brunner/Mazel.

Simon, R. (Ed.). (1990). Men nurturing men. *Family Therapy Networker, 14*, 26-58.

Spender, D. (1980). *Man made language*. Boston: Routledge & Kegan Paul.

Sternbach, J. (1989) Undoing masculinity–The men's seminar. *Proceedings 1989 Actes du Symposium*. Montreal: McGill University. Reprints available through Jack Sternbach, RFD Box 607, Vineyard Haven, MA 02568.

Stiver, I. (1984). The meanings of "dependency" in female-male relationships. Stone Center Work in Progress, No. 83-07. Stone Center, Wellesley College, Wellesley, MA 02181.

Taggart, M. (1989). Epistemological equality as the fulfillment of family therapy. *Journal of Feminist Family Therapy, 1*, 85-110.

Walters, M., Carter, B., Papp, P., & Silverstein, O. (1988). *The invisible web: Gender patterns in family relationships*. New York: Guilford Press.

Wheeler, D., Avis, J.M., Miller, L. & Chaney, S. (1985). Rethinking family therapy education and supervision: A feminist model. *Journal of Psychotherapy and the Family, 1*, 53-71.

Yogev, S. & Shadish, W. (1982). A method for monitoring the impact of sex-role stereotypes on the therapeutic behavior of beginning psychotherapists. *American Journal of Orthopsychiatry, 52*, 545-548.

PART 3: THE DIVERSITY OF FEMINIST-INFORMED FAMILY THERAPY APPROACHES

The Politics of Mood: Depressive-Caretaker Relationships

Ronald Taffel

SUMMARY. Many families we treat contain a man who has an underlying depression and a woman who is bound by socio-economic realities and emotional definitions requiring her to help regulate his moods. Men's depression is not easy to recognize. It is hidden by various "difficult man" labels, disguised by socially sanctioned mood-regulatory behaviors such as drinking and violence, and buffered by women who, for the family's survival, must keep a bad situation from getting worse. This article identifies the depressive-caretaker dynamic. It outlines several clinical interventions designed to help men regulate their own moods, thereby allowing women to focus more directly on themselves.

Ronald Taffel, PhD, is Director, Family and Couples Treatment Services, The Institute for Contemporary Psychotherapy, 1 West 91st Street, New York, NY 10024.

The author would like to acknowledge Elizabeth Carter for her generosity as both teacher and colleague. The cumulative impact of her ideas on my development as a family therapist has been immeasurable.

> It was in the middle of the night when I would find him there. Alone at the kitchen table he sat bent over a book or the daily newspaper. "What's the matter, Daddy?" I asked, already knowing what the answer would be. "Oh, it's nothing Ronnie. I just have something on my mind, so I couldn't sleep." He looked up at me, the glasses magnifying some expression in his eyes I wasn't able to name. "Don't worry," he said, "go back to bed and I'll see you in the morning." The next morning, there would be a noticeable pallor over the house. I could see that my mother hadn't slept much either; her usual concerns about getting us ready for the day had a more strident edge to them.

Though my father was definitely on the serious side, he was not that much different from the other fathers around me.

> Henry, Alan and Leon's father, was considered "very quiet." I can't remember Henry saying more than a handful of words for the twenty years I regularly saw him. It's not that he seemed unhappy. He just sat there, occasionally smiling, passively taking up space while a swirl of women and children made their commotion around him.
>
> Mickey, the father of Art, lived a block away. He stood out amongst the fathers, in that every Saturday when we played ball, he actually came out to watch Art. Week after week, through tens of thousands of innings, Mickey stood there, taking everything in. He never once smiled. He never yelled or cheered. He watched without expression of any sort. Once I asked Art, "What did your father say about that game yesterday?" He shrugged his shoulders and walked away.
>
> Walter, the father of Steve, was a man of "ritual," following the same routine every morning, every day and every night. He was so reliable that everyone said, "You could set your watch by him." Even as his son did the unthinkable by moving to California, marrying and then divorcing, even as his friends around him died, Walter's routine remained unchanged. Only as cancer got the better of him and made leaving bed impossible did Walter give in and alter his routine in

> any way. When this happened, it was clear the end was coming.
>
> Jack, Peter and Joyce's father, was considered a "wise-guy." Nothing seemed to please him. Nothing was quite right. He had an answer and a complaint about everything. Through my growing up years, I can't picture him without a scowl on his face. I can only remember him pacing back and forth like a man who was waiting around for a slow bus to come.
>
> Charlie, the father of my best friend Leo, had a "real head on his shoulders." If asked a question, he could recite point by point an unending stream of facts. Charlie didn't actually converse, he simply churned out information. It was important not to ask him any question if you weren't near a door and had to be home soon. I don't remember ever seeing Charlie and his wife in the same room together.

Probably none of the fathers in my old neighborhood would be given a diagnosis of clinical depression. True, they didn't feel very much, had no real friendships, were chronically angry or silent, had few interests other than work, didn't have fun and couldn't relate well to their wives and children. But, they had jobs, rarely went to doctors, and held up their responsibilities well enough. Yet over the years, as I have listened to clients describe their fathers' and husbands' lifelong bouts of irritability, bitterness, flatness, explosiveness or disconnection, I have begun to wonder whether we overlook significant depression in men, because men are simply acting like—*men*.

The possible underdiagnosing of depression in men should not be surprising, because its formal diagnosis is based on loss of everyday functioning or self-report of psychological pain. Loss of functioning means that job and social performance are compromised by the vegetative signs of depression—disturbances in sleep and appetite, significant changes in weight, lack of motivation and interest, inability to concentrate, and fluctuations in mood (DSM IIIR, 1980, p.210). But, I feel these criteria allow us to overlook depression in many men, since the male sex role and its concrete demands often mitigate against men admitting emotional difficulties or becoming fully dysfunctional in the workplace.

One reason the admission of psychological pain is so hard for men is the potential economic hardship. Whether it be loss of actual income, loss of career momentum, or medical insurance plans that don't protect an employee's confidentiality, a man takes some risk when he decides to seek psychiatric treatment. Another factor influencing whether a man admits psychological pain is whether he even *feels* it. Many depressed men self-medicate through socially sanctioned mood-regulatory behaviors such as drinking, gambling, womanizing and violence. At great risk to themselves and their families, these activities offer short-term relief from crippling bouts of depression.

The expense in psychological and economic terms, however, is astonishing. Billions of dollars are lost annually to alcoholism and gambling. Millions of lives are destroyed each year by family violence, the emotional consequences for the survivors lasting several lifetimes. In response, fifteen million Americans have joined self-help groups to dig themselves out from hopelessness and isolation. Yet, as Harriet Lerner (1989) and Marianne Walters (1990) observe, it is the *women* who are the prime targets of the "recovery" movement. The question of men's depression continues to be buried under rock-solid beliefs that women are sick and that men are irresponsible or bad.

Masculine identification, of course, further lessens the possibility that men will admit or experience outright depression. In the collective psyche of men, masculinity is equated with psychological toughness, taking charge, being bold, rising to the occasion—the antithesis of depressive states. The socio-political context, rightly critiqued by feminists as being controlled by men, is more precisely controlled by *a certain kind of man*. He is never openly depressed and does not let on to any of the vulnerabilities that go along with mood difficulties. For every sensitive man on "Thirtysomething," there are dozens of public figures whose lives and careers were completely ruined by the faintest whiff of vulnerability. Witness Thomas Eagleton's "exposed" psychiatric history or Ed Muskie's "breaking down" during the Canuck episode. Every bead of sweat on Richard Nixon's face during his debate with John Kennedy translated into thousands of votes in the election. George Bush spent years fighting the "wimp" factor, first "kicking Geraldine Ferrarro's ass" in their debate, then using Willie Horton, Boston Harbor and the American flag to "play hardball" against a confused, downbeat, depressive Michael Dukakis. Five seconds on "The Wide World of Sports" tells it all. The image of the skier falling wildly down the slopes in the "Agony of Defeat" has become an enduring symbol of the bottom falling out of a man's hopes and dreams. And yet, even after such disgrace, most well-schooled men would valiantly muster up an "I gave 100% . . . you just can't let these things *get you down*."

But life is full of disappointing realities, and if men can't easily experience or admit to depressive reactions, where do they go? *To women*. Women often end up being the bearers of men's depression, giving support to Jean Baker Miller's (1976) suggestion that women carry around painful issues that men and the culture at large can't resolve. Clinical observation indicates that certain gender differences begin early in life: female babies "read" other people's emotions more clearly than do males; girls try more often than boys to help a distressed mother; female infants cry more readily than boys in response to distress in other infants. Given a life-time of caretaking responsibility, it is not surprising that women are diagnosed for depression in far greater numbers than are men. As long as men have women to express their depression for them, and as long as their role is so heavily defined as the person who must go out and provide for the family, the deck is heavily stacked against men having to admit or even experience their own depression. It appears, then, that the formal clinical criteria for diagnosing depression may not adequately take into account the impact of traditional gender socialization or male-female dynamics.

FAMILY MEMBERS AS DIAGNOSTICIANS: AN INFORMAL REVIEW

On the other hand, what if we didn't have to rely on loss of functioning or the self-reports of men to diagnose depression? Suppose that we consider the descriptions of significant others as valid indicators for diagnosis? Suppose further that we would sensitize ourselves to how our biases, expectations and stereotypes *normalize* aberrant behavior in men, even as we have become aware of how we *pathologize* adaptive behavior in women? In other words, what clinical signs do we overlook in men, because our culture defines them as appropriate "male" behaviors?

With these factors in mind, I approached 125 cases seen in my practice over the last three years in the following way: Whenever a family presented with a depressed woman or child, I looked for undiagnosed depression in the man. I began to inquire about the man's affective state in detail, making sure I did not miss pathology camouflaged by gendered expectations and cliches about "the way men are."

For example, take the case of a woman client reporting a depressive undertow in the house and then describing her husband as "not being a big talker—the quiet type." Rather than saying to myself, "Well, alot of men don't talk much," I took pains to find out just what she meant. How much does he talk? Does he ever talk? When? To whom? Does he have fun? Does he have interests? Does he have friends? Can he relax? How does he relax? And so on. This included a detailed inquiry into his family of origin around the same issues: Did his father talk? With whom? Do his siblings talk? And so on.

From these reports, I learned that certain "red-flag" descriptions of family members suggested that the man of the house had difficulties with his mood. My review also indicated that a man's depression doesn't exist in isolation. As a woman described his mood or behavior, she also described her own response—be it an inner feeling or overt behavioral adaptations. In this way, I began to get clues to the interactional dances between the man and other family members around his mood difficulties.

While the general picture of depression was similar in many families, the tempo of the depressive dance seemed to fall into two groups. I labeled one group as passive, the other as agitated depression. In the passive group, the man's depression is expressed in a "nice," reserved, quiet, unexpressive manner. This is the sort of man who melts into the background of family life. The second group was made up of men whose agitated mood creates a great deal of emotional noise in the family. They demand attention, they increase the level of anxiety in the house. Their presence must continuously be dealt with by those around them. Following are sample descriptions by women of these two classes of men's depressive states. In parentheses are the women's descriptions of their own adaptative behaviors.

Group One—Passive Depression

He broods about everything, he's a worrier. (I always have to show him the bright side.)

He takes criticism badly. (I'm always careful about hurting his ego.)

He keeps his feelings to himself. (I have to pull everything out of him.)

He has no friends on his own. (I have to make all the arrangements for social events.)

He never changes his routine. Every day and every night it's the same story. (It's unbelievably boring. I keep trying to add some spice to our lives.)

Group Two—Agitated Depression

It's like living with a caged animal. Something's always eating at him. (I'm nervous all the time from trying to calm him down.)

His energy is endless. He thinks he can take on everything. (I have to bring him down to earth.)

It's like walking on eggshells around him. (I have to watch everything I say.)

He's like a little Napoleon. He always finds fault with me or the children. (It's like having a big baby on my hands.)

He wants all of me. (I have to hide from him how much I talk to my family and friends.)

While only 14% of men in the 125 cases I approached in this manner would receive a formal diagnosis of depression according to

DSM-III, 62% experienced enough disturbance in mood that they chronically affected the moods of the people who lived with them and required special treatment and monitoring by family members.

Keep in mind that almost none of the men present as depressed in the therapy interview. They fit many "difficult men" labels—obsessive, narcissistic, schizoid, workaholic, alcoholic and so on. However, beneath these labels there is a common and less pejorative thread. There is the presence of an undertow that the man has to fight against in himself and that pulls at the family's mood. Whether the undertow is sporadic or exists just below the surface of everyday life, its presence is always felt. Whether the men disappear into the woodwork with their passivity or make the foundation of the house shake with their agitation, they share a basic quality. *They cannot regulate their own moods and they depend on their partners and children to do so.*

THE DEPRESSIVE-CARETAKER PAIRING

> If ever a television program captured the depressive-caretaker pairing, "The Honeymooners" would have to be considered. Threatening abuse weekly, raging and stomping about on hopes and dreams that never saw fruition, a mountain of ego and self-absorption, Ralph's ultimate reliance on Alice for emotional stability was starkly apparent. Each week when "The Honeymooners" would come on the air, I would practically drag my father into the living room so we could watch it together. As Ralph raved on about his newest scheme to get rich quick, maybe the uranium mine in Vermont or the Handy Dandy Vegematic, my father would laugh so hard tears rolled down his face. My mother was never much interested in the show. She said there was something too depressing and too loud about it.

If an instrument had to be created to help a man maintain some equilibrium in the face of a lifetime of unattainable goals and an inability to self-nurture, what better invention than a wife? As decades of feminists have observed, a woman is socialized from birth to monitor and respond to other peoples' feelings before her own—

to adapt her behavior to the needs of others. This is particularly apparent in a family where a man has problems with his mood.

In a household whose climate is shaped by an agitated depressed man, a woman will try to calm things down, keep the kids away, protect him from daily chores, parcel out bad news, arrange dinner and the kids' bedtime to fit around his schedule—all the while asking herself: "How am I going to make it through this evening without him getting into an uproar over something?" The mood of a passive depressed man has just as much power to define the family's emotional environment. In such households, women try to maintain a positive attitude and liven things up. They try to pull or cajole him out of his shell. They set up social events and push him out of the house to try new things. They spend money and effort adding romance, intimacy and zest to the relationship.

In either case, after years of feeling responsible for changing something that cannot be changed by anyone but him, she ends up being disappointed, furious and contemptuous. She can no longer swallow his demands, his unwillingness to participate, his refusal in her eyes to grow up, and his inability to take better care of her for being "good" to him. And, in the end, she may be extremely lonely no matter how many people are crowding her in.

Her reactions are reciprocated in full by the man's complaint that his wife has been unable to improve his mood. He is depressed about the fact that life has not turned out the way he had hoped for, or even if it has, that he is still internally dissatisfied. He is resentful that despite his sacrifices—being "hemmed-in" by the demands of family and job—he is still criticized; he still feels inadequate; he still feels unappreciated at home and at the workplace. He just can't shake the depressive feeling no matter how much he succeeds in the outside world or how well his wife takes care of him.

In many relationships, then, a woman who initially idealized certain masculine qualities finds out that her partner's toughness may be hardness, his stoicism may be resignation, his contained strength may be rigidity and his decisiveness may be impulsivity. Without either partner intentionally misrepresenting themselves, they end up in a fix. She is caretaking a depression that has no name, past his being just "another difficult man." He is warding off admitting or even knowing that something is the matter—or worse, distracting himself with mood regulatory behaviors such as alcoholism, gambling, violence or compulsive sex.

When life-cycle transitions add fuel to this volatile or slow-burning mixture, we family therapists become part of the depressive-caretaker drama. And yet, even if a woman can convince her partner to show up for treatment, it's not easy for family therapists to talk about the man's underlying depression. We often don't see his inner state or question the woman's role in caretaking his depression, because therapists are caught in many of the same biases as the family. Just like other family members, we rely on the woman to intiate the treatment, to remain committed to the treatment, to become the patient, and to sacrifice her own voice for the family good (Goldner, 1985). Yet, despite our reliance on women to hold things together in the treatment, men often control the purse strings—a fact of life that has direct bearing on therapists. Much like mothers and wives who have a great deal to lose economically if the marriage breaks up, we stand to lose financially if we alienate the man by naming the depression he denies.

The rules of engagement most of us have been taught in traditional family therapy reflect these concerns and protect against exposure of the man's underlying pathology: "Approach the real therapy customer first"—usually the woman. "Push harder on the more motivated person"—again, usually the woman. "Decentralize mother, bring in father"—implying that mother or wife is the patient and father the healthy one. "Positively connote and buddy-up to the man"—by stressing action, not reflection, by using mechanistic terms rather than emotional language, by focusing on boundaries and hierarchy, rather than connectedness. When you add it all up, traditional family therapy techniques keep the couple on familiar ground, reinforcing traditional roles, and directing them and the therapist away from acknowledging the pull of his depressive undertow.

On the other hand, the feminist view that men's identity is rooted in autonomy and women's in connectedness may also protect men from looking at themselves. It has created an "idealization of relatedness" (Hare-Mustin, p. 208, 1986), which can turn therapy into an emotional re-education of the man. While many men need to learn more relationship skills (e.g., relating, sharing, empathy), this perspective may keep him too focused on the outside—on learning a new language, rather than attending to his own experience. Feminism's emphasis on his inordinate power in the socioeconomic equation can give treatment a somewhat moralistic tone and frame therapy entirely through a lense of power differences. Inequities between men and women cannot help but trigger moral outrage: the sobering post-divorce economic realities for women, the sorry record of men in providing child support, the unequal burden of household and childcare duties, the frightening statistics on wife battering, incest and other forms of male to female violence. Yet, the very truth of this analysis—that fact that men *do* have greater defining power in most relationships—makes it all too easy to leave out the genuine "angst" of many men in the emotional equation.

For both traditional and feminist family therapists, then, it's hard not to organize our thinking about men around issues of *self-esteem* and *power*, while we minimize the importance of *mood*. This is a critical oversight, because mood can be an important factor in fostering or blocking change. Like families, the way we experience our moods is both content and process, and definitely not open to easy alteration. Moods are the soupy mixture of life forces—feelings that simmer in the everyday stew of contextual pressures, thoughts that make up the muck and mire of our preoccupations, and tempermental predispositions that have been with us since birth. The psychologist Christopher Bolas (1987) believes that we develop a powerful and quite durable relationship to our basic mood states. We recreate them wherever we go and with whomever we share our lives. Family therapists intuitively understand how a person's mood shapes his context, and how the context, in turn, shapes his moods.

Yet, despite its "everydayness" (or perhaps because of it), we don't focus on mood anymore than we focus on our own heartbeat. In terms of working with men this is unfortunate. While men's emotional expressiveness often has serious limitations, it does include some capacity to report on mood. Ask a man about his *hidden* anxieties, his *real* feelings, and his *shaky* self-esteem, and he is likely to think we are after the same vulnerabilities he has had trouble verbalizing in his relationship. Ask him about his mood, however, and the question (because mood is so connected to physical experience and to everyday external situations), *may* lead you up to his preoccupations, out to his reach, into his heart, and down to his penis. A woman has a vested interest in this question, as well, because her life, especially if she lives with a difficult man, is indelibly shaped by the demands of his mood. Whether it opens things up or not, focusing on mood is a beginning, a potentially effective way to join with families. It keeps us in touch with the underlying depressive-caretaker dynamic in many couples. And, it encourages us to modify our clinical techniques when we approach something so powerful as a family's enduring blend of gender arrangements and mood.

CLINICAL TECHNIQUES

> There were essentially two fathers who came home each evening. The one I like to remember was loving and attentive. He helped me with my schoolwork, sculpted circus animals out of clay, worked with me on oilpainting by number kits and built models of airplanes and battleships. On Sundays we went to Walt Disney feature cartoons and to baseball games when I got a little older. And every night of my life, even in the midst of our wilder struggles, he would be sure to say good night to me.
>
> The other father was preoccupied. He said almost nothing, was extremely irritable and seemed always on the edge of exploding. When he did go over the edge (and this was not an infrequent occurrence), the veins in his temple looked as if they would burst, killing him on the spot for some infraction on my part.
>
> A friend of mine once commented to me, "Why is your father so serious?" I was only twelve, but from hearing my mother's explanation a hundred times before, I knew exactly what to say. "Business is slow," I answered. The fact that my father was serious regardless of business conditions did not seem to register with my mother, my friend, or me.

1. Redefining the Problem

How *does* the therapist introduce the possibility that the husband is depressed when *neither* partner may be comfortable with this idea? Most men recoil at any suggestion that they are sick, in pain, or that something is even bothering them. On the other hand, a woman's reaction may not be positive either. Many women feel despair about depending on someone so vaguely flawed as a depressed man. Alcoholism, for example, has a specific and somewhat masculine ring to it. "Depression? . . . That's what women get!" A woman may also feel rage when she finds out that something has been wrong all these years, even though he has refused to admit it, or may resist the idea of depression because it gives him an excuse and dumps another caretaking project onto her lap.

Because of these considerations, when one redefines the problem as depression, *it is essential to move slowly* (in one case, near-suicidal despondency resulted from too quick a redefinition). First describe the man's behavior using the phrases coined by the family, such as "irritable," "moody," "quiet," "restless." Later, more clinical terms can be introduced. Although many family therapists try not to use clinical terminology, it *is* my intention to pathologize what has been normalized in men. Without articulating the problem, the burden of responsibility continues to fall on the woman. This confirms the man's beliefs that things will get better once she changes, while the central issue of his mood hasn't even been touched.

Clinical Example: The "Irritable" Man

> The identified patient, an eight year old obese girl, is overly aggressive, difficult to control and a behavior problem at school. The family states that there are problems between mother and daughter. Mother is high strung, overly protective, and doesn't know how to set limits. She describes her husband as hard to live with, as he is always critical and possessive of her time, and feels caught between him and the children. When he interacts with the kids, he is one step away from being frustrated and angry at them. The family says that he is

"irritable" and "that it's like walking on eggshells around him."

THERAPIST: Fred, why do you think you're irritable so much of the time?

FRED: The pressures of work get to me, but mostly it's because they make me so irritable.

THERAPIST: You're saying that the cause of your irritability is that the family is always around bugging you, that it's never quiet?

FRED: Right.

THERAPIST: Did you start being irritable only since you met Lenore and the kids were born?

LENORE: No. He was very irritable already on our first date.

FRED: I've been irritable before. I was that way around my house growing up.

THERAPIST: So being irritable is nothing new since you got married. It sounds like you've always had a tendency towards agitation. Do you ever remember a time when you weren't?

FRED: It's funny you mention it, because once in my life I felt different. I was upset about something and my mother gave me some sort of tranquilizer. I was stunned at how calm I felt—like this is the way a person could feel. My engine stopped idling so high for a couple of hours. I can't remember a time in my life since I've been a kid when I haven't woken up in the morning thinking, what is going to go wrong today that will upset me. It's a feeling that I get in the pit of my stomach. For three hours in my life I didn't feel this.

THERAPIST: So for three hours you weren't agitated. We'd be hard pressed to say that this agitation and depressed feeling you have in your stomach every morning could possibly be the family's entire fault.

FRED: Not entirely. I suppose I've always been this way to some degree.

THERAPIST: Fred, it sounds like you've been fighting an undertow of depression for a long time. And that, Lenore, you and the kids have tried to handle it in many different ways. Fred, how do you deal with it yourself? How do you take care of your agitation and depression?

By first sticking to the family's descriptive term, "irritability," I introduced a frame that included the ruminative angst that Fred woke up with every day of his life. The focus of treatment then became the many ways that Fred's lack of self-care and Lenore's sense of responsibility for him affected their lives together. Treatment shifted to Fred assuming more responsibility for his own moods and Lenore digging herself out from three generations of caretaking women in her family—all married to depressed men.

2. Focused Family of Origin Inquiry

In many cases, the family's explanation of the mood difficulty is so naturally camouflaged in gendered stereotypes that direct attempts at reframing simply don't work. More indirect methods become necessary. At these times, it is helpful to *first* focus on depression in the man's family of origin. Discovering that his father and siblings had undiagnosed mood difficulties reduces the toxicity of the idea and allows him to accept the redefinition without as much shame. Since it has recently become clear that depression exists in many forms, it is important to get a family history of phobias and aversions, controlled alcohol abuse, sudden rage attacks, fast-cycling mood changes, obsessive-compulsive behaviors and panic attacks.

Clinical Example: The "Passive" Man

Elliot (43) and Karen (41) presented because of chronic bickering that had intensified after the birth of their first child one-and-one-half years earlier. Karen complained bitterly about Elliot's passivity—his weight, his nightly drinking, his laziness and his withdrawal into television. Elliot described Karen as irrational and never satisfied with any of his attempts at self-improvement. He was adamant that he had no problem except Karen's inability to be satisfied.

Elliot and Karen didn't budge from their positions until I did a detailed family of origin inquiry focusing on passivity and depression. Closer examination revealed that Elliot's "very quiet" father might have been very quietly depressed. Every night he had a number of drinks, retired to his room, read book after book, and rarely communicated to anyone in the family. He kept the shades drawn and Elliot barely remembered him smiling or laughing.

Defining his father as possibly alcoholic and depressed, rather than as quiet and intellectual, gave Elliot permission to admit his own chronic deadness and lack of self-care. He stopped defending himself and ridiculing Karen and began to talk about the moods he fell into that led to his nightly withdrawal. After several weeks, he decided to cut down on his drinking and made an appointment with a physician. Although he still does not view his alcohol use as problematic, he has significantly reduced his intake over the past three months.

This redefinition of the problem and Elliot's greater openness created just enough space for Karen to step back and begin exploring her own contribution to the stalemate. This was her persistent denial about seeing Elliot clearly, much as she had been unable to see her father in a realistic light. Family of origin work began to refocus Karen on her parents' unhappy and often violent marriage, further helping reduce the anger and blame in the current relationship with Elliot.

3. Reassigning Responsibility

There is a concrete denseness to some depressed men that can be extremely frustrating to a woman and therapist alike. His lack of self-awareness and her pursuit of insight represents one type of the distancer-pursuer dyad that needs to be addressed. Since our culture dictates that women teach men about their inner experience, this often results in a stuck pattern as the man resists learning about himself and the woman escalates her efforts. Unfortunately, therapists still commonly label the woman as enmeshed and convince her to "back off." In contrast, my emphasis is on encouraging the man to become the expert about his own problems with mood. Task assignments that help him become more aware of his mood changes can begin this process. Such tasks include asking a man to keep a mood log for a period of time in which he records events preceding the onset of depressive symptoms; having him get feedback about his moods from extended family members or friends; and introducing reading material about different types of depression.

Clinical Example: The "Dense" Man

Jim (47) and Chris (41), a couple in the arts, were married for 15 years with two children. They came in complaining of chronic and explosive fighting about their living arrangement. Chris contributed the lion's share to the couple's finances and childcare and was exhausted by carrying both roles. Jim complained that Chris acted as if she knew him better than he knew himself. In fact, Chris could not stop trying to teach Jim about himself. The sharper and more insistent she became, the duller he became.

Chris' own words were revealing about what it's like to live with a ruminative depressed person:

"It's like walking on eggshells. I say something to him and a shadow comes over his face and I know I'm in for it. And I won't be able to get out until something just as mysterious happens and his face clears up again. He feels okay afterwards but I feel bruised and drained and in a rage about the whole experience. The worst part is that he doesn't get it. He's dense. I can literally see the wheels of his mind turning, but he doesn't know it. I can see that he's entered certain territory and that there's no getting out until he's finished."

After several sessions, I asked Jim to write down the warning signals of a bad mood during a one week period. I also asked Chris to cease from pointing them out to him. Jim was not to show Chris his notes before the next session. It took weeks to get this to happen, with both predictably falling into their old roles. But finally, Jim came in with a list that included signals such as losing items around the house, forgetting appointments, being unable to sit still and drinking more heavily.

Upon completing the assignment, Jim began to accept how moody he was and to recognize mood changes almost as quickly as Chris. This greater capacity for self-observation allowed Chris to relax and stop monitoring him so much. Jim's obsessional mood shifts became less precipitous (though they did not disappear). In response, Chris opened up to him about items previously reserved only for her individual therapist, and Jim, being less agitated, could sit and listen. As Jim was able to attend to her, Chris started talking about her long-buried desire to begin another career. Within a few months, she reorganized her job to half-time status and started working on her new career. Jim responded well, increasing his efforts at promoting his art and feeling a good deal more confidence in himself.

3. Creating a Crisis

"Suffering" and "masculinity" can often be mutually exclusive experiences for a man. Any admission of pain may interfere with his idealized self-image and his capacity to keep pushing himself along. In order to maintain functioning, he continues to pretend that nothing is wrong—even though he may be near the point of collapse. No amount of gradual reframing, task assignment or family of origin work seems to break this stalemate. In such cases, I intensify a crisis to help the man start taking his mood problems seriously.

Clinical Example: The "Tyrannical" Man

Danny, a 40 year old businessman, believed his chronic bad mood was entirely caused by the daily demands of the household. Julie, 39, was furious at Danny's unwillingness to help with the two kids, and at his constant threats to leave the marriage if she demanded too much of him. Danny was also furious that after impossible days at the business, he was faced with the noise, commotion and demands of wife and children. After conventional approaches did not budge the couple, I attempted to precipitate a crisis. Following is a condensed version of my comments to them.

THERAPIST: I could drop dead myself anytime, so it makes me a little nervous to say this. But, of all the men in the families that I work with I worry about you, Danny, the most. You've been depressed on and off since adolescence, but you're such a well-trained man you don't even notice. You keep putting out and producing even though you're almost falling apart. You're 50 pounds overweight. You binge on junk food. You never exercise. You haven't been to a doctor in two decades. You don't know how to shut the engine of worry off in your head. You can't admit to any of it because you don't see there's anything wrong—you're simply doing your job. However I think you're at great risk to collapse soon. I find myself actually thinking about you between sessions, wondering if you're okay. So, since I think you're at such risk I suggest you do what's responsible: (1) get a bank life insurance plan—for which you don't need a physical; (2) make sure your will is in order. If Danny doesn't do his part, Julie, I think you should see a lawyer to look into estate planning.

Two weeks later, Danny arrived furious about the last session. What really disturbed him about what I said? That I worried about him between meetings. I repeated my concern and he left in a rage. Several weeks after the intervention he began individual treatment on his own. Whether it is coincidental or not, Julie applied for post-graduate training, a move she had been planning for three years, but had postponed because she had always been afraid of Danny's reaction. Though Danny hit the roof when she told him, Julie decided she had better start "getting on with her own life." Their fighting dramatically decreased and the hyperactive three year old has begun to calm down.

INTERVENTIONS WITH FEMALE PARTNERS

> When my father retired, he slid into the depression that had always seemed like a temporary mood. Not that I thought anything was wrong even then. He was just "having a hard time adjusting to retirement." It finally struck me how bad things were the day my mother blew up at him. Seemingly out of nowhere she started screaming. "You only see the dark side. I try my best to cheer you up and all you do is worry. What kind of life is this to live?" My father sat motionless. The green upholstered club chair seemed to envelop his collapsing body and, from across the room, I saw him quietly crying. Despite her fury, nobody said another word. By dinnertime some of his favorite dishes were on the table and my mother was as upbeat as ever. The rage and bitterness that momentarily pierced the family's denial had been muffled by a plate of pot roast and mashed potatoes.

A lifetime of cultural expectations and economic dependence make it threatening for many women to accept that their partners are depressed. A woman's reaction may vary from total denial at one end of the continuum to despair and contempt at the other. As the couple begins to reshape their understanding of what is going on, a period of disequilibrium often follows. During this time, the woman may become as doubtful about treatment as the man. Two factors, in particular, make the redefinition problematic for a woman: (1) she is part of an unaddressed triangle in her family of origin; (2) she is in a socioeconomically dependent position and needs her husband to be "well" in order to survive.

1. Uncovering a Hidden Triangle

Wives are often unable to caretake spouses by themselves, there may be too many other family members to look after. So, daughters are enlisted to help regulate father's mood. When dad's underlying depression is not openly recognized, it is a natural, and often unconscious, progression for daughter to find another depressed man (however different the packaging) to caretake as an adult. Redefining her partner as depressed may reveal old obligations towards father and mother that deeply affect current relationships.

Clinical Example: "The Inadequate Man"

Larry, 35, an economics graduate student, and Elaine, 35, a high school guidance counselor, had been battling for the six years of their marriage over his lack of career advancement. Larry earned a minimal salary as an adjunct lecturer. Each offered explanations for his behavior, including that he was passive, inhibited, suffering from a work block, afraid of success, guilty about surpassing his father, etc.

When I suggested the possibility of Larry's being depressed, Elaine's immediate reaction was despair and contempt. She felt hopeless about ever getting him to change, contemptuous of his character weakness, as well as enraged that she had married such a flawed person. Larry, however, knew immediately that depression was an accurate description and stopped being so defensive about something he felt he couldn't really help.

Since Elaine's character assaults were not triggering defensive reactions on his part, space was created between them to introduce family of origin work. The shadow of Elaine's father, a lifelong recluse, became more sharply defined, as did Elaine's assigned role to cheer up dad and to bring him out of his shell. A couple of letters were exchanged between them in which she expressed greater acceptance of him. Much to Elaine's surprise, he returned her letters, acknowledging his heartfelt appreciation for her efforts through the years. Elaine's contempt toward Larry gradually eased and became less of an obsession.

As Larry's self-definition changed from being inadequate to being a fighter against a long-term depressive undertow, he stopped labeling his own parents as failures. I pushed him to ask his family for financial and emotional support to help him get through graduate school. Work on his studies began to proceed for the first time in ten years.

2. Rebalancing Gender Arrangements

Sometimes the woman cannot accept a redefinition of her partner as depressed. Surprisingly, she insists on being the patient. Usually, we conceptualize this as the woman needing to be weak to be powerful. Almost without exception, however, the couple's concrete gender arrangement is an important factor in the equation. She is, *in fact*, so economically dependent, so defined as being the caretaker to several generations, that she is afraid to challenge the status quo. These cases often take years of gradual work towards self-differentiation on the woman's part—since most men in this kind of arrangement have little motivation to change the balance of power. At a certain point, however, when she has created enough self-differentiation, basic gender arrangements can be challenged. If the wife takes this risk, the man's underlying depression erupts when she stops attempting to regulate his moods for him. The longstanding depressive-caretaker dynamic becomes vividly apparent and finally open to change.

Clinical Example: The "Workaholic" Man

> Michael, 40, and Irene, 32, married for three years, complained of chronic struggles around his availability. Michael, a successful, driven physicist was angry about Irene's continuous demands to spend more time together. In fact, Irene did seem to have little else in her life other than the relationship with Michael, his family of origin and his kids from a previous marriage. After a few sessions, Michael felt he was too busy with his work schedule to continue treatment.
>
> I began individual sessions with Irene that lasted approximately a year. During this time she stopped despising her housewife, subservient mother and became less intimidated by her workaholic, intensely demanding father. She also stopped acting as mediator in her parent's troubled marriage. Irene's parents soon separated, and shortly after, Irene went back to

school to get her M.B.A. Treatment was discontinued at this time.

Five years later, both Irene and Michael came back to therapy. They had an eight month old child and Irene had become a corporate vice president, earning a salary well over six figures. Irene was exhausted from doing 95% of the childcare and household chores on top of twelve hour business days. Michael, now suddenly interested in therapy, complained that Irene was no longer as involved in his life as she had been.

During this period of treatment, Irene began demanding that Michael do equal work around the house or she would leave the marriage. Upon realizing this was no idle threat, the depression underlying his workaholic personality emerged in full force. He lost interest in his job, sex, food and the few friends he had.

The therapeutic task was to help Irene with her need to rescue Michael, and to withstand considerable pressure from her own family and Michael's family to "ease up on him." The task with Michael was to acknowledge a depression that dated back to when he was ten years old. There had been several deaths in his family, and the childcare for three younger siblings was handed over to him. He'd "never had a childhood" and forever expected women to make up for his lost years. A short course of cognitive therapy helped Michael with his black mood. Family of origin work pushed him to reconcile with his parents and siblings, further removing the entire burden of nurturance from Irene. He contributed more around the house and got more involved with their child. Irene began to make independent friends for the first time in their marriage. Their battles did not entirely disappear, but the translation of Irene's economic leverage into an effective voice, and the recognition of Micheal's neediness, moved the relationship to a more balanced place.

The referral of Michael for cognitive therapy brings me to a final point about clinical technique. The more I recognize the depressive-caretaker dynamic, the more I see limitations in using only family therapy approaches. I now regularly turn to modalities outside the domain of family therapy. These include cognitive and behavioral therapies, Twelve-Step programs, group therapy, individual therapists versed in systems theory, and psychopharmacologists.

Accepting my own limitations as a family therapist has proven to be a powerful reframe for men and women. The message, "I can't take it upon myself and supply it all . . . family therapy doesn't have all the answers," is something both partners in a depressive-caretaker relationship need to hear. And since so many of us in the helping professions grew up in families where our father's depressions were successfully camouflaged and, therefore, not usually open to change, being more realistic about our power to heal everyone makes the challenge of everyday practice a little easier to bear.

CONCLUSION

Many families we work with are likely to contain a man who has an underlying depression and a woman who is bound by socioeconomic realities and/or emotional definitions that require her to help regulate his moods. Once we take seriously interpersonal descriptions of family members, the signs of the depressive-caretaker pairing are quite apparent. It then becomes insufficient to view the man simply as controlling, withholding, tyrannical, peripheral, remote, childish, absent and so on. He may also be fighting against various forms of depression-related experiences: chronic ruminations, camouflaged obsessive-compulsive disorders, quietly managed phobias, quick-cycling mood changes, muted panic attacks and controlled substance abuse.

Almost every time I have figured out a way to speak the language of mood and to address the depressive-caretaker dynamic, the structure of the family begins to shift. The couple gets jolted out defining the woman as the patient or the teacher, and the man as being just another version of the difficult man. It then becomes possible to move the burden of change onto the man as well as the woman, so that both partners can develop a greater degree of personal responsibility.

Two years after my father retired, he died suddenly while vacationing in Switzerland. In the twenty years since then, whenever I visit the cemetery, I lean over and kiss the headstone. The rough texture of the stone always reminds me of his unshaven and tired face when he came home in the evening.

There was a long hallway in our apartment. Every night when I was a little boy I would hear the key in the door and run down the corridor as fast as I could, jumping, almost flying it seemed, so he could catch me. My mother stood off to the side a little—I used to think to give me room.

A marriage, a child, and several thousand families later I know a little better. She was looking him over, going through her own kind of hello. Between the time my feet left the ground and I landed in his arms, she already understood what kind of mood he had come home with and was already beginning to make it into her own.

REFERENCES

Bolas, C. (1987). *In the shadow of the object*. New York: Columbia University Press. pp.99-116.

Diagnostic and statistical manual of mental disorders. (1980). Washington, D.C.: American Psychiatric Association.

Goldner, V. (1985). Feminisim and family therapy. *Family Process, 24*, 31-47.

Hare-Mustin, R. & Marecek, J. (1986). Autonomy and gender: Some questions for therapists. *Psychotherapy, 23*, 205-212.

Lerner, H. Personal communication, 1989.

Miller, J.B. (1976). *Toward a new psychology of women*. Boston: Beacon Press.

Walters, M. (1990). The co-dependent Cinderella who loves too much . . . fights back. *Family Therapy Networker, 14*, 52-57.

You Never Forget How to Ride a Bicycle: Men Finding Their Mothers

Eric E. McCollum

SUMMARY. This paper proposes that a man's need to emotionally separate from his mother in childhood in order to develop a masculine identity can have a crippling effect on his relationships with women as an adult. It reinforces our cultural polarization of "masculine" and "feminine" and lays the foundation for emotional distancing to handle anxiety in intimate relationships with women. Working to develop a renewed connection with his mother can help a man develop a more balanced view of women and more tolerance of closeness in relationships, without the need to distance. Bowen's (1978) approach to therapy is one framework that can guide this work.

> Since I failed to know my mother, I was denied the gift of knowing the other women who would cross my path.
>
> –*Pat Conroy (1986, p. 110)*

Growing up male with a mother hurts, I'm afraid. At least, it did for me. A greater pain might be growing up without one but I can only guess at that. Like many men who grew up in the fifties, my mother was the center of my childhood. My father, a shadowy figure when I was small, inhabited "the office." He even went there some Sunday mornings to work for a couple of hours before we

---

Eric E. McCollum, PhD, is affiliated with the Family Research Institute, Purdue University, 525 Russell Street, West Lafayette, IN 47907.

The author wishes to thank Dr. Michele Bograd for her comments on an earlier version of this paper.

picked him up on the way to church. I was elated when he took me with him but I knew it was foreign territory. Home was with my mother.

She taught me to ride a bicycle the winter I was five. I was the youngest in the neighborhood and often left behind when the other kids rode to the park or down to the school playground on their bikes, joking when I tried to catch up on foot. We practiced in the basement, my mother and I, protected from the disparaging eyes of my friends. She held the seat of the bike to keep me upright as I learned to balance and pedal. The day she let me go all on my own, I rode around and around our old oil furnace, delighted in my prowess and her pride in me, and terrified that I couldn't stop without falling over.

"You did it," she said as I lurched past her on one trip around the furnace. "You rode all by yourself."

I practiced in the basement through the winter while my mother ironed or did laundry. When spring came and I began to ride the neighborhood sidewalks, I found I couldn't make left turns. I had ridden around and around the furnace in only one direction, always turning right. The other kids howled with laughter and easily left me behind by going left at any corner.

"Don't worry," my mother said. "You'll learn." Like any fledgling, I left the nest only half ready.

As I got older, things began to change between us. I can almost mark the day. It was raining and we stopped outside a store downtown to pick something up.

"You're old enough to go in by yourself," I remember her saying to me.

"I want *you* to go," I said. "I don't know what to do."

"Now go on," she said, irritated. We had double parked and a line of cars was beginning to gather behind us. "You're a big boy. You don't need me."

Reluctantly, I got out of the car. The message was clear. Being a big boy meant no more Mom at my side. It was the first of many pains between us.

Looking back, I've often wondered what my mother thought as I trudged across the street to pick up whatever we needed from the store. She was doing what mothers do to help their sons become men—encouraging independence and self-reliance. I'm sure she also felt my on-going need for her. At the time, though, I couldn't see her struggle. I just felt she was sending me away—and it hurt.

Leaving my mother meant entering the male world. Home and school were familiar and woman-centered but I had only glimpses of how men got along. One came when I went with my father to the barbershop every other Saturday morning, just the two of us. Barber shops were male territory then. I sat in front of the long row of barber's chairs while my father had his hair cut. The blond and brown and black clumps of cut hair scattered across the floor fascinated me. I liked the design they made when one of the barbers swept them into a pile. The special magazines kept up on a high rack also fascinated me. I'd seen one once, before my father noticed, and wondered at the bare-breasted woman on the foldout page. My father put it back on the rack, saying something to the barbers and the other customers. The men's voices and coarse laughter teased me in ways I didn't understand. It seemed there were other ways to think of women than how I thought of my mother. I looked at my father. He smiled but didn't come to my rescue, leaving me to find my way alone in the world of men.

As I got older, the push to say goodbye came more and more from me. Separation hurt badly and frightened me. Since growing up seemed to mean giving up my mother, I resolved to do it like I had learned to remove band-aids—in one swift tear. Staying too close risked being a sissy. Or worse.

When I was in junior high, my friends and I worked part-time jobs down at the dairy. Our boss, Carl, was a gentle, patient man in his early forties who still lived with his mother, helping her farm their property in his spare time. He wasn't married. We liked Carl but something was wrong.

"Do you think Carl's a fag?" Jimmy asked one day as we all walked home from work. "He's a good guy but why is he still living with his mother? I'll bet he never gets laid."

Against the gauge of teenage priorities, we diagnosed the problem. Staying close to your mother risked the loss of manhood, the loss of potency. You had to get away. At times, my own push away erupted in anger.

"I'm not your god-damned 'honey'!" I shouted at her one day

when I was fourteen or fifteen. Whatever she said in response only made it worse. She didn't deserve my anger, at least not the quantity I delivered. My anger was a tool. I became her little boy again so easily that I had to fight back, to deny that I needed her as much as I did. As time went on, our conflict turned to silence and distance. When I was eighteen, I left home, moving out one weekend while my parents were away.

* * *

I didn't think seriously about my childhood, and how it affected me as a man, until recently. It was hard to see my growing up years as anything other than the way life is. My father's preoccupation with work, my mother's life centered at home, the pain of growing away from her, the distance between my father and me, all operated beneath my consciousness as if it was part of some natural order of things. But as I listened to women talk about how they are socialized and how the family teaches a limiting view of what it means to be female, I reconsidered my own experience. Traditionally organized families give men a confining view of what it means to be male.

Nancy Chodorow (1989), Dorothy Dinnerstein (1976), and Lillian Rubin (1983) have painted the picture psychodynamically. When women are the only caretakers intimately involved with small children, boys and girls find different routes to maturity. Boys define themselves as different from their mothers and, in doing so, build their identity on the shaky foundation of separateness and emotional isolation. Giving up mother's closeness hurts, and is something to guard against in other relationships with women. We don't want to go through that pain again. Keeping women at a safe distance means emotional retreat in relationships and fosters contempt for women in the culture. What safer woman, after all, than a Playboy Playmate? She is disposable, barely out of adolescence, asks nothing from us, and is there for our every fantasied whim.

We also live in a culture that has clear rules for how to be a man and woman, a mother and son. It is an unquestioned truth, for example, that closeness between mothers and sons is dangerous or pathological. Our adolescent assessment of Carl is evidence here as is a favorite taunt I remember from grade school. When one boy beat another in a fight, he would tell his victim to "Run home to Mommy." Of course, that comfort was exactly what most of us needed when we were beaten but the taunt made our need shameful, a sign of defeat. The lesson was clear: Don't want your mother too much. Don't need her.

* * *

My mother and I didn't talk much in the years after I left home. I married at nineteen. My wife and I were each running from family tangles, hoping the marriage would solve them. It didn't work, of course, and we divorced before I was twenty-three. My mother and I both cried, I think, the night I came to tell them about the divorce. It was one small show of shared feeling in the midst of our long silence.

Somewhere in those years, I began to talk to my father. It came slowly, unplanned, as I found myself in his world of work and accomplishment. I didn't think about my mother much. It was over between us, after all. Settled. No men that I knew had anything different with their mothers. No men that I knew talked about their mothers at all.

While I was convinced I had left the troubles with my mother behind, I agonized about relationships with other women. I spent months at a time alone but craving a relationship. When romances came, they cooled quickly after the initial excitement and passion. Sometimes I was the one who initiated the split, sometimes the woman did. It only bothered me a little at first. It was the seventies. Relationships were casual and there were many unattached women out there. Other men confirmed my view.

"Hey," my friend Dale said when I was talking to him about one of my recent break-ups. "Don't mope around about it. Get back in the game. I've probably slept with fifty women in the last five years. It's great. We can settle down later. Now's the time to have some fun."

The problem was, I wasn't having fun. When I was alone, I couldn't wait for a relationship to begin. My life seemed empty without a woman to share it. When I was dating someone, I couldn't wait to get away. There were so many other experiences I wanted to have that commitment felt like prison. I couldn't win either way.

One Sunday morning I woke up with a woman, Diane, who I'd been friends with for several months. Our relationship had a lazy, comfortable feel to it. I could relax when I was with her. Sleeping together the night before had seemed the obvious next step and sex had felt familiar and good. The next morning, though, everything changed. I lay in bed beside my friend wondering how I could get away.

"C'mon," Diane said. "Let's get the paper in and make a pot of coffee. I don't have anything to do today." Her invitation felt like a demand. Something began closing in.

"I gotta go," I said, beginning to get dressed.

"Last night you said you were free all weekend," she said. "What's up?"

"I just gotta go," I said. Overnight, my friend had become a stranger I needed to stay away from. I was in my car a few minutes later. Once safely away, I felt bad, knowing that I had hurt this woman I liked, but I didn't know another way to calm my panic. Talking about it seemed impossible. We had dinner a few more times, slept together once or twice. I saw myself edging away but couldn't stop.

Solitude didn't bring comfort. The new experiences I'd longed for when I was dating someone always evaporated as soon as I was free. I no longer felt panicked by closeness, but now sat home alone wishing for someone to share my life with. I couldn't figure it out. I felt that I was suffering my own personal misery. Now I know it wasn't. Lots of other men were in the same boat but we didn't talk about it. Part of being a man was doing it all on your own, without help or a show of weakness. Feelings, especially dependent or depressed ones, felt very much like weakness. I kept my mouth shut and suffered in silence. Finally, enough broken relationships brought me to therapy, Bowen coaching, and my coach brought me back to my mother.

"Remind you of anyone?" he asked with an ironic glint in his eye after I had described a rapid exit from yet another relationship.

"What do you mean?" I said. "It reminds me of every woman I've ever known."

"I was getting an image of your mother for some reason," he said, pointing to the genogram we had drawn when I first started coming to see him. There was a big slash across the line between my mother and me, indicating cut-off.

He was right, of course. My struggle with women was a miniature version of what I'd gone through with my mother. Relationships started out intense and exciting, only to become strained and distant as I pushed away after a few weeks or months. It was an example of Bowen's (1978) thinking about the effects of emotional cut-off. Cut-off in one generation becomes the template for handling other intimate relationships and occurs over and over again. As I got close to women in my current life, the unhealed pain of leaving my mother began to stir and I pulled back. I didn't want that hurt again.

"So that's it," I said to him. "That's what this is all about." There were a few moments of silence.

"What can I do about it?" I asked, hesitant, anticipating the answer.

"Ever thought of talking to her?" he said. I took a deep breath.

"Talk?" I said. "To my mother? I don't think I could. I mean, it would just be too hard . . . "

"Just a thought," my coach said. "She is kind of involved in this, after all. She might even have some ideas about it."

After I thought about it for a couple of weeks, I realized I had to talk with my mother because I wasn't happy with how things were. Besides my conviction that something had to change, my coach's stories of his own work with his mother added to my courage to begin. It was hard, he said, but it led to real changes in his life. He also made it clear that he hadn't done it perfectly. He continued to work on that relationship and saw it as a life-long process. It was the first time I could remember hearing a man I admired, any man for that matter, talking about his effort to feel closer and more open with his mother. This was a different view of what it meant to be a man than I had heard before.

My coach suggested that the first thing I needed were facts about my mother and her family. I had trouble seeing her as a real person with her own set of childhood hurts and joys. I didn't know much about my grandparents' families or lives and how they had affected my mother. I was visiting the family for Thanksgiving in a couple of weeks so I decided to get as much information as I could. I drew up a list of questions and headed home.

If you knew my mother now, you'd think she was a nice little old lady. That's because she is. She's probably six inches shorter than I am and I outweigh her by at least fifty pounds. When the weather changes, the arthritis in her knee makes her limp a little. But in my mind, she hadn't changed from the woman who held the bicycle seat and therefore had the power to keep me steady or let me fall. As I grew up, my dependence on her, and my need to suppress it, made her nurturance feel like control, I think. Staying away had been my only protection against that power. Moving closer meant putting myself under that spell again.

I spent the entire visit dreading my talk with my mother. We managed to keep distant from one another until the last day. Then, the rest of my family went shopping and I found myself alone with her. I was petrified. My thoughts turned fuzzy and confused. I tried to think of what to say but no words would come. Finally, I gave up and left, feeling defeated.

"It's impossible," I told my coach. "I can't do it."

"You need a little better plan," he said. "Why not start by writing her a letter and telling her what you want to know? That way you won't get so anxious and she can have time to think about your questions."

I wrote the letter. Somewhat to my surprise, she responded. Haltingly, I risked talking to her, asking about her life, sharing glimpses of my own. It felt dangerous and comforting at the same time. As we communicated more, I began to learn things about my mother that I didn't expect. For one thing, physical work had filled her childhood on the farm. She told me how she had convinced her father one summer that she was strong enough to pick grapes with the crew during harvest. She earned three cents a quart, one of her few sources of spending money during the Depression. At the height of harvest, she said, she picked 100 quarts a day.

She didn't say it directly but I sensed that she hadn't gotten along so well with her own mother and that her father's support had been very important to her. I also found out that she grew up in a world peopled by extended family. Her grandmother and uncle lived with her family while aunts and uncles and cousins farmed adjoining land. They gathered often to share farm work and the pleasure of just being together. How different it was than the house in the suburbs that was home to me.

As I learned more about my mother, my opinion of her changed. Before, I had misunderstood the fabric of her life. When people asked me about her, I always said, "She doesn't do anything. She just stays home." Partly, I was blinded by our cultural notion that women's work is meaningless. I began to see, however, that my mother had many talents, many skills. She managed the family finances, helping us live well on my father's teaching salary. Her friends sought her out when they had problems. When someone told me how creative she was, I found myself agreeing. As I learned more about her past, I saw that she had been strong, physically and emotionally, and that she had struggled for independence, taking a teaching job and living on her own when other young women simply stayed at home until they married. "Getting the facts" in Bowen terms not only gave me a fuller picture of my mother as a child, it also helped me see the many strengths she has as an adult. I began to feel proud to be her son.

As my thoughts about my mother changed, so did other parts of my life. Even friends noticed. I called Diane out of the blue and asked her to have lunch. I told her I felt bad about how it had ended between us and that she was still important to me, even if I hadn't acted that way.

"What's happened to you?" she asked when I finished. "You seem a lot calmer, easier to be around. I mean, I've always liked you but now you just seem more open." I surprised myself and told her a little bit about what I was trying to do with my mother. Before, I would have kept quiet.

"It must take courage," she said. "I'm not sure I could do it."

My thoughts about relationships changed, too. It wasn't dramatic. I noticed that I was no longer desperate to find someone. As my desperation eased, a romance arose with a woman I'd known for a couple of years. I tried to go slow. I didn't want to recreate the pattern of great passion followed by panic and disillusionment that had happened so often before. I even told my new friend a little bit about my struggle. I introduced her to my parents. They liked each other and I liked being with them both. That was a big change. Relationships before had always been a refuge from my family.

I kept talking to my mother, learning more about her family, beginning to feel my connection to them. I found courage in the people in my past. My great-grandfather died when his team of horses startled and dumped a load of timber on him. He left my great-grandmother with nine children; the oldest was sixteen, the youngest, my own grandfather, was two. My great-grandmother managed to raise her family, run the farm, build a bigger house and a barn and pay off the debt for their land. I also found sorrow. Children died of diseases that doctors cure routinely now. Some lives failed. Or ended tragically. My mother's uncle died in his mid-fifties of a heart attack. He was resting from a morning's work on the farm, lying out in the yard beneath a walnut tree. His wife, in good health, died a day-and-a-half later. I don't know what the death certificate said, but it is clear to me that she died of a broken heart.

Learning about my mother's family through her eyes brought the women out of the background. My female ancestors were people of courage and strength. They had safely shepherded their families through difficult times and had worked as hard as any of the men to make a go of it. I had not realized their strength since it was subsumed under the label of "women's work"—by definition not important. But if they had been strong, perhaps I was strong, too. I also found that they were people of love and commitment, important values to me as I thought about my troubles in relationships and what I wanted to do differently.

About a year after we first met, my friend and I decided to get married. My first marriage kept coming to mind in those days and, with it, the pain of leaving home and growing away from my mother. I decided to write a letter expressing my thoughts and asking my mother to recall what my marriage and divorce had been like for her. It was an unhealed wound between us, something I never had the courage to talk about with her. I was sure that I had disappointed her and that she blamed me for making such a big mistake. I dropped my letter in the mail and held my breath. Her response came about a week before the wedding.

"I worried about you when you decided to marry so young," she wrote, "but I didn't want to push too hard for fear that I would alienate you entirely. It was a difficult time for your father and me to know what was right. I also knew that you were a bright person who could probably work things out. After you were married a little while, it was obvious that things weren't going too well for you. You were so unhappy. I was afraid you'd get lost in your unhappiness and not find a road through it. I wanted to talk to you but didn't know how to begin. We weren't talking much in those days, as you recall. The divorce, when it came, was a relief. I was sure by then that the marriage didn't have much future in it for either of you. You seemed happier after a few months. I know it was hard but I think it was better to face it and make a change than to go on in such unhappiness."

When I finished reading the letter, I felt like I had left an old, dead skin behind. The emotional distance between my mother and I had closed a little and the result wasn't fear but freedom. I could enter my new marriage with more certainty that it didn't mean losing myself.

* * *

Coming to know my mother has been a very personal journey, yet it has relevance for other men besides me. Men are turning back to look at the families that made us and how they influence our lives now. We've been rediscovering our fathers and even sounding our inner depths to find our "feminine side" and the Great Mother within. I don't think we've done much about our real mothers though—the flesh-and-blood women who raised us. Maybe it is easier to build a missing relationship with our fathers than to dig into something long-buried with our mothers. I know the anxiety I felt as I began. Maybe our culture tells us that it's more valuable to find a father than to get back in touch with dear old Mom. We can take her for granted, after all. She'll always be there, ready with a glass of milk after school or with the latest laundry trick. Despite the difficulties, reconnecting with our mothers is essential work for us to do – a further step in growing up as men.

In intimate relationships, the emotional distance we felt we had to gain from our mothers becomes a model for dealing with other people who are important to us. Men line up on the side of separateness, more often than not, choosing achievement and individual action over sustaining relationships. As family therapists, we know women's pain in the face of the silence and isolation of their male partners. We also know how misunderstood men feel when they are seen as having no feelings and not caring about their wives, children or friends. Reconnecting with our mothers is one route to changing this pattern. Breaking the silence with our mothers steadies us as husbands, as parents, and as friends. We no longer need to keep so distant if we can change the primary relationship where we learned that men should be tall, independent oaks who need no one, least of all women. Revisiting our mothers, and acting differently, opens the door to a different way of being close in many relationships, but especially with women.

On a broader level, reconnecting with our mothers can change our view of what it means to be male and female. From playgrounds to locker rooms to corporate offices, the most common insult for a man is that he is a "sissy." Suppressing those parts of ourselves that our culture defines as "feminine" begins as we move away from our mothers and fight to become "masculine." The nurturing we long for, the enjoyment of closeness, the dependency we feel, all must be denied. Coming closer to our mothers as adults is a way to regain those blocked off parts of ourselves. After years of denying any similarity, it is a surprise to find what we share with our mothers. Strength is no longer a strictly male trait when we see our mothers' strength. Emotion and relatedness are no longer for women only when we find them in ourselves. While building different relationships with our mothers, rigid definitions of male and female break down.

While I think my experience is common, it is not the only way that men relate to their mothers in adulthood. Some mothers and sons have the good fortune to maintain a solid connection without the rupture around separation that I described. Others solve the problem in a different way by completely abdicating the struggle to be different. Sons in these relationships sacrifice their own growth and independence to preserve closeness with their mothers. Finally, some men may distance so completely from their mothers that the relationship is effectively dead. Efforts to revive it make little sense to such men and will likely be ineffective.

As family therapists, several principles guide our work as we help men examine their relationships with their mothers. Primary is the issue of men's *resistance* to such efforts. It is important to remember that we are asking men to counter their anxiety about reopening the relationship with their mothers and also to counter strong societal injunctions against mother-son closeness. Therefore, this work may not be for all men who come to therapy. Men who are already questioning the effects of the male role in their lives and who seek broad change in relationships can move quickly to looking at their relationship with their mothers. For other men, especially those who enter therapy to "fix" circumscribed problems, examining how they relate to their mothers comes later, as they confront their troubles in relationships, perhaps for the first time. Finally, men who come to therapy reluctantly in a last-ditch effort to stave off their female partners' threat of divorce or separation may never be amenable to this work. The anxiety about separation in their primary relationship would need to decrease significantly before it would make sense to them to look at wider family issues.

A second principle involves *timing*. This work must go slowly. Three years passed from the time I began talking to my mother until I wrote the letter about my divorce. Encouraging a male client to go at his own pace keeps anxiety about the process from becoming overwhelming and also communicates confidence in the man's ability to judge what is right for him. It also gives his mother time to process this change in their relationship. Since our mothers have experienced pain in the process of our growing away from them, they may not welcome what seems to be the resurrection of that pain, just as it makes us anxious.

Third, therapists must communicate that establishing a new relationship with our mothers is a *process*, not a task to be accomplished as soon as possible. I sometimes use the metaphor of preventive maintenance with the car to tell men about the difference between process and product. You don't wait for a breakdown to take care of your car. You always think of maintaining it—does the oil need changing, are the tires good, is it time for a tune-up? Sadly, some of us men relate more attentively to our machines than to our family relationships. Changing a relationship is a process, though. Once started, it becomes part of life, not a discrete act.

Fourth, a therapist can point out the *power of small changes*. It isn't necessary to rehash every hurt, understand every nuance, or discuss every issue that has arisen between our mothers and us. The content of the talk may be less important than the doing. The power of small changes is especially important with men who had an abusive or very hurtful relationship with their mother. When there has been physical harm or deep emotional scarring, the process of building a new relationship must be painstaking and especially thoughtful. That doesn't mean nothing can be done, though. A Christmas card can be better than no contact at all, a letter or telephone call better than silence. Perhaps over time, the relationship will strengthen to the point that it can stand discussion of the painful past. Perhaps it won't. A man only has control over what *he* does in the relationship. I was lucky that my mother responded to me directly and quickly but there would have been value in my efforts even if she had done nothing at all.

Fifth, it is important to remind our clients that *relationships don't exist in vacuums*. A man's efforts to act differently in his relationship with his mother will reverberate throughout the family system. We must continually help our clients monitor the many triangles in which the mother-son relationship is embedded. If our client has been a prodigal son, brothers and sisters who stayed close may fear that his return will displace them. A father may fear that new closeness between his wife and son will increase his isolation in the family. It is important to help our clients maintain contact with all parts of the family as they work on their relationship with their mothers. To neglect this can result in crisis as other family members attempt to move mother and son back to their accustomed roles.

Reconnecting can also affect current marriages. A woman may feel threatened as her male partner moves closer to his mother. If the marriage is based on keeping distant from families of origin—"Us against them," in other words—increased closeness will seem to threaten the foundation of the marital bond. If mother and son learn to get along, what role will be left for a wife? Ironically, by changing his cut-off stance with his mother, a man will become a more intimate marital partner, not a more distant one. However, this runs counter to the emotional logic of interpersonal triangles, and we need to help male clients anticipate their female partners' responses. The goal is for the client to keep trying to reconnect with his mother while not distancing himself from his partner's emotional reactions. The therapist's calm encouragement can be a real asset in maintaining this stance.

Underlying these principles is the *therapist's role*. The therapist's own work on his or her family system is a distinct advantage. It takes a therapist who has begun this process to understand the fits and starts, the need for periods of rest and incubation, the necessity of a clear plan. Asking for help is not easy for men, but the male ideal of going it alone isn't useful here. This work stirs powerful feelings that are tempting to run from. A male therapist's stories of his own work can help a client appreciate this perspective. It was helpful to me. Just as we are teaching our male clients, we may need to remind ourselves that sometimes just being there, not doing something, is what's needed.

* * *

I'd like to say that my life has gone perfectly since I got that letter from my mother. It hasn't. I still struggle with the parts of being a man that I wish would magically go away. The old fear of closeness creeps in. I retreat into silence to get my thoughts straight when my wife and I fight. Sometimes, it feels more satisfying to dive into work and not think about relationships. I'm not always perfectly there with my mother, either.

"Do you glow in the dark yet?" I asked her a couple of days ago when I called to see how she felt after beginning a series of radiation treatments. We both laughed. I knew the joke covered my sadness and worry at realizing she was fragile and could not be the unwavering figure in my life I once thought she would be. I hope she knew it, too. The burden of building a different relationship with my mother is that I must ultimately give her up again. A few years ago, I would have thought it didn't matter.

REFERENCES

Bowen, M. (1978). *Family therapy in clinical practice*. New York: Aronson.

Chodorow, N.J. (1989). *Feminism and psychoanalytic theory*. New Haven, CT: Yale University Press.

Conroy, P. (1986). *The prince of tides*. New York: Bantam.

Dinnerstein, D. (1976). *The mermaid and the minotaur: Sexual arrangements and human malaise*. New York: Harper & Row.

Rubin, L.B. (1983). *Intimate strangers: Men and women together*. New York: Harper & Row.

Working Affirmatively with Puerto Rican Men: Professional and Personal Reflections

Victor De La Cancela

SUMMARY. The family therapy literature has generally ignored the sociopolitical realities of men of color in prescribing treatment approaches for families of different racial and ethnic backgrounds. Therapists of a feminist persuasion, though often more aware of the influence of larger systems on women and men, are unfortunately not as familiar with recent developments in research, theory and praxis as these apply to Puerto Rican males. This article will outline some of my work in this area as well as attempt to present some personal reflections on my experiences in "the movement."

Contemporary pro-feminist treatment models often attempt to provide "how to" approaches responsive to the pathogenic aspects of "normal" male socialization. Ironically, these theoreticians and practitioners emphasize the influence of gendered world views while addressing masculinity in universal terms that neglect racial and ethnic variations. Even efforts to include cultural sensitivity or minority issues often lack socio-political contextualization, leading at times to the creation of new negative stereotypes about men of color.

The present contribution aims to provide a corrective to these practices by recommending a framework contextualizing family therapy with men of color from a systemic, pro-feminist and explicitly political perspective. Emphasis will be placed on experiences

---

Victor De La Cancela, PhD, is Assistant Vice President, Mental Hygiene Services, New York City Health and Hospitals Corporation, 125 Worth St., New York, NY 10013.

with Puerto Rican clients given my own culture and gendered world views. Based on my personal and professional experience with African American and Latino men in families, in groups, and as individuals, examination of sexist issues beyond the therapy setting will also occur, as I give some personal testimony regarding contradictory patterns and oppression I have experienced.

For the most part, "Anglo" mental health workers active in men's studies have committed the conceptual error of assuming that all U.S. males hold the same masculine values across different social class levels. This has been true in other transcultural psychological excursions (Leighton, 1972), as the economics, social organization, individual lifestyles and ethnic characteristics of large groups of people have been ignored (Brody, 1966; De La Cancela, 1986). For example, the sociocultural diversity of Latin American peoples with their origins in European colonization, Indo-mestizo roots, varied African influences as well as socioeconomically polarized existences (Brody, 1966) has been neglected, leading to monolithic views of Latin Americans. Similar to charges levelled against the women's movement and "white" feminism, it can be argued that the "men's movement" has failed to address the concerns of ethnic and Third World men in U.S. society. Left unexplored, for example, are the endangered species status of Native American males, the overrepresentation of African Americans and Latinos in prisons and mental hospitals, or the increased mortality, morbidity and unemployment rates of these males of color when compared to whites (Blakey, 1974).

It is shortsighted to speak of "Men's Liberation" in the face of racism, classism, and discriminatory popular and social science images of colored men as "Black studs," "Don Juans," or hotheaded "machos." A young Puerto Rican woman states: "Our men don't have equal rights or equal pay. We are all fighting for the same thing; both male and female are oppressed" (Miranda King, 1974). Indeed, the particular situation of African American and Latino males in the U.S. includes experiences of minority women often having had greater access to employment than men because sexism facilitated the hiring of women at lower wages (Miranda King, 1974). It appears necessary, therefore, to examine that which is sexist among Latino and African American males from both a cultural perspective and its class-related origins and material conditions. For example, Ramirez Boulette (1975) states that severe and long lasting poverty leads to conditions such as father absence that are often incorrectly attributed to machismo. In her view, lack of local jobs, abandonment due to poverty, or imprisonment, rather than victim-blaming charges of "machismo"–better explain the marginal position of Mexican-American males. Staples (1971) similarly writes that, under capitalism, economically impoverished Black families are forced into welfare systems in which "it makes sense" from a daily economic stability perspective for Black men to leave their families.

I believe that feminist family therapists need to increase their awareness of the oppressed minority male's sociopolitical realities and the ways in which women and men of color are both struggling against white male capitalist culture. Through such awareness, feminist mental health practitioners can be catalysts who aid ethnic minority and low-income men to unravel "layers of imposed otherness" (Gendzier, 1974). Men of color also need consciousness-raising to explore how all women and men are oppressed by sex role conditioning. I suggest that use of an aggressive outreach and engagement approach with men of color by feminist family therapists will be of great utility in meeting these requirements. This will be illustrated through description of socio-culturally sensitive ways of working with Puerto Rican males, that might be generalizable to other men of color.

PUERTO RICAN MEN AND DIALECTICAL THERAPY

Most Anglo therapists appear to organize their understanding of Puerto Rican men under the construct of *machismo*. Rendon (1984) defines the Anglo myth and stereotype of *machismo* to be the behavior of "blindly proud" men who "have to prove" their manliness both sexually and aggressively no matter the cost. In my view, the construct is bandied about in Anglo circles to describe Latinos and all men without any understanding of its specific cultural connotations (both positive and negative), and without understanding any of its contradictions or relation to the material (socioeconomic and political) conditions of Latinos' lives. This has led to negative stereotypes of all Latino males and of Puerto Rican men in particular and to a view that their culture is a specific barrier to therapeutic engagement. I believe this to be a clearly ideological point of view that "blames the victim" and operates from a deficit/pathology model.

Previously, I have questioned the validity of definitions and theoretical premises employed by social scientists when the topic of inquiry was Puerto Rican *machismo* (De La Cancela, 1981). Based on a critical review of the prevalent literature and in-depth interviews with 40 U.S. mainland-residing working class Puerto Rican males and females, I see three perspectives existent in the conceptualization of machismo. These perspectives are: (a) *Traditionalist*—based on psychodynamic theories that see "machismo" as psychopathological; (b) *Culturalist*—a socio-cultural paradigm critiquing intrapsychic views of "machismo" while suggesting positive cultural affirmation through "machismo"; and (c) *Dialectical*—a perspective viewing "machismo" as both progressive and reactionary, and intimately related to the social economic historical forces maintaining the colonization of Puerto Ricans. A dialectical examination of the Puerto Rican male gender role reveals that it is neither a Latino malady that must be eliminated nor a healthy cultural value that must be reinforced. Instead it is both and, contradictory as this conclusion may seem, this analysis provides us with a more hopeful picture for our Puerto Rican clients. For example, a positive value related to *machismo* is self respect which is socially oriented and based on the idea of responsibility to one's family. Hence, some Puerto Rican *machos* strive to both upgrade the family's economic and moral standing, and to remain loyal to the family sense of propriety. However, this family loyalty and responsibility can be negative when they lead to possessive demands that all family decisions/activities be condoned by the man as moral leader. Other negatives include some *machos* feeling a need to maintain their self-respect by abandoning the family when they perceive themselves to be economic burdens, i.e., unemployed, rather than providers.

The necessity of a dialectical perspective is imperative, when one recognizes that the conceptualization of phenomena from a particular philosophical perspective has profound implications for our family therapy practice. Specifically, exclusively intrapsychic conceptualization of "machismo" as a stumbling block to growth engenders practices and policies that alienate the client, e.g., not reaching out to Puerto Rican men because it is believed that they will avoid therapy due to their being threatened by exploration of their inferiority feelings. Similarly, a culturally syntonic view of Puerto Rican male gender roles may lead to further mystification of the client's realities through well intentioned but misguided respect for the client's culture, i.e., emphasizing adherence to moral leader/family provider roles when socioeconomic and political realities are such that there is a scarcity of jobs and training for men to effectively support their families. However, by dialectically viewing these roles, we can (a) reduce the client's alienation from his personal and group history; (b) avoid blaming the client or his ethnic culture for what are socioeconomically related behaviors; and (c) empower the client such that reality testing is enhanced. Additionally, a dialectical framework provides the family therapist a view of gender roles that is sensitive to the negative and adaptive function of behavior, increases the possibility of favorable outcomes, and decreases stereotyping of clients. An illustration would be those contemporary urban Puerto Rican males seen in therapy who question their roles as economic providers and the cultural dictates of appropriate masculine behavior (De La Cancela, 1988). These men explore their contradictions given changing social norms and economics that require dependency on women as wage earners and the undue pressures and limited opportunities for self-worth associated with attempting to be the main breadwinner.

CONCEPTUALIZING A DIALECTICAL TREATMENT MODEL

My research subjects generally held dialectical views of "machismo": their popular notions of *macho* indicated awareness of socioeconomic problems and contradictory behavior and ideology. Seventy two percent of the sample reported that "good things" came from being *macho*, while 85% reported "bad things" come from being *macho*. Fully 82% of the sample reported that the greatest worry Puerto Rican men are faced with is related to their future economic condition. The sample also reported regional differences in *macho* behaviors as well as a sense of alienation from U.S. society. These findings support the premise underlying a dialectical counseling/therapy model, in which behavior is not seen as predetermined but as situational and where behavior changes in the Puerto Rican man are expected, sought out, and encouraged. This model should be empowering and not encourage dependency. It should legitimize the Puerto Rican man's role in the family by encouraging his participation in family matters and include outreach services that are not impersonal or that conflict with work schedules. Technically, the use of cultural metaphors, poetry, film/video, and songs are integrated into the model in order to promote discussion, clarity and engagement. These artistic expressions can lead to confidence, insight, understanding, and paradoxical interventions related to gender role behaviors among Puerto Ricans. Treatment should be time-limited, goal-oriented, contracted for, and should include self-revelation on the part of the therapist. Attention to the contradictory aspects of being *macho* would be paramount in this model, and would be noticeable by the attention paid to the danger of displacing employment related conflicts onto his mate; the utilization of the family, sex and substance use as a refuge from the world; the distinction between protection of the family and paternalism; how social institutions like welfare and schools encourage displacing the Puerto Rican man; and the oppression of women (De La Cancela, 1986).

Dialectical feminist-oriented work with the Puerto Rican male begins with the acknowledgment that he may not easily self-refer for treatment or even see himself as in need of counseling, given past negative experiences with so-called expert helpers. Rather the model suggests appealing to his sense of familial or even racial group responsibility by inviting him to participate in concert with other men of color in addressing a problem specific to their community. One method I have found useful in such explorations with Black, Puerto Rican and other men of color is the time-limited group focused on how they can collaborate with and be supportive of women. Such groups generally begin with the men introducing themselves to each other, then the facilitator defines the group's task as discussing the positive and negative ways that men can aid women. As the men engage in discussion and ask questions, the facilitator stimulates them to consider how they differ from non-colored men by examining their childrearing beliefs, their work histories, their reproductive practices, their substance use and their resolution of differences with females. The emphasis in these groups is to provide participants with less stereotyped views of themselves and of women. Men are asked to question whether what they previously defined as part of their culture might be better understood as a response to oppression or buying into sexist/racist or ethnocentric myths. The ultimate goal is to encourage participants to speak with other men and women about their fears and sense of responsibility. Parham and McDavis (1987) similarly suggest the use of topical group or individual discussions with Black men towards helping them resist involvement in behaviors detrimental to their family. These authors exhort counselors to organize groups for young Black men that focus on confronting role definitions of manhood. They believe that Black men can be taught to develop respectful healthy relationships with women.

Obviously, in dialectical therapy there is a potential for social analysis which other perspectives lack. A family therapy fashioned on this model would owe something to Kornilov's (1930) call for a "*class psychology*. This would aim at the study of the behavior of definite social groups in relation to the position held by them in the system of production" (p. 267). This psychology would differ from other family psychologies inasmuch as it would encourage examination of how male family roles are related to labor and the external social world of the Puerto Rican. It would lead to analysis of how these social relations lead to *macho* beliefs, and how *macho* behavior changes and contradicts itself. It would also encourage further exploration of those behaviors that indicate that not *all* Puerto Rican males are hard-core *machos*. In exploring these tendencies, one may recognize the development of different forms of *machismo* as a result of changes in the material conditions and consequent interpersonal relationships of Puerto Rican males. Looking at Puerto Rican "machismo" from the vantage point of the different class levels of Puerto Rican family life, this therapeutic model would address the connection between the institution of the family as the unit where reproduction and socialization of the work force occurs, and how that family role has been modified, changed, or negated by a changing social economic and political situation for Puerto Ricans. For example, the Puerto Rican agrarian society of the past demanded a large family; however, current post-industrial society makes a large family a liability for the poor. A class psychology more succinctly explains the changes evident in the contemporary Puerto Rican male's greater acceptance of household and child caretaking/responsibility and the role of Puerto Rican women in the labor sphere, than do psychodynamic or cultural conceptualizations. A class perspective and labor role analysis might also be of use in exploring the marital/family relationship of gay male Puerto Rican couples where both partners struggle with the legacy of *macho* inculcations and, hence, both compete for a coveted "real man" status (Ramirez, 1982). This model adds the critical dimension of class to conventional "ethnicity" models that tend to lump individuals together without real examination of economic and material factors that contribute to cultural development. Additionally, it informs the socially-conscious mental health provider of the shortcomings of traditional psychodynamic, behavioral, and systemic theories in understanding Puerto Rican male behavior and consciousness. Indeed, it challenges the feminist family therapist to form his/her theory through praxis with Puerto Rican men versus making assumptions about Latinos (and especially Puerto Rican men) that negatively shape how therapy is done with them.

Generalizing this critical perspective to Black males and family work with them is necessary given that they too have been alienated by therapists who ignore their socio-economic realities. Some therapists view Afro-American males as trapped inextricably into "macho" patterns because of their culture, and unwittingly recreate detrimental experiences these men have had in social service settings by expecting them to be uninvolved in family sessions. Similar to assumptions about Puerto Rican men, the oversimplified portrayal of Black men in the literature states that they express themselves through sexuality and gender roles in ways that impact negatively on childrearing, marital relationships and employment patterns (Bernard, 1966; Harper, 1981). Psychoanalytically, the African American man is viewed as being insecure about his manhood and engaged in reaction formation thereby exaggerating the most obvious external signs of masculinity (Arnez, 1972; Majors, 1986). From a sociological viewpoint, he is also forced to prove his manhood in capitalist society by being an economic provider and, since this is often impossible, he allegedly tends to abandon his family (Staples, 1971).

In closing this necessarily brief discussion of the dialectical analytic framework, let it be said that the model is important to family therapists not only because of the changing demographics of the U.S. population leading to greater cultural diversity in the workplace and mental health work, but because it may have much to offer all of us in valuing other modes of being. For example, there is much for white males to learn from in the flexibility of sex roles among Black families (McAdoo, 1977), from the greater tolerance of touching, hugging, kissing and lesser intra-male physical distance among many Latino cultures, and from the social prescription for Puerto Ricans to be noncompetitive/and giving, and to evaluate life success in terms of personal worth and interpersonal and familial obligations. That men from these cultures and certain class backgrounds might express both these positive, socially-valued attitudes, beliefs and practices as well as negatively valued tendencies gives us a contradictory but more real model of their potential than do traditional analyses.

CONCLUSION

This discussion of work with Puerto Rican men from a family oriented theoretical and practice model views men of color within their specific social context. I have emphasized the need for self-disclosure and challenged stereotypical approaches to therapy with so-called *macho* men, that are based on flawed theoretical models that see Puerto Rican males only in negative terms and which psychologize their social realities. In contrast, a dialectical model offers a fluid view of the reality of men of color in which their values, goals and aspirations are seen as, at times, contradictory given differential social reinforcement. A therapy model is advocated, which is clearly pro-feminist, includes analysis of a man's self expectations as well as how society and women view his role, and which defines class as a factor along with culture as contributory to the *macho* role. The model addresses strengths or assets held by Puerto Rican males towards establishing working alliances or engagement for problem solving. My hope is this model contributes to a consciously progressive counseling practice that integrates sociopolitical and economic concerns with a commitment to help men out of their personally limiting roles.

PERSONAL IMPACT OF BEING A DIALECTICAL THERAPIST

The feminist critique has particularly emphasized the psychological harm sustained by women in being socialized and sociopolitically relegated to an inferior status (Thomas, 1977). Men have also been damaged by their socialization into power and alleged superiority. Some analyses of oppressed-oppressor, slave-master, and colonized-colonizer relationships suggest both parties in the relationship are negatively impacted by it (Fanon, 1968; Mannoni, 1966; Memmi, 1965). The therapist who identifies as a feminist, or who is a progressive dedicated to empowerment, typically also calls for changes in the traditional relationship between counselor and counseled especially in so far as self-disclosure is concerned (Thomas, 1977). Hence, as a therapist who is particularly interested in working with men, I endeavor to break down the competitiveness and mistrust they have been socially conditioned to feel towards each other. But even as I pursue this goal as a therapist, as a product of male conditioning, I find myself wishing for the "good old days." Difficult as it is to admit that there are times when "I liked it better before the questions were asked" (Pilsecker, 1977), it has to be done in order to engage us all in the recognition that this is a struggle we are involved in. This is about contradictions, self-confrontation and acknowledging that our work applies to us as well as to our clients. Pro-feminist therapy is not about we the enlightened raising the consciousness of our therapeutic "charges," but about analyzing our collective madness and socialization into limiting roles. When I realize the enormity of the task, I am humbled and recognize that the nonfeminist men I see in the consulting room are not the enemy. I see that their fractured modes of relating must be criticized yet not belittled, for they are only the result of what has shaped all of us—few affectionate male models (Lewis, 1978).

Feminist therapists bring a sociological perspective to their work that cautions against quick psychiatric labelling of clients. They also encourage reassessment of and a focus on same sex relationships as opposed to only heterosexual relationships (Radov, Manshick and Hauser, 1977). Both of these views of feminist work with females are applied to my work with Puerto Rican men (De La Cancela, 1988). In particular, I question how it is that we are enriched in relationship with other men. Why is it that it appears at times that we lack such relationships? And how do heterosexual men avoid falling into the socially encouraged trap of thinking that a relationship with a woman must be central to our lives?

This type of questioning has led to some professional and personal oppression for me, inasmuch as it is accurately seen as a challenge to the field's and society's traditional definition of what is appropriate for a man or therapist to think/feel/do. Sometimes, my debating traditional ideas, or my dissenting and having different opinions, have been met with accusations of countertransferential investments in men's issues (leveled at me during the oral defense of my doctoral thesis by a member of my dissertation committee). I have also been accused of having political interests, rather than clinical or therapeutic ones. These charges have been leveled at me innumerable times as a graduate student, administrator, clinician, researcher and author regarding this topic and especially in regards to my work on ethnic issues (De La Cancela, 1978). The final charge in the personal arena has been the "accusation" of being gay because I wear an earring. Such charges are familiar ones to feminist females who as therapists and assertive women have been accused of being bitches, man-haters or lesbians (Habib and Landgraf, 1977). Indeed, given the reality of an "ole boy" network in the mental health field, publication of this article may amount to be a "CLR," a Career Limiting Remark (Cardona, 1989).

As a believer in the unconscious, I have sought out therapy to understand if I was self-defeating or self-destructive in my efforts to blend political and clinical work. I have taken my conflicts with my male ways of being to male and female therapists, some white and some black. I have worked on relationship issues both in short-term and long-term group or individual therapies. I grieved the loss of my father who died just as I was beginning to enjoy closeness with him. I grieved the loss of the premature birth, the ectopic pregnancy and miscarriage that I was the father in. I discussed my discomfort with the performance on demand expectations of past sexual partners. I realized my attempts at stepfathering sometimes translated into traditional, aloof, and distant breadwinning behaviors with little involvement with my stepson, Manny. I was not well prepared for the realities of surrogate fathering. My nurturing was limited by what I imposed upon myself, what my partner ideally envisioned, and what my stepson wanted. In this regard, I gain some solace in learning that many other men are in the same straits (Fein, 1978). I was not simply an ogre in my stepson's life. I also modeled nonsexist behavior, gave positive advice and have negotiated a relationship with him that is independent of my involvement with his mother.

In self-disclosing as a Puerto Rican man, client, and therapist, I am sensitive to the fact that though I wish to counter prevailing negative views of men of color, I am not representative of the majority of these men. I have educational credentials, job skills, work experiences, income, and a middle class status (until my career limiting remarks catch up with me) that most African-American and Latino men don't share (Staples, 1978). Nevertheless, I do share with them a history of racism, ethnocentrism, sexism and a past history of working class poverty that has made me both a perpetrator and victim of sexism in conscious and unconscious ways, as well as a survivor that affirmatively seeks to work with "the brothers."

FRAGMENTS FROM AN ILL KEPT JOURNAL

In this section of the article, I would like to self-disclose some to highlight the importance of connecting my professional work with my personal development—a development that has included being both a client of traditional and feminist therapists, as well as a "political" person highly aware of his Puerto Rican and masculine identity. The journal entries that follow provide a glimpse of how my development as a Puerto Rican man is fluid, contradictory, sometimes reinforced and sometimes undermined by the dominant Anglo culture. Hopefully, this brief disclosure will show how social realities are sometimes psychologized or pathologized.

Circa 1979: I had just sat down on a park bench to eat a Syrian salad when this white woman walked across the yard, sat down next to me, and struck up a conversation. At the end of an hour of pleasant talk, we exchanged names, occupations, etc. before saying goodbye. Two days later, I received a call at work from her. (How did she get my number? I didn't give it to her.) She wanted to go swimming together sometime. I was both flattered and suspicious, feeling this was a "pick up" that I wasn't quite sure I liked. While talking to my compañera Iris I realized that my sexist introjects (read as: it's the man who should make the first move) were being challenged. Although I considered myself "liberated," I was still taken aback having roles reversed. Indeed I would probably not have related in the same direct manner to any woman for fear of being seen as a sexist male on the make. Even worse, would this white woman see me as a "Latin Casanova" coming on to her? But hold it, this whole analysis is based on the assumption that the woman had indeed wanted to pick me up. Maybe she was just a friendly person making human contact as opposed to getting into my pants. Or maybe my reaction had to do with her being a white woman. ¡*Ay dios mio*!

Circa 1987: I have always remembered with anger witnessing a mother reacting to her son's and daughter's scraped knees in a sexist manner. The daughter was pampered while the little boy's wailing was silenced by his being told that he had to learn to be a man and not cry. Though I witnessed that differential treatment when I was about 12 years old, I clearly recollect feeling even then that parents should spend more time raising their sons. I recently read a paper by two psychologists that says that in many Black families, boys don't receive the nurturance girls do. I agree. I think it's true for Puerto Ricans males and other men. It's as if we are supposed to somehow automatically or naturally know how to fend for ourselves from an early age on. No wonder many of our decisions are so screwed up. It's no wonder we trust so little given our not having been fully comforted due to some oppressive notion of what we're supposed to be.

And while I'm expressing anger here's an offering for the white man's culture which sometimes is so overbearing that I, just like my clients, fear being contaminated by its anti-Puerto Rican bias. At those times, I also refuse to play the "dual identity" game that middle-class Black men confronted with the pressures of working in places controlled by whites engage in. Their need to prove competence, to work doubly hard in racist settings, and to achieve recognition is something I'm too familiar with. I won't let this professional stuff get to me. I refuse to assimilate or compromise my Puerto Ricaness the way I've seen other brothers do. I'll use this anger well.

Circa 1989: I was born in the South Bronx in an Irish, Italian, Latino and Black community and raised by a full time "housewife" mother who socialized me while my "provider" father sailed the seas as a merchant marine. After parochial schools, I attended an urban public university. My oral presentation for the required freshman speech course was entitled "UP AGAINST THE WALL, FEMINIST SWINE!" It was a provocative title aimed at drawing attention to my felt oppression as a male and Puerto Rican. I spoke to how my class, cultural, religious and heterosexist background prepared me to look down on homosexuality, to protect my sister even if she was bigger and stronger than me, and to act the Don Juan. I also spoke of my confusion that being *macho* also meant to be dignified, just and loyal. By my junior year, these contradictions engendered much questioning and laborious attempts to disentangle myself from stereotypes like "Men love from the groin and not the heart." The growing consciousness among women, Blacks and Puerto Ricans, and my kinship with "brothers and sisters" proclaiming their human rights against phallic cultural shackles led to my identification with national liberation and women's movements. I married shortly before finishing college, but the marriage dissolved over conflict regarding my male aspirations to succeed in graduate school and Puerto Rican "cultural" dictates for us to start a family. Our sexual politics played themselves out in my hanging out with "my boys," her being jealous, and neither of us really knowing what we were supposed to do in the required roles of Puerto Rican "man and wife." The gender and cultural pressures were such that I was constantly put on the spot by my peers and family members with questions about whether I was impotent, infertile or gay because I had not yet produced the required symbol of adult masculinity—a child. However, these same forces came to my defense when we separated since all concluded that my "ex" was short-sighted in "nagging" about pregnancy and not realizing what a "good thing" she had going in a Puerto Rican male who was "bettering the race" by getting an education. Obviously, we were both double-binded!

Circa 1990: Blanca has said over and over again that I have to write about this stuff in a non-academic way. Elsie supportively challenges me and calls me a "feministo" as she encourages me to give "testimony" regarding my work in the area. Guys like Steve, Richard and my brother Edwin agree that men's voices must be heard, yet they admit to the difficulty they have in forming the necessary words. Sometimes I think we're making headway in our longwinded, often painful talks about how men are objectified sexually, how we experience masculine sports mania in an oppressive manner, our discomfort in being victims and perpetrators of "male bashing," and of how difficult it is to relate to women and men in non-sexist ways when it's so easy to fall into automatic power scripts. Then there are those days when I just want to give up, times I want to get into a closet and not have to challenge other men on their sexism or admit to my own. There are efforts to keep me in my place. Some women still try to gain increased power in our interaction by using their sexuality. Some men use direct and informal verbal and non-verbal ways to impress upon me my status as a man if it appears to them that I've forgotten what I am. Indeed, there are days when I realize how much easier it is as a therapist to speak to other men about these issues, than it is to bring the discourse into my daily non-therapy activities. In the office, I can be supportively confrontative of male clients and persistently pursue aspects of their and my "male stuff," yet outside of the room, I sometimes tire of examining the contents of the baggage. It's just so much easier and more familiar to carry the bags around, rather than stopping to see what's in them. Getting tired of being a man in these times even occurs when I am speaking with Latinos like Yohel, Jorge and Emilio, compañeros with whom I have struggled and worked with for over a decade. Men who care for me and whom I care for, "fellers" whose ups and downs I have been witness to and "bros" with whom I can let go. And then the talks with Maria, Milly J. and my sister Milagros impress upon me my responsibility to be honest and accountable, as well as to break down stereotypes of Latino men as not sensitive.

"Sucede que me canso de ser hombre"

(It so happens I'm tired of just being a man.)

Pablo Neruda (1974, p. 28)

REFERENCES

Arnez, N. (1972). Enhancing Black self-concept through literature. In J. Banks & J. Grambs (Eds.), *Black self concept*, (pp.93-116). New York: McGraw-Hill.

Bernard, J. (1966). *Marriage and family among Negroes*. Englewood Cliffs, N.J.: Prentice-Hill.

Blakey, W.A. (1974). Everybody makes the revolution: Some thoughts on racism and sexism. *Civil Rights Digest*, *6*, 11-19.

Brody, E.B. (1966). On the psychiatry of Latin America. *American Journal of Psychiatry*, *123*, 475-477.

Cardona, C. (1989). Personal Communication.

De La Cancela, V. (1978). On being a minority student in clinical psychology. *Journal of Contemporary Psychology*, *9*, 178-182.

De La Cancela, V. (1981). Towards a critical psychological analysis of machismo: Puerto Ricans and mental health. *Dissertation Abstracts International*, *42*, 368-B.

De La Cancela, V. (1986). A critical analysis of Puerto Rican machismo: Implications for clinical practice. *Psychotherapy*, *23*, 291-296.

De La Cancela, V. (1988). Labor pains: Puerto Rican males in transition. *Centro de Estudios Puertorriqueños Bulletin*, *2*, 40-55.

Fanon, F. (1968). *The wretched of the earth*. New York: Grove Press.

Fein, R.A. (1978). Research on fathering: Social policy and an emergent perspective. *Journal of Social Issues*, *34*, 122-135.

Gendzier, I.L. (1974). *Frantz Fanon: A critical study*. New York: Vintage Books.

Habib, M., & Landgraf, B.J. (1977). Woman helping woman. *Social Work*, *22*, 510-512.

Harper, F.D. (1981). Alcohol use and abuse. In L.E. Gary (Ed.), *Black men*, (pp.169-170). Beverly Hills, CA: Sage.

Kornilov, K.N. (1930). Psychology in the light of dialectic materialism. In C. Morchison (Ed.), *Psychologies of 1930*. Worcester: Clark University Press.

Leighton, D.C. (1972). Cultural determinants of behavior: A neglected area. *American Journal of Psychiatry*, *128*, 1003-1004.

Lewis, R.A. (1978). Emotional intimacy among men. *Journal of Social Issues*, *34*, 108-121.

Majors, R. (1986). Cool pose: The proud signature of Black survival. *Changing Men: Issues in Gender, Sex and Politics*, *17*, 5-6.

Mannoni, O. (1966). The decolonization of myself. *Race*, *7*, 337-346.

McAdoo, H. (1977). Family therapy in the Black community. *American Journal of Orthopsychiatry*, *47*, 75-79.

Memmi, A. (1967). *The colonizer and the colonized*. Boston: Beacon.

Miranda King, L. (1974). Puertorriqueñas in the United States: The impact of double discrimination. *Civil Rights Digest*, *6*, 20-27.

Neruda, P. (1974). *Five decades: A selection (Poems 1925-1970)*. New York: Grove Press.

Parham, T.A., & McDavis, R.J. (1987). Black men, an endangered species: Who's really pulling the trigger? *Journal of Counseling and Development*, *66*, 24-27.

Pilsecker, C. (1977). Vive la difference. *Social Work*, *22*, 484-486.

Rado, C.G., Masnick, B.R., & Hauser, B.B. (1977). Issues in feminist therapy: The work of a woman's study group. *Social Work*, *22*, 507-509.

Ramirez, R. (1982). Personal communication.

Ramirez Boulette, T. (1975). Group therapy with low-income Mexican Americans. *Social Work*, *20*, 403-405.

Rendon, M. (1984). Myths and stereotypes in minority groups. *International Journal of Social Psychiatry*, *30*, 297-309.

Staples, R. (1971). The myth of the impotent Black male. *The Black Scholar*, June, 2-9.

Staples, R. (1978). Masculinity and race: The dual dilemma of Black men. *Journal of Social Issues*, *34*, 169-183.

Thomas, S.A. (1977). Theory and practice in feminist therapy. *Social Work*, *22*, 447-454.

Treating the Absent Man: Is It Possible? Is It Ethical?

Karen Gail Lewis

SUMMARY. Men are an important part of many women's therapy, yet they often do not attend any sessions. In seeing women individually, feminist family therapists are indirectly providing therapy for the man. This paper presents suggestions for a direct therapy with the absent man and raises some of the ethical dilemmas this poses for the therapist.

Men are an important part of many heterosexual women's therapy, yet often they do not attend the sessions. A woman's personal growth most likely will lead her to expect more from her husband or partner and to expect a more equitable and satisfying relationship. Therefore, even if the man is not present in the therapy, he will be greatly affected by what happens there. Therapists may make an effort to invite the man to the sessions, but if he refuses, the woman is seen individually. He and the relationship, either directly or indirectly, may still remain a major part of the therapy.

Although family therapy has a sizable body of literature on working with only one member of the family, the focus usually is on the systemic, interactive behavior patterns, emphasizing triangles, complementarity and symmetry. It does not address the ethical repercussions of seeing one part of a couple nor does it offer a feminist conceptualization of this type of treatment. The feminist therapy literature focuses on women's personal issues and the political, philosophical, and sociocultural factors that negatively impact on their role in society today. There is a developing body of literature

---

Karen Gail Lewis, ACSW, EdD, is in private practice, 560 N Street, SW, #N505, Washington, DC 20024.

on therapy with men (Meth & Pasick, 1990; Myers, 1989) which focuses on the uniqueness of male ways of expressing feelings and relating. However, there is no literature bridging these theories, providing a feminist, systematic analysis of the couple's relationship when one half of the couple does not participate in the therapy.

As feminist therapists, we may say we are doing individual therapy, but as family therapists we know it is not possible to effect change on only one part of a relationship; the woman's change is bound to impact on her partner's behavior and on their relationship. This article, then, offers a way to conceptualize what we, in fact, are already doing, only making it more explicit—providing treatment to the "absent man." As this work becomes more explicit, two important questions are raised: Is it *possible* to help a man when he does not come into the therapy sessions, and is it *ethical* to try to impact a relationship when only one partner is requesting the help? Feminists must begin discussing the implications and the ethics of providing such therapy.

MEN AND THERAPY

Women seek therapy far more frequently than men. Informal discussions with directors of American mental health clinics suggest that from 80-95% of referrals for therapy are initiated by women. Unfortunately, there are no adequate statistics on how many men agree to conjoint therapy versus those who refuse to participate, but we can speculate that a large percentage of women in committed relationships are in therapy without their partners. Why is it that men so often do not seek therapy? One answer may lie in how they have been indoctrinated to think about themselves as men and about therapy.

Men's prescribed gender roles have left them poorly equipped to deal with women's personal changes. As a result of the Women's Liberation Movement, many women have become more self-aware, found and developed their personal power, and demanded more emotionality from their partners. They now want and expect men to take more responsibility for their relationships. Although the Men's Liberation Movement started around the same time as the Women's, it never gained the same momentum, despite a rash of professional and popular books (Cooke, 1978; Dubbert, 1979; Farrell, 1974; Nichols, 1975). In many couples this precipitated an unbalancing with the women better able to state their needs, and their male partners retreating to familiar coping mechanisms, e.g., anger, withdrawal, defensive accusations.

While one goal of feminist therapy is to empower women, one goal of "masculist therapy . . . strives to empower men relationally through the desensitizing to and teaching of intimacy . . . " (Scher, Stevens, Good, & Eichenfield, 1987, p. 28). For most men, addressing feelings and relationships is a foreign concept that dramatically conflicts with the stereotypical image of a man – autonomous, cognitively oriented, competitive, and fearful of intimacy (Scher et al., 1987).

> Therapy threatens that identity with its inherent intimacy and relatedness, and it is often viewed therefore as feminine, something the male must "not be." The expression of vulnerability, emotional needs, pain, and confusion are the antithesis of maleness. . . .
>
> – *Carlson, 1987, pp. 40-41*

It is no surprise, then, that men do not easily turn to therapy, rather they seek help only when their current pains are greater than their fears of change. A considerable amount of research reveals that married men are emotionally and physically healthier than married women (Bernard, 1972; Chesler, 1972; Guttentag, Salasin, & Belle, 1980). If there is no discomfort, why change? The therapeutic challenge is finding a way to reach the man in a way he can accept. It is a particularly difficult challenge because so often therapists never see the man – he refuses to participate in the therapy.

THERAPIST'S ETHICAL DILEMMAS

Many women begin individual therapy when their partners refuse to join them. This should raise many ethical issues for feminist family therapists. These can be arbitrarily grouped under three headings: issues in working with women, impact on the absent man, and impact on the couple system.

Issues in Working with Women

There are at minimum three key ethical issues that need to be considered in working with only the female half of a couple. The first is how to help free the woman from her rigidified roles and to help her free her partner in a way that does not lay responsibility on her for his behavior changes. Can the woman learn to teach her partner to be more emotionally available and to take a more mutual role in the relationship without it sounding like "If only you do the right thing, the man will be able to respond."

The second ethical issue relates to the possible conflict between the woman's wish to help "change" her partner and the therapist's political/philosophical stance that women should not caretake men. Therapists need to be clear about the distinctions around caretaking. There is the stereotypical caretaking which some women do out of a "moral duty" (Gilligan, 1982) or woman's obligation. However, the caretaking can also be motivated by a personal benefit: "I owe it to *me* to help Steve grow; if he does not change then I may have to leave him. So it is in my best interest to do whatever I can to help him." Some women derive a great source of satisfaction from nurturing and caretaking, their lives enhanced by utilizing their sensitivities with those they love. Ethically, therapists must be careful that their own beliefs do not blind them from seeing differences in behaviors that look familiar.

The third ethical dilemma is related to the systemic awareness that the partner will be effected by what happens in the therapy. As the woman becomes more assertive and less bound by gender roles, she may become dissatisfied with the relationship, particularly if her partner is not changing in similar ways. Should a therapist tell a female client that her benefits from therapy are likely to unsettle her relationship—causing more tension or even causing her to outgrow him?

Impact on the Man

Even though the man is not in the session, as systemic therapists we know the woman's treatment will have an impact on him. Is it ethical to provide therapy without a contract? Must he agree to the indirect effect on him? When the woman is the identified client, she hires the therapist, she requests the treatment, and she pays the bill. But the man is not a willing participant. Do the same rules for a contract hold? And, what are the therapist's confidentiality obligations when the woman talks about her partner? The therapist is privy to private information about the absent man. Must she have his permission to discuss him? If not, must he be told what the therapist knows about him?

The question of forewarning the woman of possible danger to the relationship of her individual therapy has been raised, but it is equally relevant for the man. Does the therapist have an ethical duty to inform the man of the potential damage if he does not participate in the therapy? Does he need to understand that she may make changes that will be disruptive to their status quo and perhaps become dissatisfied with their current style of relating? If he still refuses to attend and the woman later leaves him as a direct result of her therapy, will he feel he was duly warned?

Impact on the Couple

As a woman becomes more empowered, more able to directly express her needs, and more aware of the inequality in the relationship, she may experience increased anger. In addition, in supporting her efforts to challenge conventional roles, the therapist knows there will be increased conflict and tension between the couple. Does the therapist have an obligation to warn each partner? How does she monitor the rising tension level? What should she do if she sees it getting dangerously out of control?

Clearly the above questions have no easy answers, but it behooves us to carefully consider them. A feminist individual therapist must focus on helping the woman identify her own needs, not have to caretake men, and to empower herself. Yet, the feminist therapist must also incorporate the woman's realistic fear that her self-empowerment, without her partner's concomitant changes, may drive an irrevocable wedge between them. The therapist must find a way to help both partners that does not reinforce traditional sex roles, but one where the woman does not do the relational work for the absent man. One possible avenue – for those women willing to invest the energy (out of self-benefit not moral duty) – is for them to work simultaneously on their own issues in the relationship *and* on teaching their partners how to be more emotionally responsive.

TEACHING THE WOMAN TO TEACH THE MAN

Many men are more invested in their relationships than they demonstrate; therefore, "teaching" them may be one way to meet the therapeutic challenge of helping them break through the "masculine mystique" (Allen & Gordon, 1990). The question is how to do this without their feeling threatened. Therapists need to remember that the women's integrity must not be compromised by their doing the ground work for the relationship and that the men must be treated with respect; this can not be a man-blaming process.

The first lesson must cover the different communication styles of men and women. In my practice, I regularly hear women asking their partners, "Why don't you talk to me? Please tell me how you feel." Conversely, just as often, I hear exasperated men complain, "What does she want!" Couples do not understand that some of their problems result from gender based communication styles (Gilligan, 1982; Lerner, 1985). Generally stated, women want to talk about their feelings while men want to take action. Typically, when a woman expresses her feelings about a situation, the man may respond with a suggestion for what to do, but may turn off to her emotions. The result is a symmetrical escalation as the woman increases her emotionality and the man further distances himself. Her initial concern, even if minor, becomes lost in their gender based stylized patterns. If the woman asserts herself and does not give in as she has in the past, the man may defend himself by denigrating her new found power and/or patronizingly withdrawing from her "when you are like that."

While there is nothing intrinsically wrong with the woman's emotional style, if she wants to engage her partner in a discussion of their relationship, she *initially* may have to talk his language. She may have to present her needs or concerns in cognitive terms, using facts and specific examples. Undertaking this endeavor requires full awareness on the woman's part that, at least at the beginning, she will carry the major burden for making the communication happen. This is all the more reason why the therapist needs to help her understand the distinctions between investing in this effort out of a "moral duty" or out of an awareness of her own benefit.

Part of the therapy includes teaching the woman that some of what she does not get from her partner may not be her inadequacy; he may not be able to respond to her emotional needs. Too often, women personalize men's emotional unavailability, rather than seeing it as a result of how men have been socialized. Some of the more debilitating messages men have incorporated include

- decreased sensitivity to own and others' feelings
- intolerance of other's expression of feelings
- rationality too highly valued
- disguised feelings
- avoidance of intimate, committed relationships
- use of addictive substances to avoid unpleasant feelings
- restricted emotions resulting in stress-related disorders

—Pasick, Gordon, & Meth, 1990

If the woman understands how the man is also bound by his gender, it may free her from personalizing and blaming herself for his unavailability. It sometimes is useful to ask the woman if she believes, in her heart, that her partner wants a better relationship with her. Hearing her own answer may further help her see her task in a less personalized, and hence constructive light, so she can find alternative methods of confronting him.

Once the woman is ready to teach her partner about this world of feelings, she needs to start in a safe and non-threatening way. She should choose a time when there is a calm mood between them. She might start with an academic discussion based on an article or a newspaper story. They might discuss a movie, such as Moonstruck, Accidental Tourist, or even Fiddler on the Roof. In each case, they could look at how the gender roles inhibit each of the people involved. By discussing people unrelated to them, there is a better chance they can look, less emotionally, at how gender roles limit *both* men and women. If discussions about unrelated people prove fruitful, she can initiate a discussion about how these roles have limited their parents. This is particularly useful after a family visit, when they can identify specific behavioral interactions, such as distance and closeness or demonstrations of love that are based on role definition. They can speculate how each parent loses from the rigidity of the roles, as well as how they both have absorbed styles and expectations from their parents' relationship. Obviously, the timing for these discussions needs to be well chosen so that the man will not feel "attacked." For men who like to read, the woman may recommend some readings about gender roles and feminism. Books like *The Dance of Anger* (Lerner, 1985) are non-threatening and often present ideas with which men can identify.

The woman may first have to understand how her partner developed his relational style before she can begin teaching him to communicate with her. This may entail the therapist asking the woman about her partner's family of origin and then making "professional guesses" about why he may be reacting in a certain way. This does three things: it frees the woman from taking the blame for a particular interaction; it validates her reaction to a given situation; and it helps her understand why her partner is behaving in such a manner. Free from self-blame, supported by the validation of her perspective, and armed with insight, the woman is in a better position to approach her partner in a potentially more successful manner.

THERAPIST INVOLVING THE MAN

The examples above will help the woman behave differently and confront her partner more productively. However, the therapist herself can engage the man, even if he never attends a session. Because of confidentiality, many therapists are hesitant to contact the partner. Yet, sometimes women are eager for their partners to know what is happening in the therapy and may already be discussing the sessions with them. For those women afraid of their partners' anger at being discussed, keeping the men attuned to the issues and progress in the therapy may alleviate the men's anger. Engaging the absent man would also address the therapist's ethical concerns about warning the partner of the potential danger to the relationship without his participation and warning the woman that her individual therapy may possibly lead to her outgrowing him. In addition, it is a way to handle the contract with the non-participating man. If he is included in the process, the woman will no longer be talking about an absent person.

There are many ways to include the non-present man:

1. The therapist stays available to the man by periodically suggesting the woman invite him to a session. If appropriate, the therapist contacts him directly by telephone or letter.
2. The therapist offers to make a home visit to give the man a chance to meet her—on his own territory.
3. After each session, the therapist and woman draft a summary letter to him so "you'll not be left out about the progress that is occurring." The use of the letters, the timing, and the wording should be carefully personalized for each couple. This can be started by the therapist sending him an initial letter explaining her intent to keep him informed after each session.
4. The therapist sends him (directly or through the woman) articles or newspaper clippings that relate to the woman's issues or that exemplify the gender roles that limit each of their behavior.
5. Audio or video tapes of the sessions are sent to him to keep him abreast of the treatment issues and progress.
6. The therapist writes him suggesting he write her (or send a tape) presenting his perspective on a given issue.

Sometimes, the results from any of these actions serve to desensitize the man enough that he can begin participating more directly in the therapy. However, even if that does not happen, it is likely that the indirect effect will have positive ramifications on the couple's relationship.

CLINICAL EXAMPLE

Lou and Sally had been together for 18 years. Sally finally wanted to marry; Lou could not explain why he was "not yet ready." Sally suggested couple's therapy, but Lou refused; she decided to come anyway. Her affection for him, though, was quite apparent, and it sounded like it was mutual. She was torn, thinking she should leave him, yet knowing she had invested so many years of her life in this relationship and did not want to start over; however, she could not wait much longer. Sally said they had never really shared feelings together but, in recent years, Lou was even more distant; this coincided with her efforts to begin expressing her needs more directly.

The first step was helping Sally understand how she became so silenced. She saw the connection with her caretaking oldest child role in her Native American family. By contrast, Lou is an only child of two elderly German parents cut off from their families of origin; he was not used to taking charge. I suggested Sally was personalizing Lou's lack of expression and reminded her he had spent most of his childhood silently keeping out of his parents' way. He had good reasons for "his emotional limitations" and his never taking the initiative. She needed to distinguish between his issues and her own.

After each session, Sally shared our discussions with Lou. Since he showed some interest, I suggested Sally invite him to write his reactions to each session. He wrote me a letter, first showing it to Sally, agreeing with her comments about his family's impact on him. That precipitated a long discussion about his relationship with his parents. He made the connection between his obediently doing what he was told, making no waves, and his difficulty now in taking initiatives. He wondered if his fear of commitment was related to his never having taken a definitive stance.

The letter was so successful that I suggested, for a while, they have non-verbal discussions. This would equalize their ability, since Sally was a verbal heavy-weight and he was a lightweight. I suggested they assign a specified period of time each week and talk through letters. I explained this in a letter to Lou.

The letter writing led to more direct communication, but Sally's anger, repressed for many years, fueled long arguments. She was proud to be able to express herself, but he would silently listen to her; she never really felt better afterwards. I validated her anger and suggested she ask him if their long talks helped him understand her hurt or if it immobilized him. Since we periodically videotaped the sessions, I spoke directly into the camera, asking Lou if he would prefer to set a time limit on their discussions. I asked him if his silence was a result of feeling verbally blocked. The next week, Sally reported that Lou suggested 45 minute talks. At first, Sally was hesitant about the time-limit, but she noticed he seemed more involved than during the longer ones.

Sally liked that they were sharing more, but she needed him to show his affection for her. She had given him numerous suggestions how to do that, but he never followed through. Given what we three were learning about Lou's style, I told her I imagined he would never take that initiative on his own. With that information, Sally decided to give Lou a list, with a time frame, of things he could do that would help her feel he cared, e.g., like putting her picture on his desk or bringing her flowers. He responded, "Now I have some idea what it is you want from me." In therapy, she was furious: "I must have told him that 1000 times before!" I explained that it seemed he only heard suggestions when they were concrete, in writing, and with a deadline. I validated her efforts and reminded her not to personalize his not hearing her before. By the end of the three weeks, Lou had, in fact, done 6 things, including telling Sally, with words, how much she meant to him. Shortly after that, he got tired of "writing to that therapist of yours," and suggested he come to the sessions.

CONCLUSION

Men are not as likely to seek therapy as women yet, willingly or not, they are recipients of women's treatment. Therapists know that the absent man is powerfully present in the therapy. When seeing a woman individually, they may feel conflicted, though, between a systemic understanding that her changes impact her partner and a feminist belief that she can no longer take responsibility for him.

While there are many ways to provide treatment from an integrated perspective, this paper offers one avenue: helping the woman look at her own role in the relationship while also helping her to teach the man how to respond more relationally. While this paper focuses on the woman's treatment, the emphasis is on ways to help the man grow along with the woman, which decreases the danger of her outgrowing him. Clearly, any changes the woman makes in a feminist treatment may cause more dissension for the couple. Therefore, specific therapeutic attention must be paid to both the possible disruption for the couple and the danger of laying responsibility on the woman for making the changes happen.

The purpose of this type of therapy is not just to teach the man about intimacy and emotional expression. This therapy must be seen as a mutual learning process where one partner takes the lessons and passes them on to the other. It is crucial that the woman learns to check for signs that her teaching is useful. Pursuing her efforts without the rewards is futile and can become abusive to her.

This article has raised two broad questions: is it possible to treat a man who is not in therapy, and is it ethical to do so? The suggestions presented here, for both the woman and the therapist, offer an affirmative answer to the first question: yes it is possible, as a systemic, feminist therapist, to treat an absent man. The partner may or may not ever decide to join the therapy, but by utilizing his "presence" in the treatment, he may well benefit from it.

This paper has highlighted the ethical issues therapists face each time we work individually with a woman. Because of the complexity of working with only the woman, we may overlook the indirect relevance of these questions to the non-present partner. There are no easy answers to ethical questions; however, some of the dilemmas may be resolved by including the absent man in the treatment. Hopefully, the questions raised here about the feasiblity and ethics of treating one half of a couple will be a beginning of an active discussion of these complicated yet vital issues.

REFERENCES

Allen, J.A. & Gordon, S. (1990). Creating a framework for change. In R. Meth & R. Pasick, *Men in therapy: The challenge of change.* New York: Guilford.

Bernard, J. (1972). *The future of marriage*. New York: World Publishing.

Carlson, N. (1987). Woman therapist: Male client. In M. Scher, M. Stevens, G. Good, & G. Eichenfield, (Eds.), *Handbook of counseling and psychotherapy with men*. Newbury Park, CA: Sage.

Chesler, P. (1972). *Women and madness*. Garden City, NJ: Doubleday.

Cooke, C. (1978). *The men's survival resource book: On being a man in today's world*. Minneapolis: R.B. Press.

Dubbert, J. (1979). *A man's place: Masculinity in transition*. Englewood Cliffs, NJ: Prentice Hall.

Farrell, W. (1974). *The liberated man*. New York: Bantam.

Gilligan, C. (1982). *In a different voice: Psychological theory and women's development*. Cambridge, MA: Harvard University Press.

Guttentag, M., Salassin, S., & Belle, D. (Eds.). (1980). *The mental health of women*. New York: Academic Press.

Lerner, H. (1985). *The dance of anger*. New York: Harper & Row.

Meth, R. & Pasick, R. (1990). *Men in therapy: The challenge of change*. New York: Guilford.

Myers, M. (1989). *Men and divorce*. New York: Guilford.

Nichols, J. (1975). *Men's liberation: A new definition of masculinity*. New York: Penguin.

Pasick, R., Gordon, S., & Meth, R. (1990). Helping men understand themselves. In R. Meth & R. Pasick, *Men in therapy: The challenge of change*. New York: Guilford.

Scher, M., Stevens, M., Good, G., & Eichenfield, G. (Eds.). (1987). *Handbook of counseling and psychotherapy with men*. Newbury Park, CA: Sage.

PART 4: MEN AND VIOLENCE

Abuses of Power by Father-Daughter Incest Perpetrators in Treatment: The Necessity of the Therapist-Family Coalition

Vincent Fish

SUMMARY. Father-daughter incest perpetrators abuse power and impede progress in their therapy by (1) using treatment to avoid consequences while maintaining a responsible image; (2) concealing details of their abuse of the victim; (3) minimizing the extent of their sexual deviance; and (4) continuing attempts to dominate their families. The role of a therapist-family coalition, based on the therapist's support and empowerment of the mother, in blocking these tactics is discussed.

Kings are earth's gods; in vice their law's their will;
And if Jove stray, who dares say Jove doth ill?

. . . for wisdom sees those men

Vincent Fish, MSSW, is affiliated with the Family Therapy Center of Madison, 6400 Enterprise Lane, Suite 211, Madison, WI 53719.

> Blush not in actions blacker than the night
> Will shun no course to keep them from the light.
>
> *Pericles, Prince of Tyre. I.i.11.103-104, 134-136 (Shakespeare, 1951, pp. 1241-1242)*

> The informants described their fathers as perfect patriarchs. They were, without question, the heads of their households. Their authority within the family was absolute, often asserted by force. They were also the arbiters of the family's social life and frequently succeeded in virtually secluding the women in the family. But while they were often feared within their families, they impressed outsiders as sympathetic, even admirable men.
>
> *–Herman, 1981, p. 71*

The link between patriarchal power and father-daughter incest in Western cultures is clear and longstanding. The position of King Antiochus, described in the first quotation above, is typical of incestuous fathers and stepfathers. The introduction to Scene I. of *Pericles, Prince of Tyre* tells us:

> This king unto him took a fere,
> Who died and left a female heir,
> So buxom, blithe, and full of face,
> As heaven had lent her all his grace;
> With whom the father liking took,
> And her to incest did provoke.
>
> *–11.21-26 (Shakespeare, 1951, p. 1240)*

When his daughter reaches marriageable age, Antiochus attempts to discourage suitors, and keep his daughter silent, by making solving a riddle a condition of their proposing marriage. An incorrect answer means death. Pericles accepts the challenge of solving the riddle (which points directly to Antiochus' incest) in sight of the numerous corpses of his predecessors. Recognizing the riddle's answer, he is faced with a fearful dilemma: To pretend he can't solve it means execution, but to reveal the answer openly exposes

Antiochus. As Pericles puts it to Antiochus, "Who has a book of all that monarchs do, He's more secure to keep it shut than shown. . . ." (11.94-95, Shakespeare, 1951, p. 1241). Antiochus, perceiving that Pericles has unraveled his secret, attempts to have him killed.

The figure of Antiochus personifies the issues of power we face in treating incest perpetrators. Typically, these men try to control their families, information about their criminal sexual behavior, and treatment. Like Antiochus, the perpetrator regards the therapist as an unwelcome, dangerous intruder, and will go to great lengths to negate the therapist's influence on himself, the family and the larger system. While the perpetrator's abuse of power within his family has been recognized and discussed (see, for example, Herman, 1983, and Sommers-Flanagan & Walters, 1987), the nature of the perpetrator's ongoing abuse of power during treatment has not been systematically examined.

The perpetrator's abuse of power in the treatment context usually includes: (1) his use of treatment as a means to avoid consequences, such as jail and losing access to his family; (2) his keeping information from the therapist about his past and present abusive behavior toward the victim(s); (3) his minimization and distortion of the nature and extent of his sexual deviance; and (4) his continued attempts to control his family and block their alliance with the therapist. When successful, these moves by the perpetrator subvert the therapy and are accompanied by, or set the stage for, further sexual abuse.

This paper discusses how therapists must work with perpetrators in a context where such abuses of power are countered.[1] The therapist's part in helping create such a context, by supporting a radical shift in the distribution of power in the perpetrator's family, will also be indicated in relation to each of the four ways in which perpetrators abuse power in treatment.

THE PERPETRATOR'S MOTIVATION IN THERAPY

As long as the perpetrator is secure in his dominant role with his family, his motivation to change will be minimal to nonexistent.

Generally this is true even when the perpetrator is physically removed from his family and facing harsh penalties, such as prison time, if he does not cooperate in treatment. Without real motivation, the perpetrator relates to the therapist as a target for manipulation to gain or maintain access to the family, or to appease or avoid the legal system.

A perpetrator's treatment may continue on these terms for months or sometimes years without the therapist realizing that the perpetrator has never really entered therapy. One way the illusion of "successful therapy" may be shattered is when it is later learned that the perpetrator has been reabusing his daughter or other children simultaneously with treatment. The perpetrator will have discovered how to meet his therapist's expectations by saying the right things. He may even demonstrate some surface insight about the nature and consequences of his abusiveness and, with little therapeutic prodding, offer that he is remorseful and guilty about his harmful behavior. Meanwhile, the perpetrator usually provides the therapist minimal or misleading information about his real abuse history and pattern, especially when he believes the therapist is not already well-informed in this area.

When the perpetrator's control over his family is disrupted, his efforts to misuse treatment will be clarified, and his motivation may change. The larger system, including the perpetrator's therapist, must support and ally with the mother and children in ways that enable them to withdraw from the perpetrator's agenda of denial and false front of "family togetherness." We must remember that the perpetrator has punished, and continues to punish, his family for any moves which challenge his denial or otherwise go counter to his wishes. Through his abuses of power within the family, the perpetrator has severely compromised the family's ability to function. The mother, at a minimum, has been grievously misled, disempowered and isolated. Her role with her children, particularly the victim, has been chronically and often purposefully undercut by the perpetrator. Additionally, the mother herself will frequently have been physically and sexually abused, and otherwise intimidated by him.

The illusory nature of the perpetrator's progress in individual treatment is frequently demonstrated when conjoint couple and/or family sessions are begun. When the therapist has not formed a strong alliance with the family, any initiative in conjoint sessions to examine the reality of the incest and its effects will elicit tactics from the perpetrator designed to obfuscate the issue and block the therapist's access to his family. Some offenders exert control through sophisticated techniques of verbal mystification that can leave the therapist perplexed and vaguely anxious. One such technique is, when confronted by the therapist, to attribute the incest to some other problem, such as drinking, which the perpetrator then claims to have resolved or to be working on in another setting. He thus indicates that the therapist is irrelevant, while overtly seeming to take responsibility for his difficulties. If the therapist is undeterred by this parry, the perpetrator may next appear hurt and misunderstood, seeking support from his family against the therapist, whom he now portrays as unfair to him. Another typical tactic is to join the concern about the victim's safety by trying to shift attention to potential perpetrators outside the family. Again, the perpetrator attempts to appear responsible while eluding therapeutic focus. (This may also reveal a continued sexual preoccupation and intrusiveness toward the victim.) Other perpetrators, having been uniformly obsequious to the therapist in individual work, may react with remarkable belligerence in the presence of the family, both to the therapist and the family. Still others may have coached family members on how to act and what to say in the therapist's presence. The therapist is usually quickly made aware of just how peripheral and inconsequential the individual therapy has been, and how central and dominating the perpetrator's project of controlling his family remains.

When the larger system has successfully allied with the mother and children, so that the perpetrator's control over them is reduced, the perpetrator will begin to experience others, such as the therapist, as possible sources of support and guidance. As the perpetrator's control of his family is eliminated, his extreme emotional dependency on them remains. Typically, once the family successfully allies with the treatment and not with the perpetrator, he will not react with anger, but will transfer some of this dependence to the therapist and become more genuinely cooperative and self-disclosing.

DEFEATING THE PERPETRATOR'S CONTROL OF INFORMATION

A primary problem in therapeutic work with perpetrators is the therapist's lack of information about the abuse. Like Antiochus,[2] a perpetrator operates to keep knowledge of his incest to himself and his daughter. Therapists come to understand, with Pericles, that perpetrators have no wish for us to know their secrets and are intent on rendering us impotent to affect them in what they regard as their personal domain. The overwhelming majority of perpetrators misrepresent their sexual behavior with children at almost every opportunity throughout the beginning of treatment. Most continue to dissemble even past the first few months, and many lie through the entire therapy.

In the initial stage of therapy, some of this seems due to an acute denial related to the shock of having been found out and to a need to defend against a precipitous loss of self-esteem. In some rare instances, repression may temporarily occur. However, for the most part, the perpetrator lies as an act of power. This is a well-known phenomenon in perpetrator treatment (Groth, 1982; Herman, 1981; Wheeler, 1989). Groth (1982) has summarized typical styles of perpetrators' denial and minimization, along with possible therapist responses (pp. 232-234). As Groth remarks: " . . . it is important . . . in confronting the offender that the clinician also operate from a power base. Knowledge is power and it is therefore necessary to obtain a dependable account of his incestuous behavior. It is essential to know the victim's version of the offense" (p. 232).

From the start, then, we are in a battle with the perpetrator over control of information. It is important that we prevail, since it is unlikely that therapy will be useful if we do not. This is especially so if the perpetrator surreptitiously continues to sexually abuse the identified victim or other unknown victims while therapy is proceeding. If we depend on the perpetrator, we are automatically defeated. We are the weaker party here, and our recourse is to others, especially the victim and anyone to whom the victim has given her story.

There are at least three potential difficulties here. First, the victim may not be able to give the information we need because she is very young, or was when some or all of the abuse occurred, or because of some psychological or physical infirmity, or because she is not available to us, directly or through intermediaries. Second, the victim may not have all the information we need because she is not the only victim, and does not know of the others or cannot speak for them. Third, the victim may not give us all the information we need because she does not want to. The victim is frequently intimidated by the perpetrator into silence, or is moved to protect him because of her or her mother's attachment to him. To the extent that the perpetrator can bring about any or all of these difficulties, or prevent their resolution, he is at an advantage.

As with the problem of the perpetrator's motivation, the therapist must look beyond the individual work with the perpetrator and form coalitions. This is another point at which we must carefully examine our relationship with the victim and the family, and temporarily shift our interest away from the perpetrator. If we cannot do this, therapy with the perpetrator is effectively over, no matter how many sessions occur subsequently. When the therapist is empowered by the family by being given more information about the perpetrator's abusive behavior, perpetrator treatment can take a dramatically positive turn. Just the fact that the family is endorsing the therapist by providing details of his behavior often cuts through much of the perpetrator's motivation for denial. Information from the victim and other family members is also crucial in establishing the extent of the perpetrator's sexually deviant behavior and formulating an adequate treatment plan.

THE PERPETRATOR'S MINIMIZATION OF SEXUAL DEVIANCE

One source of perpetrators' power in treatment, especially over information, is the confusion in the field over what it is that needs to be treated: is the perpetrator's behavior an abuse of power or sexual deviance? In the area of incest, proponents of the first view emphasize the perpetrator's normality: "There is nothing all that unusual about the incest offender" (Sommers-Flanagan & Walters, 1987,

p. 170). The response of those advocating a sexual deviancy approach is typified by Berlin's (1983) remark that: " . . . the assumption that paraphiliac behavior is little more than misbehavior is a conceptually invalid oversimplification" (p. 92).

The position taken here is that the abuse of power is a means to a usually sexually determined end. Most men who abuse power in other circumstances do not target children as sex partners. Some men who sexually abuse children do not routinely abuse power in ways unrelated to carrying out the offense and keeping it secret. The willingness of the perpetrator to abuse power is a necessary condition for incest to occur, and this willingness must be dealt with in treatment. But it is unlikely to be a sufficient cause of incest. What most incest perpetrators have in common is a sexual compulsion toward children and a habit of acting on it. Although they are like other men in many regards, incest perpetrators often have a deviant sexual arousal pattern.

The explanatory constructs of deviant arousal pattern and abuse of power are not mutually exclusive. For example, Groth (1983) presents a view which includes both sex and aggression as explanatory concepts in sexual abuse, but gives priority to aggression:

> By definition, sexual assault is an interpersonal act involving both sexuality and aggression. It is the sexual abuse of power and the sexual expression of needs, motives, and issues that are predominantly nonsexual. It is the sexual expression of aggression rather than the aggressive expression of sexuality. (p. 166)

Contrary to Groth, I think the more general truth is that sexual assault is "the aggressive expression of sexuality." Referring to the idea that " . . . sexual abuse isn't really sexual at all," Conte (1986) has remarked:

> There are a number of problems with this notion. Virtually all sexuality, deviant and nondeviant, contains both sexual and non-sexual dimensions. Indeed, one of the mental health implications of sexuality is that it can be a means of expressing

> anger, closeness, dependence, caring, or affirmation. There is no reason to assume that sexual abuse of children does not include sexual and non-sexual dimensions. (p. 119)

He suggests: " . . . [N]ot treating the problem, at least in part, as a sexual one, is to not directly help the client with the problem which places him at legal and social jeopardy" (p. 120). Unfortunately, the common conception that the sexual nature of incest is somehow secondary to the abuse of power may lead some clinicians to underfocus on the sexual determinants of the perpetrator's abusive behavior.

This matter has been complicated for individual clinicians and for the field at large by the perpetrator's tendency, discussed above, to lie about and minimize his transgressions. Perpetrators as a group have successfully left us, until recently, with the false impression that their offenses have been almost exclusively targeted at their children. In their study, Abel and his colleagues (1988) were able to guarantee perpetrators of sex crimes complete anonymity. Under these conditions, they found that 49% of the incest perpetrators whose victims were girls had also been sexually abusing girls outside the home, and 12% had also been sexually abusing boys. Rape was acknowledged by 19% of incest perpetrators, and 20% admitted to exhibitionism. Other paraphilias were mentioned by smaller proportions of the sample. Only 28% of the sample of incest perpetrators who targeted girls said they limited their sexual deviance to abusing female relatives. Seventy-two percent said they had offended in more than one category of paraphilic behavior. For incest perpetrators targeting boys, this figure was 95%.

As therapists of incest perpetrators, we need to raise this sort of finding with our clients, their families and other members of our incest treatment teams. To the extent that confusion about the sexual component of the abuse leads the therapist to neglect this crucial issue, the perpetrator will take advantage of the lapse. For the most part, perpetrators would rather talk about anything but their sexual motivation for the incest and other sexual crimes they have committed. Also, if we do not indicate a readiness to deal with this topic, the victim and other family members may be reluctant to bring it up, thereby compromising our alliance with them and leaving us uninformed. Perpetrators must be asked repeatedly and persistently about other victims and additional sexual deviance. As part of treatment, evaluations which include laboratory measures of sexual arousal patterns should be routinely utilized.

If the therapist is the only person concerned about the perpetrator's possible sexual deviance, there will be no motivation for the perpetrator to go beyond the victim's initial story, if that far. While the therapist should never be gullible, it is not a useful role for the therapist to be the person in the system who is always most suspicious of the perpetrator. Also, it is generally vain for the therapist to attempt to motivate him to tell the truth. Mothers must be invited to share our burden of concern about the perpetrator's treatability if aspects of his sexual deviance, which is likely to be farther ranging than is indicated by the contents of the police report, are hidden. This invitation should be combined with whatever support is required to help family members assimilate this potentially devastating new information. Attention should be given to the mother's possible need to grieve the loss of an idealized picture of the perpetrator or the abuse (as represented, for example, by ideas such as "He only did it once, because he was extremely stressed," or "It wasn't really very sexual – he was just trying to feel close"). When mothers are aware of the sexually compulsive aspect of perpetrators' behavior, this perspective may help them cope with blame levelled against them by perpetrators and others. Sexual compulsiveness almost always begins in men long before they are married, and functions independently of the man's relationship, sexual and otherwise, with his wife. There is nothing the wife can do to help with this problem, except support her husband in seeking treatment, even if she knows about it – and she almost never does. Blaming mothers for incest is always untenable, but within a framework that includes the perpetrator's sexual compulsiveness, it is clearly absurd.

If the mother and the legal system, in cooperative combination, press the perpetrator for more information, they may convince him that they are prepared for the truth, and that it is in his interest (as well as that of his family and other actual and potential victims) for him to address the true extent of his sexually abusive behavior. When this pressure is consistent, a perpetrator's continued assertion that his abusive behavior has been circumscribed becomes somewhat more believable. When it is not, and the perpetrator is admitting only to what is in the initial police report, there are strong reasons to disbelieve him.

THE PERPETRATOR'S CONTINUING ATTEMPTS TO CONTROL THE FAMILY

Detaching the perpetrator from the family, by requiring him to reside out of the home for at least some months, is almost always required to protect the victim and to allow for a restructuring of the family (Fish & Faynik, 1990). This intervention is an essential aspect of perpetrator treatment. However, as necessary as this step may be, it should not be assumed that accomplishing it automatically shifts power to the mother or adequately blocks the perpetrator's influence. Separating the perpetrator will certainly not reduce his attempts to gain control of the situation, but will intensify them. Paradoxically, the perpetrator's real or apparent vulnerability after his departure, combined with the financial and emotional trauma his absence occasions for the rest of the family, often increases his influence with them. The mother's position will not improve without additional interventions, such as therapy, group support, social services, and financial help. In fact, it is usually more precarious, given the increased stress she is likely experiencing and the escalating demands on her resources that the father's absence entails.

In a previous article (Fish & Faynik, 1990), an example was given of a family which relocated in order to follow the perpetrator, who had been sentenced indefinitely to the forensics unit at a state mental hospital. No therapy or other interventions had been offered to the mother and children. Although this father did not see his children for almost three years, and saw his wife only every few weeks, he maintained an astounding amount of control over his family through his weekly half-hour phone calls home. Simultaneously, he remained impervious to the intensive treatment program in which he was confined.

We must always assume, therefore, that the perpetrator is endeavoring to influence his wife and family, and strive to learn how this is happening and what are the effects. This information about ongoing interaction is as important to treatment as the details of the past, explicitly sexual, abuse. Perpetrators routinely feel threatened by the possibility that the family will ally with the therapist and not with them. They will take pains to discourage both the family and the therapist from joining together. It is important, therefore, for the therapist to remember that, even after legal intervention, the perpetrator's hold over his wife and family may be significant. He is likely to lie to them about the abuse (vilifying the victim and the authorities); play on their fears about his well-being (for instance, by threatening suicide); attempt to intimidate them verbally; threaten violence; encourage them to focus on the financial cost to the family of his separation; and otherwise pressure them directly and through others in anyway he can. His efforts will often be reinforced by societal and institutional factors that favor fathers and stepfathers at the expense of mothers, for example, by enabling him superior earning power, leading to greater control of financial resources. When the perpetrator does exert illegitimate influence with his wife, therapists or child protective workers who confront or penalize the perpetrator without involving the mother will usually do nothing more than to unite him further with his spouse against the larger system. Instead, elements of the larger system need to engage with the mother, understand the dilemmas which bind her to the perpetrator, and act toward the perpetrator with her consultation and, whenever possible, her assent. Ideally, the larger system offers her sufficient protection and support to increasingly challenge the perpetrator herself, establishing autonomy in her own way and leading, rather than following, the larger system in its efforts to heal the family, including the perpetrator.

When the perpetrator's illegitimate tactics are highlighted and blocked, the legitimate influence of the wife is shown to be formidable. It is an extraordinarily powerful experience for perpetrators to be confronted by their wives in sessions, under circumstances where the wives cannot be shouted down, ignored, distracted or mystified. Mothers need not be particularly forceful or eloquent or sophisticated, although they often are. When she is sufficiently supported by the larger system, the participation of the mother in the perpetrator's treatment can catalyze the therapy, intensifying the emotional impact of sessions as she represents her daughter's story and confronts the perpetrator's denial.

THE NATURE OF THE THERAPIST'S ALLIANCE WITH THE FAMILY

With each perpetrator we treat, we must continuously examine how to best ally with his family members. Too often, we assume they feel we are on their side. We frequently find that we do not have a solid coalition with the family, despite their attendance at sessions and apparently cooperative manner. The family often remains more under the perpetrator's influence than we acknowledge, and frequently perceives the community's intervention as making matters worse instead of better, with no positive end in sight. Some of the family's discouragement may result from the hard, painful work of the therapy per se. But it usually arises from the seemingly senseless burden of decreased income following the perpetrator's removal; time taken up with one meeting after another; the grinding work of trying to function as a single-parent family with extreme boundary ambiguity in regard to the perpetrator (Boss, 1977); the effects of stigma; a loyalty, however ambivalent, to the perpetrator; pressure from the perpetrator, extended family and social network; and a continuous sense of dislocation and anxiety about the future. When we do have a real alliance with the family, it is often because they have found or been provided with the emotional, financial and social resources that make it possible for them to somewhat disentangle themselves from the perpetrator's influence and to be more optimistic, or at least grimly determined, about surviving our treatment.

Herman (1981) has stated: ". . . a favorable outcome [of incest treatment] requires a drastic change in the balance of power within the family, in favor of the mother" (p. 153). From the very beginning of treatment, it is incumbent on each therapist treating any part of the family (but especially the perpetrator) to ally with the mother and to enhance her power within the family and the larger system. It is ironic and unfair that mothers must single-handedly be responsible for so much of the healing required by their families. Given this, it is imperative that they be provided the resources they require to act in support of themselves and their families.

For this reason, the therapist should actively monitor how the larger system engages with her. For instance, the legal system often mandates mothers' involvement in treatment. Sanctions that directly or indirectly impact on mothers, which are not balanced with tangible support, will be unproductive and gratuitously punitive. The therapist should use her or his influence in the larger system to assure that sanctions which affect the mother are adequately balanced by real help.

For example, the therapist and larger system should try to protect mothers who attempt to influence the perpetrator's cooperation with treatment. Any risks the mother may run in confronting the perpetrator should be carefully assessed and neutralized as completely as possible. The mother will usually be the best judge of whether she is safe. Also, any treatment program that the mother is expected to participate in should be planned, whenever feasible, so that her preferences are respected and her time, energy and other resources are conserved.

CONCLUSION

The willingness of the perpetrator to habitually abuse power is a prerequisite for the occurrence of incest. This habit of abuse of power does not disappear when the perpetrator enters treatment, but continues unabated. The therapist must assess and counter the perpetrator's misuse of power from the beginning for treatment to proceed. To do so, the therapist must form a coalition with the perpetrator's family, based on the therapist's empowerment and support of the mother. Because the community institutions which intervene in families where incest has occurred often operate on patriarchal assumptions, it is also the therapist's role to influence these systems to enhance the mother's status and resources.

NOTES

1. This is the case even when the mother and perpetrator separate and divorce during treatment, or were already divorced when the abuse was discovered. However, divorce introduces some additional complexity into these dynamics. For

purposes of simplicity, this paper will focus on the situation where the mother and perpetrator intend to remain together, however ambivalently.

2. The nature of Antiochus' riddle appears inconsistent with this principle. However, in having Antiochus ask a revealing riddle, Shakespeare repeats an element of the older stories from which he borrows his plot. Referring both to this play and the Oedipus legend, Taylor (1982) comments:

> The association of riddles with incest in the stories of Oedipus and Antiochus appears to be neither coincidental nor accidental. Since in many societies incest is the great taboo, the one truly inadmissible sin, all references to it must be veiled in the language of the riddle. In *The Elementary Structures of Kinship*, Levi Strauss describes cognate stories in Greek and Cambodian folklore "in which the king symbolically reveals his incestuous desires toward his daughter. . . . " (p. 71)

Taylor actually identifies two taboos here: incest, and admitting incest. As a social constraint, the latter is much more generally adhered to than the former, including in perpetrator treatment.

REFERENCES

Abel, G. G., Becker, J. V., Cunningham-Rathner, J., Mittelman, M. S., & Rouleau, J. L. (1988). Multiple paraphilic diagnoses among sex offenders. *Bulletin of the American Academy of Psychiatry and the Law*, *16*, 153-168.

Berlin, F. S. (1983). Sex offenders: A biomedical perspective and a status report on biomedical treatment. In J. G. Greer & I. R. Stuart (Eds.), *The sexual aggressor: Current perspectives on treatment* (pp. 83-123). New York: Van Nostrand Reinhold.

Boss, P. (1977). A clarification of the concept of psychological father absence in families experiencing ambiguity of boundary. *Journal of Marriage and the Family*, *39*, 141-151.

Conte, J. R. (1986). Sexual abuse and the family: A critical analysis. In T. S. Trepper & M. J. Barrett (Eds.), *Treating incest: A multiple systems perspective* (pp. 113-126). New York: Haworth Press.

Fish, V. & Faynik, C. (1990). Treatment of incest families with the father temporarily removed: A structural approach. *Journal of Strategic and Systemic Therapies*, *8*, 53-63.

Groth, A. N. (1982). The incest offender. In S. M. Sgroi (Ed.), *Handbook of clinical intervention in child sexual abuse* (pp. 215-239). Lexington, MA: Lexington Books.

Groth, A. N. (1983). Treatment of the sexual offender in a correctional institution. In J. G. Greer & I. R. Stuart (Eds.), *The sexual aggressor: Current perspectives on treatment* (pp. 160-176). New York: Van Nostrand Reinhold.

Herman, J. (1981). *Father-daughter incest*. Cambridge, MA: Harvard University Press.

Shakespeare, W. (1951). *William Shakespeare: The complete works (The players edition)*, P. Alexander (Ed.). London: Collins. (Originally published 1623 & 1664).

Sommers-Flanagan, R. & Walters, H. A. (1987). The incest offender, power, and victimization: Scales on the same dragon. *Journal of Family Violence*, *2*, 163-175.

Taylor, M. (1982). *Shakespeare's darker purpose: A question of incest*. New York: AMS Press.

Wheeler, D. (1989). Faulty fathering: Working ideas on the treatment of male incest perpetrators. *Journal of Feminist Family Therapy*, *1*, 27-48.

Sponsorship: Men Holding Men Accountable for Domestic Violence

Rhea V. Almeida
Michele Bograd

SUMMARY. In spite of feminist analyses of domestic violence that emphasize the social roots of battering, interventions with batterers are primarily conceptualized within the framework of the private psychotherapeutic encounter. Furthermore, it is still often women—be they battered women's advocates, shelter workers, or feminist clinicians—who hold batterers accountable for their violence. This article presents an alternative framework that suggests links between domestic violence and the social values of the privacy and autonomy of the family, as well as with male rites of passage organized around themes of violence or the devaluation of women. From this frame of reference, a central component to ending violence against women entails men holding men accountable for battering. The development of a community based male sponsor program that functions in conjunction with more conventional psychotherapy of batterers is described.

How can men assume the burden of responsibility for other men's violence and join the professional community in protecting women's lives in the privacy of their homes? Numerous articles on domestic violence have emphasized it is crucial to intervene from a gender sensitive perspective (Bograd, 1982, 1984; James & McIn-

---

Rhea V. Almeida, ACSW, is in private practice in Somerset, NJ 08873. She is Founder/Director for the Institute of Family Services and Adjunct Faculty at the Graduate School of Social Work, Rutgers University, 536 George Street, New Brunswick, NJ 08873. Michele Bograd, PhD, is a psychologist and marital therapist in private practice in Cambridge, MA. Correspondence may be sent to 63 Stowecroft Road, Arlington, MA 02174.

tyre, 1983; Pressman, 1989). Central to this thinking is that treatment of the battered woman or abusive man cannot occur within the patriarchical context of viewing psychological/interactional dynamics in isolation from the supporting societal/cultural context. Family life is viewed by society as a private matter. Therefore, treatment strategies aimed at shifting the power imbalance within the family alone, without accompanying social sanctions, run the grave risk of entering into a covert alliance with the abuser. For instance, when clinicians only investigate and reconstruct past psychological traumas of abusive men, they beg questions of the men's social responsibility for their violence. It is the societal context of the abuser that must also be addressed and restructured. This societal context is composed in part by the values and institutions that define family life and tacitly support violence against women, at least until recently. In and out of the family, power is distributed according to the hierarchy of men over women and children. Power is "control over choices and decisions concerning one's own life; control over the definition of one's relationships; the ability to influence others, especially one's mate; and access to resources and opportunities–economic, educational and vocational" (Avis, 1989, p. 5). This context of unequal power between men and women is further supported and perpetuated by patriarchal definitions of the family as a private and relatively autonomous unit (Eisler, 1987; Hare-Mustin & Maracek, 1986). These values promote an ideology of separatism between the public and private domains, between the community and the intimate lives of men and women. Thus, until recently, what transpired within the privacy of the home went unexamined. In this way, among others, our society tolerated husbands' physical oppression of their wives.

Through the efforts of the women's movement, there are growing sanctions against batterers (Schecter, 1982). Yet, although there now exist some legal channels for prosecuting batterers, domestic violence is commonly defined as a clinical problem where individual men seek therapy within relatively protected psychotherapeutic settings. Due to the separation of public and private life, the codes of ethics and morality that define criminal behavior in the public domain do not apply to domestic life. Additionally, it has been primarily women that have held batterers accountable for their domestic violence. Although there are a growing number of male-run programs for batterers (Adams & McCormick, 1982; Purdy & Nickle, 1981), it is the voices of feminist activists and battered women shelter advocates that most loudly speak out against male violence (Bograd, 1986; Controneo, 1988; MacKinnon & James, 1987). But men are crucial to the process of reordering patriarchal structures (Cath, Gurwitt & Munder, 1982; Taggart, 1985). A strong community response is crucial to breaking down the separation between the public and private domains that helps maintain wife battering. Non-clinical interventions are crucial for defining battering as a social and political problem.

In this article, we examine how domestic violence is perpetuated by social values concerning the privacy and autonomy of family life and by traditional male rites of passage. After a brief examination of the dangers of "psychologizing" a social problem, we suggest how clinical approaches to batterers can be significantly strengthened by *sponsors*, or the inclusion of non-violent men from the community as part of the intervention plan. Description of a model sponsors program is provided.

THE PRIVACY AND AUTONOMY OF FAMILY LIFE

"A man's home is his castle" is not simply a familiar dictum. It captures prevailing social beliefs that a man's home and the people within it are his private and personal domain, over which he wields legitimate control (Dobash & Dobash, 1977, 1978, 1979). Until recently, what transpired within the home was not open to public scrutiny. Although a man would be criminally prosecuted for beating a stranger, less than 100 years ago, he could legally physically chastise his wife, who could not press charges against him (Fields, 1978; Gelles, 1981; Lane, 1976; Lystad, 1975). Even now, although we have seen an important increase in the support laws for restraining orders against batterers and in regulations mandating police reporting of domestic violence, physical assaults against wives are still seen as less objectionable than crimes against strangers (Gil, 1986). In this way, although recent years have witnessed significant changes in attitudes about wife battering, we still witness hesitancy about public involvement in the "private" matter of domestic violence.

MALE BONDING, RITES OF PASSAGE, AND THE DEVALUATION OF WOMEN

Why communities and, specifically, men in the community have remained silent on husbands' violence against wives is a complicated issue. We want to emphasize one facet. Historically, men have promoted group solidarity with each other through the devaluation of women (Doyle, 1983). "Being men together" is often accomplished by verbally objectifying or degrading women, or bragging about sexual exploits. Too often, the devaluation of women is not simply symbolic: witness gang rapes, "wilding," or boys going to brothels together. In these acts, domination of women, sexuality and violence are joined. Gerzon (1984) speaks to the interrelationship between masculine identity, rites of passage, and negation of the feminine:

> For every pro-feminist, there is his counterpart. . . . Until the seventies, Americans of all ages and of all educational and income levels were in wide agreement about what traits are masculine. . . . men are expected to be very aggressive, not at all emotional, very dominant, not excitable, very competitive, rough, and unaware of others' feelings. And women are expected to be more or less the opposite.
>
> If this is what maleness is, then a young man must find ways to demonstrate those traits. Without a rite of passage, he can only prove what he is not. Not a faggot, a pussy, a queer. Not a pushover, a loser, or a lightweight. Not a dimwit or a dunce. Not a jerk or a nobody. Not a prick or a pansy. Not, above all, anything that is feminine. Indeed, without clear rites of passage, the only way to be a man is essentially negative: to not be a woman.
>
> A 16-year-old who lives in a comfortable suburb throws a large rock from a freeway overpass through the windshield of a car. The victim, a 31-year-old housewife, suffers a concus-

> sion but survives. "You do it for the thrill," the boy says. "It's a boring town," says one of his classmates. (p. 8)

While Gerzon paints a universal portrait of manhood, how masculinity is defined and manifested depends on ethnic and class differences. For instance, how violence is played out within the particular ecological and cultural milieu necessitates a range of complex therapeutic solutions (Griffith & Jones, 1978; Jones & Korchin, 1982). Black men who exist within a history of oppression, are already stressed from their membership within the black community (Moritsugu & Sue, 1983). Consequently they enter treatment with considerable distrust of a largely white therapeutic context. Similarly, Asian Indian men, who not only carry a burden of minority status in this culture but come with a history of poverty and oppression, are also more disadvantaged than their white counterparts (Rabkin, 1979). In as much as we are informed about the ethnic variants that are relevant to the way in which numerous problems present themselves (Gibbs & Huang, 1989; McGoldrick, Garcia-Preto, Hines & Lee, 1989; Staples & Mirande, 1980), we need to acknowledge these variations in the meanings attributed to the violence. It is essential that assumptions about men and their violence be tempered with great sensitivity to issues of class, ethnicity and race.

If it is true that many men bond with other men through the devaluation of women or through group rites of passage that victimize women (Dobash & Dobash, 1979), then we can begin to understand why many men have remained silent as others have physically assaulted their wives. But we also can see the seeds for healing here. Men can provide men with ways of bonding and being masculine that do not rest on the negation and brutalization of women.

PSYCHOTHERAPY AS A PRIVATE SOLUTION

Separate public and private domains and how male solidarity is accomplished co-exist with current conceptualizations of battering as a clinical, not a social, problem. In other words, psychotherapy is seen as the intervention of choice with batterers as notions of rehabilitation take prominence over those of punishment—in spite of the fact that research has shown that the most effective way to stop battering is through legal or criminal sanctions (Sherman & Berk, 1984). Psychotherapeutic interventions maintain the split between private actions and public accountability, as the batterer disappears into the community mental health center offices, often without any outside monitoring of his commitment to therapy. In fact, although some batterers are legally mandated to attend therapy, it is not uncommon that legal action is dropped once the batterer seeks therapy. In therapy, violence becomes a private individual affair—often in ways that neutralize the social consequences of the man's violence.

What can happen in therapy? In spite of the development of models for treating batterers, the man's domestic violence is often minimized or misdiagnosed (Penfold & Walker, 1983). His current violence disappears in clinical formulations of "explosive personality" or other character disorders. His treatment then entails medication, assertiveness training for the "appropriate" expression of anger, self-exploration of past history of losses, substance abuse and family-of-origin issues. Sometimes he is referred to substance abuse programs that may or may not address his ongoing violence. In these ways, personality problems are deemed more clinically important than the ongoing violence; past traumas take precedence over current behaviors; and de-emphasizing the violence covertly sanctions it. When the major focus is on the batterer's private inner emotional states or clinical symptoms, it negates the necessity for social accountability—a public matter (Stark, Flitcraft, & Frazier, 1979).

As importantly, many batterers who are referred to therapy do not feel compelled to address their violence against women. Because follow-through is often voluntary, these men either refuse treatment or drop out prematurely. Many batterers reject the idea of accepting treatment for their violence by mostly female mental health professionals. When men stay in therapy, they are often treated by well meaning clinicians who lack special training in domestic violence. Because of the volatility and complexity of these cases, many mental health centers lack the mechanisms for managing the man's violence. Since most family service agencies run on a structure of weekly appointments and no night call, the violence cannot be monitored. Therapists are often unavailable at critical times in the abuse cycle. Also, therapists, male or female, carry very little leverage with violent men. In fact, police and court action—not therapy—have shown promise in controlling men's violence (Wardell, Gillespie & Leffler, 1983). Therefore, holding the batterer accountable for his violence solely within a therapeutic milieu, with the professional restrictions of ethics and confidentiality (Hines & Hare-Mustin, 1978), limits the effectiveness of eradicating domestic violence.

NEW DIRECTIONS

How then can we intervene with men who batter in ways that simultaneously address the violence and the structure of the family, social norms and male solidarity, the private and public? First, as long as domestic violence is addressed only within the privacy of the home or in therapeutic settings, our interventions are weakened, if not ineffective. Second, we must reconceptualize the patriarchal values of privacy and domination that still define contemporary family life. Third, we must define assault against wives as a social problem that requires community intervention and social consequences that support and amplify the power of conventional clinical interventions.

Non-violent men are crucial to this process of transforming patriarchal structures. Men must begin to take responsibility for other men's violence against wives in the interest of human consciousness, rather than experiencing their involvement as a form of betrayal of other men. When men from the society at large are involved in the treatment of men who batter, this sanctions the therapeutic process within the public domain (Kaufman, 1987). This does not mean that women cannot effectively treat batterers. But women clinicians possess limited status at the societal level and must also guard against carrying, once again, the burden of change for abusive men.

Another level of accountability is enforced when men of the community are involved in the clarification and redefinition of the problem. In this way, a different kind of male bonding and rite of passage are enacted. Instead of men connecting together around the negation and victimization of women, they are joined in a compassionate and collaborative effort to find and preserve human integrity. This new kind of male connection between the batterer and men of the community expands the relevant intervention context beyond the largely feminine and private context of therapy, while replacing restrictive standards of maleness with different values about relational responsibility and public accountability (Goldner, 1985, 1987; Imber-Black, 1988; Wheeler, 1989). Through a different quality of connection, with other men, batterers can learn to be powerful but not at the cost of others, and to feel masculine without a rite of passage of violence. The inclusion of men from the community combats the common social isolation of batterers. It also challenges the social values that maintain that battering is a personal affair of private family life, and suggests instead that it is a social problem of legitimate public concern.

SPONSORSHIP: A MODEL PROGRAM

In one mental health setting, these ideas have been put into practice through developing a program where non-violent men from the community are a crucial part of the intervention efforts aimed at eradicating domestic violence. The objective of our program is to protect women and children from the unrelenting violence that pervades their lives. (For specifics of this comprehensive treatment program for battered women and their partners, see Almeida, 1987.) In this program, violence is defined as physical abuse, but also includes any sort of enforced social and psychological subordination such as financial hostage-taking, control of social relationships, and demands that the woman be unquestionably accepting of family life and responsibility as defined by her male partner. Treatment combines family and group therapy. Children are included in much of the treatment process because they suffer the consequences of violence long after it has ceased (Elbow, 1982; Gil, 1970). Central to our program is the concept of a "sponsor," derived from social networking theory (Klein, 1984; Litwak, 1985; Tolsdorf, 1976), and the Alcoholics Anonymous Model (AA).

Definition of Sponsorship

In the AA model, a sponsor is someone (well into his or her own recovery) who provides a symbol of permanent support for the alcoholic while he obtains sobriety and beyond. For our purposes, however, a sponsor is a man outside of the treatment context who does *not* have a history of violence, who "adopts" a violent man in treatment. We use a sponsor because it is our belief that we need to include representatives from the community in order to alter societal structures that sanction violence against women and children. Treatment offered only within the privacy of our offices colludes with the patriarchical oath of silence regarding the violence against women. Other non-violent men need to dialogue with abusers about the relationship between power, ownership and violence. We have experimented with sponsors with abusers in voluntary out-patient care, but our sponsor program is also feasible with abusers in mandated treatment or inpatient units as well. Sponsors are especially important when women refuse the services of a shelter because the sponsors are crucial in the monitoring of the violence at critical times in the abuse cycle. Additionally, sponsors can reinforce the importance of therapy for the abuser, insuring that he remain in treatment. As members of the batterer's community, a sponsor has more leverage than does the therapist alone.

Process of Sponsor Selection and Criteria

We have found that sponsors are particularly effective when the batterer and his partner are still living together and refuse to separate or use a shelter. Even when the couple decide to separate we try to persuade the batterer to remain in therapy with the sponsor, to deter yet another relationship of violence. The couple together with the sponsor are the central focus in treatment. The sponsor is a man that may be chosen by the couple or by our staff. The couple is told that violence cannot be addressed through therapy alone and that the use of a sponsor holds great promise. Most couples enter treatment voluntarily when the women threaten to leave, or a physician insists that the couple seek therapy after treating the woman for battering injuries. This disclosure leaves the abuser temporarily vulnerable. It is this emotional discomfort of the abuser that is capitalized upon to convince the abuser to use a sponsor for a limited period. The couple is offered the opportunity of speaking with abusers who have successfully completed the program to help alleviate their fears of exposure. Sometimes, segments of videotapes of other couples and sponsors are employed to reassure the couple of the process.

We encourage the couple to make the selection. Sometimes they choose a man from their social circle, church, or family. Guidelines for this selection are made clear to the couple. The woman's participation through selection and evaluation of sponsor is encouraged. This is to ensure that she is an active partner in this process, that her best interests are represented, and that she remains engaged in the process necessary to motivate the batterer to change. When the couple is able to solicit a sponsor that meets the criteria of the program, he is accepted. Potential sponsors with past histories of violence, mental illness, and involvement with drugs or alcohol are excluded. Sponsors who have major difficulties in their relationships with their wives or women in general are not suitable candidates. Specific criteria as well as clinical judgment are used to assess which sponsors would be beneficial role-models for the batterer. This sometimes requires dismissal of a sponsor after treatment has begun, when ambivalences towards verbal abuse might surface. We are concerned that sponsors with histories of past violence could easily enter into a camaraderie with batterers about violence as a form of male bonding, disconnected to the lives of the women. The sponsors are matched with the abusers according to ethnicity and religion when possible.

Frequently, couples cannot come up with a choice. In this instance, the program has a pool of sponsors made available through networking with fire departments, churches, men's auxiliary organizations, or off-duty policemen. Such contacts result from dedicated outreach and networking with these and other primarily male organizations. When preliminary information is available, attempts are made to avoid matches of policemen with drug abusers as this heightens the paranoia of the abusers and creates a conflict of interest for the police sponsors. Sponsors are also obtained from AA, when the abuser has a history with alcohol. With these sponsors, there has to be a philosophical reorientation to the burdens of violence that are quite different from alcoholism. Sponsors from AA endorse the forgiveness ethic in recovery. Women frequently complain this places an additional burden on them in their own struggles of giving up the co-dependent dance and entitling themselves to new options. When men in recovery become violent, there is a tendency on the part of male sponsors from AA to be forgiving of the violence as it is attributed to the stress of recovery. It is initially difficult for these sponsors to differentiate the process of addiction from that of social responsibility.

Training the Sponsors

Following the screening process, a female leader provides training for the sponsors through a consciousness raising group experience about violence and its political context. This is done through discussion groups, videotapes, role-plays and readings. The initial training including the screening interview lasts 3-4 hours. This process has to move quickly as treatment cannot begin without a sponsor. Much of the training continues in a parallel process to the treatment as issues emerge. For example, most sponsors initially believe that violence is something engaged in only by immoral men or men with deep seated problems. There is a total denial regarding the prevalence of male violence towards women as a traditional rite of passage. In spite of these common attitudes, the training builds on the fact that violence against women is not a part of the conscious experience of these men and is not tolerated by them in their private lives. They are also given didactic information to better comprehend the women's experience of violence and feminist perspectives on its treatment (Davidson, 1980; Dinnerstein, 1976).

During the training, discussions are structured to elicit information about their lives and personal values. This orientation sometimes creates a guardedness on their parts until they are more familiar with the process. Like most men, many sponsors are not used to personal sharing among men. Others have become extremely angered by how abusers intimidate women. We help them understand the connection between violence toward women and predominant definitions of masculinity. We try to assist them to shift their anger from individual batterers towards the societal structures that endorse male violence against women.

The Sponsor's Contract

Sponsors are expected to commit to the program for approximately six months. Frequently the sponsors stay connected to their sponsorees even when they take on new ones. The sponsor is expected to be on 24-hour call during the first 4-6 weeks of the treatment. Whenever there is a threat of violence, he is called by the abuser, his partner and sometimes the therapist. Telephone contact is the primary way the sponsor tries to calm the abuser and to discuss alternatives. If this does not diffuse the threat of violence, the sponsor is required to contact the police and proceed to the batterer's home. If the woman has been assaulted, a restraining order is obtained, and the abuser goes to the sponsor's or a relative's home. If the abuser has managed to control his physical assaultiveness, the sponsor takes him away from the home for a brief period and "talks him down." They return to the home, and the sponsor discusses strategies with the couple for resolving the conflict or managing the tension until the next therapy appointment.

The sponsor is educated by our program to the typical sorts of outbursts to expect with abusive men. These men usually do not constitute a threat to the sponsor and, if they do, the batterers are forewarned about our policy of police action. This policy states that the sponsor will press charges if he is assaulted at any time. Sponsors are also required to sign a release stating that they have volunteered to assist a citizen in the process of recovery from violence and to maintain confidentiality. The agency and therapists are exempt from any legal liabilities. The sponsors are usually adamant about their own self protection, and reassure us that they will contact the police if they are threatened.

Contract with the Batterer and His Partner

Therapists are always walking a tightrope between establishing a supportive treatment environment while, at the same time, defining the rules of social responsibility. The process of negotiation has to be carefully handled to avoid the possibility of the abuser gaining too much control and intimidating the therapist. Following the initial consultation with the abuser and his partner, an appointment is set up for the batterer and his partner to meet with the sponsor. In cases where the couple select the sponsor, he is brought in to meet with the therapist. In that session, the sponsor explains that he is willing to be of assistance to the abuser in ending the violence towards his family. It is in this session that we elicit more detailed information about the abuser's history of violence at work and social settings (the public domain), and within both partners' families of origin (the private domain). It is more common to find that violence occurs only within the home and not in any public setting. This punctuates the context of domestic violence and offers the opportunity to dialogue about society's definition of criminality, and therefore sanction of domestic violence. In order to minimize a hierarchical positioning between the sponsor and abuser, general political and personal information in the life of the sponsor are also shared with the abuser and his partner.

Whenever possible, the couple is required to set up a "safe room" that includes a telephone and a strong door lock as an intermediary protection for the woman. If the structure of the home permits it, we recommend that the woman have a room with a door leading to the outside. The woman is also encouraged to telephone the sponsor any time a violent episode is anticipated, in the event that the abuser does not. When this occurs, the sponsor is required to assume the responsibility of contacting the abuser on the telephone or in person. All of these contractual arrangements are made in the presence of the couple, the therapist and the sponsor, and jointly signed.

The Sponsor vis-à-vis the Therapeutic Context

The sponsor becomes an integral part of the therapeutic context that slowly shapes new choices in relationships between men and women. He collaborates with the therapist team through helping the batterer disconnect from his violence while supporting alternate types of relationships. These include assisting in the art of negotiation in personal relationships, and sharing anecdotes from his own relationships around problem-solving experiences.

In soliciting sponsors, we go to organizations where we anticipate some support. An appeal is made to the sense of courage and integrity that men value and like to share with others. We also attempt to choose men who have some understanding of the confidential nature of some of the material to which they will be privy. While they are permitted to publicly talk about their role as sponsors, they are requested to keep other specifics about the family private. Just as with any therapy group, within the group of sponsors that evolve over time, there is no guaranteed way of maintaining confidentiality. Sponsors are cautioned against keeping any secrets that abusers might choose to share with them. The sponsor and couple meet weekly, sometimes twice weekly depending on the frequency of the violence. When there are several couples entering treatment at one time, then they are seen in different subgroups. While there is no fixed pattern as to how the subgroups are seen, usually the therapist meets with the sponsors and abusers, while the women observe through the one-way mirror. During this process, there is an intense tracking of any instances of verbal/physical violence and alternatives to it. Within the same session the therapist meets with the couple and retraces "hot" issues in order to desensitize the abuser to the new context of control and negotiation. The abuser is permitted to request that his sponsor, who is observing from behind the mirror, enter the room whenever he feels unable to discuss an issue with his partner without an expression of violence. Issues such as work difficulties, money management, parenting, in-law relationships, drug and alcohol histories, and neighborhood problems are routinely discussed.

CONCLUDING COMMENTS

The prominence of feminist scholarship has raised our consciousness in the field of family therapy. It has offered new horizons in extending our therapeutic visions. Ideas over the last decade have redefined the context of therapy as needing to bridge women's personal lives with their political position in the larger societal context. Attempts to bring these analyses into treatment contexts have been problematic. This is largely due to how many therapeutic contexts still maintain a traditional value structure based on beliefs about the privacy and autonomy of the nuclear family and about conventional roles for men and women.

In articulating the link between social values of privacy and autonomy around family life and therapeutic contexts, as connected to male rites of passage that honor violence and devaluation of women, new ways of male bonding and new definitions of masculinity seem imperative. These new male rites of passage must include social values of public accountability and connectedness. When the system of therapy is no longer viewed as an autonomous healing system, but rather as one embedded within multiple complex systems that hold the power to sanction such healing, personal and public accountability for battering are joined. In this spirit, the use of male sponsors in the treatment of male batterers is one way to create structures that honor the human experience of connectedness and the physical and emotional protection of women.

REFERENCES

Adams, D.C. & McCormick, A.J. (1982). Men unlearning violence: A group approach based on the collective model. In M. Roy (Ed.), *The abusive partner*, (pp. 170-197). NY: Van Nostrand Reinhold.

Almeida, R. (1987). *Families in violence: A new treatment perspective*. Unpublished Manuscript. Available at 3 Clyde Road, Suite 101, Somerset, NJ 08873.

Avis, J. M. (1989). Integrating gender into the family therapy curriculum. *Journal of Feminist Family Therapy*, *1*, 3-26.

Bograd, M. (1982). Battered women, cultural myths and clinical interventions: A feminist analysis. *Women and Therapy*, *1*, 69-77.

Bograd, M. (1984). Family systems approaches to wife battering: A feminist critique. *American Journal of Orthopsychiatry*, *54*, 558-568.

Bograd, M. (1986). Family therapy and violence against women. In M. Riché (Ed.), *Women and family therapy*, (pp. 34-50). Rockville, MD: Aspen Systems.

Cath, S., Gurwitt, A., & Munder, J. (1982). *Father-son: Developmental and clinical perspectives*. Boston: Little Brown & Co.

Controneo, M. (1988). Women and abuse in the context of the family. In L. Braverman (Ed.), *Women, feminism and family therapy*, (pp. 81-96). NY: Haworth Press, Inc.

Davidson, T. (1980). *Conjugal crime: Understanding and changing the wifebeating pattern*. NY: Ballantine Books.

Dinnerstein, D. (1976). *The mermaid and the minotaur: Sexual arrangements and human malaise*. NY: Harper & Row.

Dobash, R.E. & Dobash, R.P. (1977-78). Wives: The "appropriate" victims of marital violence. *Victimology, 2*, 426-442.

Dobash, R.E. & Dobash, R.P. (1979). *Violence against wives: A case against the patriarchy*. NY: The Free Press.

Doyle, J. (1983). *The male experience*. Dubuque, IA: Wm. C. Brown.

Eisler, R. (1987). *The chalice and the blade: Our history, our future*. San Francisco: Harper and Row.

Elbow, M. (1982). Children of violent marriages: The forgotten victims. *Social Casework, 63*, 465-471.

Fields, M. (1978). Wife-beating: Government intervention policies and practices. In U.S. Civil Rights Commission (Ed.), *Battered women: Issues of public policy*. Washington, DC: U.S. Government Printing Office.

Gelles, R.J. (1981). Violence and the family: A review of the research in the seventies. *Journal of Marriage and the Family, 42*, 873-885.

Gerzon, M. (1984). *A choice of heroes: The changing faces of American manhood*. Boston: Houghton Mifflin.

Gibbs, J.T. & Huang, L.N. (1989). *Children of color: Psychological interventions with minority youth*. San Francisco: Jossey-Bass Inc.

Gil, D. (1970). *Violence against children: Physical child abuse in the United States*. Cambridge, MA: Harvard University Press.

Gil, D. (1986). Sociocultural aspects of domestic violence. In M. Lystad (Ed.), *Violence in the home: Interdisciplinary perspectives*, (pp. 124-149). NY: Brunner/Mazel Publishers.

Goldner, V. (1985). Feminism and family therapy. *Family Process, 24*, 31-47.

Goldner, V. (1987). Instrumentalism, feminism, and the limits of family therapy. *Journal of Family Psychology, 1*, 109-116.

Griffith, M. & Jones, E.E. (1978). Race and psychotherapy: Changing perspectives. *Current Psychiatric Therapies, 18*, 225-235.

Hare-Mustin, R.T. & Maracek, J. (1986). Autonomy and gender: Some questions for therapists. *Psychotherapy, 23*, 203-212.

Hines, P.M. & Hare-Mustin, R.T. (1978). Ethical concerns in family therapy. *Journal of Marital and Family Therapy, 9*, 165-171.

Imber-Black, E. (1988). Rituals of stabilization and change in women's lives. In M. McGoldrick, C. Anderson, & F. Walsh (Eds.), *Women in families: A framework for family therapy*, (pp. 451-469). NY: W.W. Norton.

James, K. & McIntyre, D. (1983). The reproduction of families: The social role of family therapy? *Journal of Marital and Family Therapy, 9*, 119-129.

Jones, E.E. & Korchin, S.J. (1982). *Minority mental health*. NY: Praeger.

Kaufman, E. (1987). *Beyond patriarchy: Essays by men on pleasure, power, and change*. NY: Oxford University Press.

Klein, E. (1984). *Gender politics from consciousness to mass politics*. Cambridge, MA: Harvard University Press.

Lane, R. (1976). Criminal violence in America: The first hundred years. *Annals of the American Academy of Political and Social Science, 423*, 1-13.

Litwak, E. (1985). *Helping the elderly*. NY: Guilford Press.

Lystad, M. (1975). Violence at home: A review of the literature. *American Journal of Orthopsychiatry, 45*, 328-345.

MacKinnon, L., & Miller, D. (1987). The new epistemology and the Milan approach: Feminist and socio-political implications. *Journal of Marital and Family Therapy, 13*, 139-155.

McGoldrick, M., Garcia-Preto, N., Hines, P.M., & Lee, E. (1989). Ethnicity and women. In M. McGoldrick, C. Anderson, & F. Walsh (Eds.), *Women in families: A framework for family therapy*, (pp. 169-199). NY: W.W. Norton.

Moritsugu, J. & Sue, S. (1983). Minority status as a stressor. In R. Felner, L. Jason, J. Moritsugu, & S. Farber (Eds.), *Preventive psychology: Theory, research and practice*. Elmsford, NY: Pergamon Press.

Penfold, P.S. & Walker, G.A. (1983). *Women and the psychiatric paradox*. Montreal: Eden Press.

Pressman, B. (1989). Wife-abused couples: The need for comprehensive theoretical perspectives and integrated treatment models. *Journal of Feminist Family Therapy, 1*, 23-43.

Purdy, F. & Nickle, N. (1981). Practice principles for working with groups of men who batter. *Social Work and Groups, 4*, 111-222.

Rabkin, J. (1979). Ethnic density and psychiatric hospitalization: Hazards of minority status. *American Journal of Psychiatry, 136*, 1562-1566.

Schecter, S. (1982). *Women and male violence*. Boston: South End Press.

Sherman, L.W. & Berk, R.A. (1984). Deterrent effects of arrest for domestic assault. *American Sociological Review, 49*, 261-272.

Staples, R. & Mirande, A. (1980). Racial and cultural variations among American families: A decennial review of the literature on minority families. *Journal of Marriage and the Family, 42*, 887-903.

Stark, E., Flitcraft, A. & Frazier, W. (1979). Medicine and patriarchal violence: The social construction of a "private" event. *International Journal of Health Services, 9*, 461-493.

Taggart, M. (1985). The feminist critique in epistemological perspective: Questions of context in family therapy. *Journal of Marital and Family Therapy, 11*, 113-125.

Tolsdorf, C. (1976). Social networks support and coping: An exploratory study. *Family Process, 15*, 407-417.

Wardell, L., Gillespie, D. & Leffler, A. (1983). Science and violence against wives. In D. Finkelhor, R. Gelles, G. Hotaling & M. Straus (Eds.), *The dark side of families*, (pp. 69-84). Beverly Hills, CA: Sage.

Wheeler, D. (1989). Faulty fathering: Working ideas on the treatment of male incest perpetrators. *Journal of Feminist Family Therapy, 1*, 27-48.

PART 5: NEW DIRECTIONS IN TRAINING

Family Therapy Training Issues of Male Students in a Gender-Sensitive Doctoral Program

Roberta L. Nutt

SUMMARY. Gender bias has been strongly demonstrated in counseling/therapy services in general and family therapy in particular. The counseling psychology doctoral and master's programs at Texas Woman's University emphasize family therapy and women's/gender issues. As the programs integrated the feminist critique of family therapy theory and practice, it became clear that both women's and men's sex-role stereotyping must be addressed if students were to be effective change agents working with families. This paper describes training issues involved in male student reactions to feminist family therapy perspectives and outlines course content for coverage of male issues in the training program.

Historically, gender bias has been strongly demonstrated in counseling/therapy services (Broverman, Broverman, Clarkson, Ro-

Roberta L. Nutt, PhD, is Professor of Psychology and Director of Counseling Psychology Doctoral Program, Department of Psychology and Philosophy, Texas Woman's University, P.O. Box 22996, Denton, TX 76204.

senkrantz, & Vogel, 1970; Chesler, 1972; Hare-Mustin, 1983; Sherman, 1980) and several sets of guidelines for gender-fair counseling/psychotherapy have been developed (Feminist Therapy Institute, 1987; Fitzgerald & Nutt, 1986; Gilbert, 1980, Rawlings & Carter, 1977; Task Force on Sex Bias and Sex Role Stereotyping, 1978). More recently, the issues of sexism and feminism in family therapy are being widely addressed (Ault-Riché, 1986; Goldner, 1985; Goodrich, Rampage, Ellman, & Halstead, 1988; Hare-Mustin, 1978, 1983, 1986; Luepnitz, 1988; McGoldrick, Anderson, & Walsh, 1989; Taggart, 1985, Walters, Carter, Papp, & Silverstein, 1988). Unfortunately, it is still true, however, that most textbooks and sourcebooks in family therapy lack references to feminist models and even fewer address special issues of men in families, particularly changing roles for men (Meth & Pasick, 1990). There is a growing body of literature on both counseling men and feminist psychology in counseling psychology but most of that information is not yet familiar to family therapists. Men's studies courses and programs are also developing in universities around the country.

The Department of Psychology and Philosophy at Texas Woman's University offers doctoral and master's degrees in counseling psychology which emphasize family therapy and women's/gender issues. The emphasis on family therapy/psychology neatly fits the developmental perspective of counseling psychology and the emphasis on women's/gender issues is very compatible with the goals of a woman's university. As our program began to integrate the feminist critique of family therapy theory and practice, it became clear that both women's and men's sex-role stereotyping must be addressed. Pittman (1985) suggests family therapists become "gender brokers" who help families sort out their gender roles and values, where they got them, and which ones they wish to retain and discard. By training students in sex-role analysis of both genders, this brokering becomes possible. While women's and feminist issues had been discussed in a variety of courses, little attention had been given to companion men's issues. It was also much more difficult to locate resources for teaching men's issues. Twenty years of the women's movement and women's studies had produced a large body of writing. The men's movement is much younger, so fewer materials are available (Bule, 1990).

Related to male issues in general is the reaction of male graduate students to the gender structure of the counseling/family psychology programs at TWU. The director of the program, half of the departmental faculty, and most of the administrators of the university are women. Therefore, male students are not only expected to address sexist issues in therapy in particular and the culture in general, but many of their professors and supervisors are women, and they are attending a university which historically has focused on the needs of women. For some, this has created feelings of sex-role reversal and minority group status. A training challenge is how to use positively the numerical minority group status of the male students while giving them greater understanding of women's experience.

This paper details training dilemmas of male students in their initial exposure to feminist family therapy issues. I will examine differences between male and female students, stresses between female faculty and male students, and male struggles to understand female perspectives. To facilitate curriculum development in family therapy regarding men's issues and their relevance to feminist family therapy, an outline of pertinent topics and key references are presented.

RESPONSES OF MALE STUDENTS TO FEMINIST CURRICULUM

In general, males students respond thoughtfully and positively to feminist family therapy perspectives. We suspect that an initial self-screening occurs in men who chose to matriculate in a family therapy oriented graduate program that emphasizes women's/gender issues at a women's university. Women graduate students frequently comment on the woman-positive attitudes of their male peers. That is not to suggest, however, that there are no struggles or stresses.

Little concern was expressed by male students regarding being supervised by female faculty which seems related to the efforts of the faculty to role model equity. Occasionally, there is a tendency for students to go to male faculty for decisions and female faculty for nurturing/understanding. We attempt to emphasize the power of the female faculty, particularly by noting the areas in which they are in charge, and the caring of the male faculty. That several male faculty are very involved in the lives of their children helps this balance.

Male students experience some feelings of role reversal. While some have felt welcomed and attended to, others have felt some anger expressed toward them as males and reported their ideas had been ignored or discounted by female students. One reported, "With female peers, I find that humor is often prejudiced against men: men's lack of sensitivity toward women; sexual humor with men as victim, inept actor, bungling idiot, cuckold, etc. This humor is often the reverse of 'locker room humor.'" When I perceive what one student called "male bashing" in the classroom, I acknowledge the anger but challenge the linear thinking involved in blaming men. Just as Rawlings and Carter (1977) point out that neither men nor women are the enemy, it is important to examine how cultural stereotypes victimize and damage everyone. Male issues are often then addressed as companion or counterpoint issues.

These students also described these encounters as positive learning experiences: "(they) were discomforting and led to . . . introspective questioning"; "I have the beginnings of an understanding of the feelings many women must have when these things happen to them." None reported feeling discriminated against by faculty, but one did feel challenged to have "an instant understanding of women's issues, gender bias" and was concerned that he could risk "a major faux pas in . . . conversation . . . with a faculty woman." He did go on to "wonder if this is how a woman feels in a male oriented environment." One student described situations in which "female persons take the position of 'protector' or 'mentor' and seem to watch over the guys. At times, this becomes a case of mama watching over the little boy(s)." Again, this was viewed as a lesson in understanding women's experiences in other situations.

Discrimination is partly averted through feminist pedagogy which emphasizes student participation, use of first names and absence of hierarchy, and use of student's own experience as a primary source of learning (Andersen, 1987; Boxer, 1982; Bricker-Jenkins & Hooyman, 1987; Klein, 1987; Perreault, 1983). It also aims to train students to be change agents.

One male reaction to feminist material, particularly topics that relate to male violence against women, is male guilt. One male student burst into tears at hearing how constantly vigilant the female students in the class were in taking precautions against rape. He had not realized the continuous burden of the problem.

Relationships with women were reported to have changed. "No longer is there an underlying sense of attraction or seduction. Rather, I find that my relationships are more open and honest with equality rather than one-up/one-down. My relationships with men have also changed. I find that there is more sharing among my male friends and less competing." Said another, "I became so much more aware—and accepting—of my own feminine and masculine parts." Another challenged his former emphasis on masculine "antidependence" and found himself moving toward interdependence in his marriage. While another described finding himself "expecting more of women (intelligence, personality, etc.) and being somewhat perturbed when women in my life allow, accept, and welcome subservient roles." Fathers described trying to respect their daughters more and a greater commitment to their development and opportunities.

Male students expressed appreciation for being challenged on their gender biases and for being required to examine gender bias in family therapy. Stated one, "I have not been as aware as I thought I was." Said another, "I have seen how the family unit is enmeshed in the culturally defined stereotyped roles" and how that relates to "dysfunctional activity." And another related, "women's/gender issues . . . became more and more relevant—and useful—as I began to take my therapy *seriously*. I realized what an integral part these issues play in performing therapy effectively and with sensitivity." Another was "much more in touch with issues of 'power' in families (e.g., power differential)—much greater understanding of relationships (e.g., how men and women view intimacy, autonomy, separation, etc.)."

The coverage of women's issues seemed to awaken interest in and sensitivity to their own concerns about growth and change in their societal roles. In our feminist context, male students have requested a separate psychology of men course. Although we address these issues in a variety of other courses, the men felt a course that focused specifically on men's issues would help broaden their understanding of themselves, their clients, and families. They were excited to see how women's and men's issues fit together in creating a healthier family environment. This growing attention to changing male awareness has been a logical progression, given the feminist emphasis of the program. As Hare-Mustin (1986) pointed out, "Family systems therapy, including structural and strategic approaches, is characterized by beta prejudice, ignoring differences when they do exist" (p. 20). The danger of ignoring gender differences is that the therapist supports the societal status quo of differences in power, resources, needs, and interests of family members. Our program is committed to the belief that sex-role stereotyping injures individuals and families and that only by examining and challenging them can healthy families develop.

MEN'S ISSUES AND FAMILY THERAPY: MAJOR THEMES AND READINGS

While the request for a separate course in the psychology of men has been proposed and accepted by the department, it is critically important that these issues, like those of women and feminist approaches, be integrated into the entire curriculum. This section will highlight major themes that may be addressed in these courses and provides key readings that might be used. Some general texts have relevant sections for several themes and may be repeated. References under counseling men may also summarize major themes.

Masculinity: Advantages and Disadvantages

The beginning of consciousness-raising is definitional, as we ask male and female students to describe what they mean by masculinity. Students easily generate lists that include strong instrumental adjectives like ambitious, competitive, autonomous, competent, confident, unemotional, powerful, logical, leader, etc. Understanding the impact of the descriptions takes much more work. Women students often easily identify the advantages of the male sex-role. Pittman (1985) suggests that most women are aware of gender issues because of the limitations they feel in their gender role, while men often do not think specifically about their roles. Sattel (1976) suggests men maintain the power inherent in their sex role through inexpressiveness and lack of awareness.

Next, we examine the hazards of male socialization. Health issues are usually the most readily apparent to students, since data reveal that men die younger and suffer more heart attacks and stress disorders than women. Less obvious to students are the costs in quality of life. Male difficulties with intimacy, attachment, and commitment (related to their early socialization that emphasizes autonomy and individuation) have serious consequences for the quality of personal and family life (Chodorow, 1974, 1978; Erikson, 1968; Gilligan, 1982).

SUGGESTED READINGS

Carter, S., & Sokol, J. (1987). *Men who can't love*. New York: Berkley Books.

David, D. S., & Brannon, R. (Eds.). (1976). *The forty-nine percent majority: The male sex role*. Reading, MA: Addison-Wesley.

Farrell, W. (1974). *The liberated man*. New York: Bantam.

Farrell, W. (1986). *Why men are the way they are*. New York: McGraw-Hill.

Fasteau, M. F. (1974). *The male machine*. New York: McGraw-Hill.

Fine, R. (1987). *The forgotten man: Understanding the male psyche*. New York: Harrington Park Press.

Goldberg, H. (1976). *The hazards of being male*. New York: New American Library.

Meth, R. & Pasick, R. (1990). *Men in therapy: The challenge of change*. New York: Guilford.

Moyers, B., & Bly, R. (1990). A gathering of men. New York: Public Affairs Television and Journal Graphics. (Air date: January 8, 1990).

O'Neil, J. M. (1981). Male sex role conflicts, sexism, and masculinity: Psychological implications for men, women, and the counseling psychologist. *The Counseling Psychologist*, *9*, 61-80.

Pittman, F. (1990). The masculine mystique. *The Family Therapy Networker*, *14*, 40-52.

Pleck, J. H. (1984). *The myth of masculinity*. Cambridge, MA: MIT Press.

Pleck, E. H., & Pleck, J. H. (1980). *The American male*. Englewood Cliffs, NJ: Prentice-Hall.

Rubin, M. (1980). *Men without masks*. Reading, MA: Addison-Wesley.

Sattel, J. W. (1976). The inexpressive male: Tragedy or sexual politics? *Social Problems*, *23*, 469-477.

Witkin-Lanoil, G. (1986). *The male stress syndrome*. New York: Berkley Books.

Relationships with Other Men

It is important to examine the father-son relationship, especially its characteristic distance or content. In a culture that expects men to be good providers, there is often little time for quality relationships with spouse, children, and friends. A boy's wish to identify with his father is made difficult by the father's often shadowy existence in his world, and he is left vulnerable and wounded when the father is often absent, or inexpressive and distant when home. Helping male students examine their relationships with their fathers makes them better therapists and better fathers, while witnessing that examination aids female students in treating men and living with the men in their own lives.

Men's relationships with other men have been criticized as activity-oriented and not emotionally sharing and supportive. Often men report that they only turn to their wives to share their feelings and seek emotional support. This has a devastating effect on marriage as it places the emotional burden on the female partner and also deprives many men of the pleasure of close male friendships. The use of rituals by leaders in the men's movement is aimed at strengthening that connection.

SUGGESTED READINGS

Bliss, S. (1986). Beyond machismo: The new men's movement. *Yoga Journal* (Nov.-Dec.), 36-40, 56-58.

Bliss, S. (1986). The men of the wound. *The Men's Journal*, (summer).

Bly, R. (1986). Men's initiation rites. *Utne Reader* (April/May), *15*, 42-43, 45-49.

Chesler, P. (1978). *About men*. New York: Simon and Schuster.
Cosby, B. (1986). *Fatherhood*. New York: Berkley Books.
Druck, K., & Simmons, J. C. (1985). *The secrets men keep*. New York: Ballantine Books.
Garfinkel, P. (1985). *In a man's world: Father, son, brother, friend, and other roles men play*. New York: New American Library.
Keen, S. (1986). The rites of manhood. *GQ* (August), 164-167.
Merton, A. (1987). Father hunger. *New Age Journal*, *13*, 25-29, 72.
Naifeh, S., & Smith, G. W. (1984). *Why can't men open up*? New York: Warner Books.
Neubauer, P. B. (1986). Reciprocal effects of fathering on parent and child. In G. I. Fogel, F. M. Lane, & R. S. Liebert (Eds.), *The psychology of men: New psychoanalytic perspectives*. New York: Basic Books.
O'Connor, T. (1990). A day for men. *The Family Therapy Networker*, *14*, 36-39.
Osherson, S. (1986). *Finding our fathers*. New York: Fawcett Columbine.
Pasick, R. S. (1990). You've got a friend. *The Family Therapy Networker*, *14*, 46-47.
Pittman, F. (1990). The masculine mystique. *The Family Therapy Networker*, *14*, 40-52.
Thompson, K. (1982). What men really want: A New Age Interview with Robert Bly. *New Age Journal*, *7*, 30-37, 50-51.

Sexuality and Relationships

Male sex-role stereotyping also encourages men to treat women as sex objects rather than intimate partners. Masculinity is still measured by sexual prowess and performance, creating standards that are usually impossible to meet. Zilbergeld (1978) described the male fantasy model of sex as a penis "two feet long, hard as steel, and can go all night" (p. 21). Men fear admitting to other men and women that they do not live up to this model. This programming also creates hostility in men toward women because men believe women expect the impossible. Good dialogue between male and female students in class helps explode some of these myths and can focus as well on how sex-role stereotyping inhibits intimacy and ways to develop better communication patterns and equity in relationships. This leads naturally to a detailed study of family therapy approaches and the need to explore issues of gender within family patterns.

SUGGESTED READINGS

Farrell, W. (1986). *Why men are the way they are*. New York: McGraw-Hill.

Fasteau, M. F. (1974). *The male machine*. New York: McGraw-Hill.

Goldberg, H. (1979). *The new male: From self-destruction to self-care*. New York: New American Library.

Goldberg, H. (1983). *The new male-female relationship*. New York: New American Library.

Goldberg, H. (1987). *The inner male: Overcoming roadblocks to intimacy*. New York: New American Library.

Pittman, F. (1990). The masculine mystique. *The Family Therapy Networker, 14*, 40-52.

Real men do do housework. (1990, Spring). *People Weekly*, 103-104.

Skjei, E., & Rabkin, R. (1981). *The male ordeal: Role crisis in a changing world*. New York: G. P. Putnam's Sons.

Walls, C. (1987). Back off, buddy. *Time* (October 12), 68-73.

Zilbergeld, B. (1978). *Male sexuality*. Boston: Little, Brown.

Work, Career, and Success

Our culture evaluates masculinity by success in career, status of occupation, and financial standing. We emphasize that each individual needs to specify his or her own definition of success. Students are encouraged to take an individualized look at the definition of success and to examine the relative importance of job satisfaction, family life, hobbies and leisure, money, and status. Since both men and women work for the same basic motivation of survival, pleasure, and contribution (Astin, 1985), we assume any gender differences are a function of sex-role socialization and the perceived structure of opportunity.

The structure of sports and the military have been described as a proving ground for masculinity and as the model on which American business is built. Both promote competition with clear-cut winners and losers (Loden, 1985; Melia, 1986). The costs of competition versus cooperation warrant examination.

Related to work, career, and success issues is the phenomenon of midlife career change. One common reason for men changing careers is that the initial career was not the person's own choice, often a result of family and sex-role expectations. Sensitivity in dealing with the issues of changing self-definition and the accompanying doubt, sadness, and anxiety are important. The term midolescence has been coined because this life stage resembles adolescence in that it upsets all aspects of a man's life—mental, physical, emotional, and spiritual.

SUGGESTED READINGS

Bernard, J. (1981). The good-provider role: Its rise and fall. *American Psychologist*, *36*, 1-12.

Borman, C. A., & Guido-Dibrito, F. (1986). Strategies for midlife career counseling. *Texas Association for Counseling and Development Journal*, 5-11.

Brenton, M. (1976). The breadwinner. In D. S. David & R. Brannon (Eds.), *The forty-nine percent majority: The male sex role*. Reading, MA: Addison-Wesley.

Coleman, J. S. (1976). Athletics in high school. In D. S. David & R. Brannon (Eds.), *The forty-nine percent majority: The male sex role*. Reading, MA: Addison-Wesley.

Farrell, W. (1976). Super bowl. In D. S. David & R. Brannon (Eds.), *The forty-nine percent majority: The male sex role*. Reading, MA: Addison-Wesley.

Fasteau, M. F. (1974). *The male machine*. New York: McGraw-Hill.

Finnegan, R., Westefeld, J., & Elmore, R. (1981). A model for a midlife career-decision-making workshop. *The Vocational Guidance Quarterly*, *30*, 69-72.

Goldberg, H. (1976). *The hazards of being male*. New York: New American Library.

Gould, R. (1976). Measuring masculinity by the size of a paycheck. In D. S. David & R. Brannon (Eds.), *The forty-nine percent majority: The male sex role*. Reading, MA: Addison-Wesley.

Isaacson, L. E. (1981). Counseling male midlife career changers. *The Vocational Guidance Quarterly*, *29*, 324-331.

Perosa, S. L., & Perosa, L. M. (1983). The midcareer crisis: A description of the psychological dynamics of transition and adaptation. *The Vocational Guidance Quarterly*, *32*, 69-79.

Roach, J. (1972). Confessions of a househusband. *Ms*, *1*, 25-27.

Sagal, K., & DeBlassie, R. (1981). The male midlife crisis and career change. *Journal of Employment Counseling*, *18*, 34-42.

Violence and War

Related to the toughness of sports is the image of man as soldier. We teach men that masculinity means being a hero, even at the price of sacrificing life. Television and movies are filled with scenes of violence that suggest it is the normal, manly way to live. Douglas MacArthur repeatedly said, "that the greatest thing a man can do is die in battle" (Fine, 1987, p. 116). This programming for aggression also defines feeling and expressing fear as unmasculine which creates another way in which men are cut off from feeling and expressing their feelings. Feminists suggest that the cultural attitude toward male violence also encourages the high rate of sexual and physical abuse in the country. When feelings are cut off and aggression is idealized, it is easier to abuse a victim that one perceives as an object.

SUGGESTED READINGS

Broyles, W. (1984). Why men love war. *Esquire*, *102*, 55-58, 61-62, 65.

Eisler, R. (1987). *The chalice and the blade*. San Francisco: Harper & Row.

Fasteau, M. F. (1974). *The male machine*. New York: McGraw-Hill.

Fine, R. (1987). *The forgotten man: Understanding the male psyche*. New York: Harrington Park Press.

Komisar, L. (1976). Violence and the masculine mystique. In D. S. David & R. Brannon (Eds.), *The forty-nine percent majority: The male sex role*. Reading, MA: Addison-Wesley.

Stouffer, S. A. et al. (1976). Masculinity and the role of the combat soldier. In D. S. David & R. Brannon (Eds.), *The forty-nine percent majority: The male sex role*. Reading, MA: Addison-Wesley.

Homosexuality

Examination of stereotypes and personal prejudices precedes readings aimed at equipping students to better understand and counsel homosexual clients, couples, and families. Our program supports the American Psychological Association, in particular, Division 44—Lesbian and Gay Issues, stance that homosexuality is an alternative life style. A number of gay and lesbian students have matriculated in our graduate program and been open about their sexual preferences. Some students express discomfort with homosexual issues, but acceptance of their backgrounds and socialization and the openness of classroom discussion are designed to allow for self-examination and growth. Gay psychologists in the area are also available for consultation and supervision.

SUGGESTED READINGS

Bozett, F. (1985). Gay men as fathers. In S. Hanson & F. Bozett (Eds.), *Dimensions of fatherhood*. Beverly Hills, CA: Sage.

Bozett, F. (1987). *Gay and lesbian parents*. Westport, CT: Praeger.

Bozett, F. (1989). *Homosexuality and the family*. New York: Harrington Park Press.

Bozett, F., & Sussman, M. (1989). *Homosexuality and family relationships*. New York: Harrington Park Press.

Brown, L. (1989). Lesbians, gay men and their families: Common clinical issues. *Journal of Gay and Lesbian Psychotherapy, 1*, 65-77.

Carl, D. (1986). Acquired immune deficiency syndrome: A preliminary examination of the effects on gay couples and coupling. *Journal of Marital and Family Therapy, 12*, 241-247.

Cass, V. (1979). Homosexual identity formation: A theoretical model. *Journal of Homosexuality, 4*, 219-236.

Coleman, E. (1987). *Integrated identity for gay men and lesbians: Psychotherapeutic approaches for emotional well-being*. New York: Harrington Park Press.

Gochros, J. (1989). *When husbands come out of the closet*. New York: Harrington Park Press.

Malyon, A. K. (1982). Psychotherapeutic implications of internalized homophobia in gay men. *Journal of Homosexuality, 7*, 59-70.

McWhirter, D., & Mattison, A. (1982). Psychotherapy for gay male couples. *Journal of Homosexuality, 7*, 79-92.

McWhirter, D., & Mattison, A. (1984). *The male couple*. Englewood Cliffs, NJ: Prentice-Hall.

Paff, B. (1985). Sexual dysfunction in gay men requesting treatment. *Journal of Sex and Marital Therapy, 11*, 3-18.

Stein, T., & Cohen, C. (Eds.) (1986). *Contemporary perspectives on psychotherapy with lesbians and gay men*. New York: Plenum.

Ethnic Minorities

Understanding ethnic minority male issues and how they differ from white male issues has significant impact on counseling/therapy. This is the area that needs the most enhancement. While substantial literature exists on female minority group members, less is published on men of color, especially in the family therapy literature. It also seems that what literature exists on minority males focuses on black men and occupational issues. More is needed to understand unique developmental issues of men of color and their impact on their families.

SUGGESTED READINGS

The Black Male: Critical Counseling, Developmental, and Therapeutic Issues. (3 Special Issues) Part I. (1985). *Journal of Non-white Concerns in Personnel and Guidance, 13*(2), (whole issue). Part II. (1985). *Journal of Multicultural Counseling and Development, 13*(3), (whole issue). Part III. (1986). *Journal of Multicultural Counseling and Development, 14*(1), (whole issue).

Coelho, R. J., & Wilkins, D. M. (1980). Evaluation of occupational literature: A guide for use with minorities. *Journal of Non-white Concerns, 9*, 3-9.

Dean, S. A. (1984). External locus of control and career counseling for black youth. *Journal of Non-white Concerns, 12*, 111-116.

Franklin, C. W. (1986). Conceptual and logical issues in theory and research related to Black masculinity. *Western Journal of Black Studies, 10*, 161-166.

Griffith, A. R. (1980). Justification for black career development. *Journal of Non-white Concerns, 8*, 77-83.

Lee, C. C. (1987). Black manhood training: Group counseling for male blacks in grades 7-12. *Journal for Specialists in Group Work, 12*, 18-25.

Lockman, P. (1984). Ebony and ivory: The interracial gay male couple. *Lifestyles, 7*, 44-55.

McDavis, R. J., & Parker, W. M. (1981). Strategies for helping ethnic minorities with career development. *Journal of Non-white Concerns, 9*, 130-136.

Miles, L. (1981). Midlife career change for blacks: Problems and issues. *The Vocational Guidance Quarterly, 30*, 5-13.

Osipow, S. H. (1983). *Theories of career development*. Englewood Cliffs, NJ: Prentice-Hall.

Parham, T. A., & McDavis, R. J. (1987). Black men, an endangered species: Who's really pulling the trigger? *Journal of Counseling and Development, 66*, 24-27.

Reisman, B. L., & Banuelos, D. (1984). Career fantasy in the barrio. *Journal of Non-white Concerns, 12*, 99-104.

Weltner, J. S. (1990). The lost generation of Japanese men. *The Family Therapy Networker, 14*, 35.

Williams, J. H. (1979). Career counseling for the minority student: Should it be different? *Journal of Non-white Concerns*, *7*, 176-182.

Williams, W. (1986). *The spirit and the flesh: Sexual diversity in American Indian culture*. New York: Beacon Press.

Wooden, W., Kawasaki, M., & Mayeda, R. (1983). Lifestyles and identity maintenance among gay Japanese-American males. *Alternative Lifestyles*, *5*, 236-243.

Counseling Men

There is a growing variety of resources about counseling men. Students are asked to examine male resistance to therapy/counseling, including men's discomfort at seeking help, discomfort with feelings, fear of own performance, fear of dependence on the therapist, fear of weakness and loss of control, competition with the therapist, and suspicion of the therapy process. We encourage male and female graduate students to become active in organizations that promote sex role change such as the National Organization for Changing Men ("Real men," 1990) and the Men's Studies Association (Kerr, 1990) or to join special interest groups in their professional associations such as the Standing Committee for Men of the American College Personnel Association and the task force on men's roles in the American Psychological Association (Bule, 1990). Subscriptions to publications such as the *Men's Studies Review* (Kerr, 1990) also support growth.

SUGGESTED READINGS

American Personnel and Guidance Association. (1981). Counseling males. *The Personnel and Guidance Journal*, *60*, (whole issue).

American Psychological Association. (1978). Counseling men. *The Counseling Psychologist*, *7*, (whole issue).

Bograd, M. (1990). Women treating men. *The Family Therapy Networker*, *14*, 54-58.

Fogel, G. I., Lane, F. M., & Liebert, R. S. (Eds.). (1986). *The psychology of men: New psychoanalytic perspectives*. New York: Basic Books.

Good, G. E., Dell, D. M., & Mintz, L. B. (1989). Male role and gender role conflict: Relations to help seeking in men. *Journal of Counseling Psychology*, *36*, 295-300.

Lee, J. H. (1987). *The flying boy: Healing the wounded man*. Deerfield Beach, FL: Health Communications, Inc.

Meth, R., Pasick, R., Gordon, B., Allen, J., Feldman, L., & Gordon, S. (1990). *Men in therapy: The challenge of change*. NY: Guilford.

Scher, M., Stevens, M., Good, G., & Eichenfeld, G. (1987). *Handbook of counseling and psychotherapy with men*. Newbury Park, CA: Sage Publishers.

REFERENCES

Andersen, M. L. (1987). Changing the curriculum in higher education. *Signs*, *12*, 222-254.

Astin, H. (1985). The meaning of work in women's lives: A socio-psychological model of career choice and work behavior. *The Counseling Psychologist*, *12*, 117-126.

Ault-Riché, M. (Ed.). (1986). *Women and family therapy* (Family Therapy Collection series). Rockville, MD: Aspen Systems.

Boxer, M. J. (1982). For and about women: The theory and practice of women's studies in the United States. *Signs*, *5*, 661-695.

Bricker-Jenkins, M., & Hooyman, N. (1987). Feminist pedagogy in education for social change. *Feminist Teacher*, *2*, 36-42.

Broverman, I. K., Broverman, D. M., Clarkson, F. E., Rosenkrantz, P. S., & Vogel, S. R. (1970). Sex-role stereotypes and clinical judgments of mental health. *Journal of Consulting and Clinical Psychology*, *34*, 1-7.

Bule, J. (1990). 'Men-only' therapy programs emerge. *APA Monitor*, *21*, 16-17.

Chesler, P. (1972). *Women and madness*. Garden City, New York: Doubleday.

Chodorow, N. (1974). Family structure and feminine personality. In M. Rosaldo & L. Lamphere (Eds.), *Women, culture and society*. Stanford, CA: Stanford University Press.

Chodorow, N. (1978). *The reproduction of mothering*. Berkeley, CA: University of California Press.

Erikson, E. (1968). *Identity: Youth and crisis*. New York: Norton.

Feminist Therapy Institute. (1987). *Feminist therapy ethical code*. Davie, FL: FTI.

Fine, R. (1987). The forgotten man: Understanding the male psyche. New York: Harrington Park Press.

Fitzgerald, L. F., & Nutt, R. L. (1986). The Division 17 principles concerning the counseling/psychotherapy of women: Rationale and implementation. *The Counseling Psychologist, 14*, 180-216.

Gilbert, L. A. (1980). Feminist therapy. In A. M. Brodsky & R. T. Hare-Mustin (Eds.), *Women and psychotherapy*. New York: Guilford Press.

Gilligan, C. (1982). *In a different voice: Psychological theory and women's development*. Cambridge, MA: Harvard University Press.

Goldner, V. (1985). Feminism and family therapy. *Family Process, 24*, 31-47.

Goodrich, T. J., Rampage, C., Ellman, B., & Halstead, K. (1988). *Feminist family therapy: A casebook*. New York: W. W. Norton.

Hare-Mustin, R. T. (1978). A feminist approach to family therapy. *Family Process, 17*, 181-194.

Hare-Mustin, R. T. (1983). An appraisal of the relationship between women and psychotherapy. *American Psychologist, 38*, 593-601.

Hare-Mustin, R. T. (1986). The problem of gender in family therapy theory. *Family Process, 26*, 15-27.

Kerr, R. (1990). We've studied everything else, so how about men? *Dallas Morning News* (May 4), 1C-2C.

Klein, R. D. (1987). The dynamics of the women's studies classroom: A review essay of the teaching practice of women's studies in higher education. *Women's Studies International Forum, 10*, 187-206.

Loden, M. (1985). *Feminine leadership or how to succeed in business without being one of the boys*. New York: Times Books.

Luepnitz, D. (1988). *The family interpreted: Feminist theory and clinical practice*. New York: Basic Books.

McGoldrick, M., Anderson, C., & Walsh, F. (Eds.). (1989). *Women in families: A framework for family therapy*. New York: W. W. Norton.

Meth, R. & Pasick, R. (1990). *Men in therapy: The challenge of change*. New York: Guilford.

Melia, J. (1986). *Breaking into the boardroom*. New York: St. Martin's Press.

Perreault, G. (1983). Contemporary feminist perspectives on women and higher education. In C. C. Gould (Ed.), *Beyond domination*. Totowa, NJ: Rowman & Allanhild.

Pittman, F. (1985). Gender myths. *The Family Therapy Networker, 9*, 25-33.

Rawlings, E., & Carter, D. (Eds.). (1977). *Psychotherapy for women: Treatment toward equality*. Springfield, IL: Charles C Thomas.

Sattel, J. (1976). The inexpressive male: Tragedy or sexual politics? *Social Problems, 23*, 469-477.

Sherman, J. A. (1980). Therapist attitudes and sex-role stereotyping. In A. M. Brodsky & R. T. Hare-Mustin (Eds.), *Women and psychotherapy*. New York: Guilford Press.

Taggart, M. (1985). The feminist critique in epistemological perspective: Questions of context in family therapy. *Journal of Marital and Family Therapy*, *11*, 113-126.

Task Force on Sex Bias and Sex Role Stereotyping in Psychotherapeutic Practice. (1978). Guidelines for therapy with women. *American Psychologist*, *33*, 1122-1123.

Walters, M., Carter, B., Papp, P., & Silverstein, O. (1988). *The invisible web: Gender patterns in family relationships*. New York: Guilford Press.

Zilbergeld, B. (1978). *Male sexuality*. Boston: Little, Brown.